THE SQUEEZE

To Jean Gottmann
Géographe de l'homme dans le paysage

Foreword

It is an undeniable fact that, throughout the long history of this earth, environment has been a dominating influence upon the existence and development of all living things—plant, animal, and, of course, man himself. This forceful book therefore deals with a subject of utmost importance. It is addressed especially to the people of the United States, but it contains much of interest to people in other countries at a time when the constant increase of urbanization is a universal trend. As for the United States, it is no exaggeration to say that what we now do, or fail to do, in planning and molding the physical environment of America will have a profound effect, for good or ill, upon our nation—physically, psychologically and spiritually.

It can justifiably be said that our country in many respects is becoming less and less *habitable*. The meaning of the word "habitable" can be simply defined. It connotes a living place that is practical for the purposes of both work and leisure, that is healthful and that, finally, contributes to a sense of happiness. There are few Americans today who are not conscious of the effect on their own lives of what the author, dramatically but still accurately, calls "the squeeze." While the increasing concentration of ever greater numbers of people in the congested urban areas is indeed a world-wide social phenomenon, in no other country is the metamorphosis so rapid and so revolutionary in its character.

Several years ago an article appeared in one of our scientific journals citing how similar the tendency of human beings to concentrate their numbers in a limited space is to the social behavior of ants and certain other insects. This observation suggests that the evolution of modern man could eventually prove a fatal one in that gradually all individuality will disappear and the ultimate of human society will be that of a huge insensate robot state. We of course are not prepared to recognize the possibility that our destiny will take that shape, yet the tantalizing thought persists that a theory projecting such a bleak outlook may not be completely imaginary. "The squeeze" is upon us. Of that there is no doubt, with consequences we cannot yet measure.

This book is a powerful presentation of what needs to be done to make the United States a habitable place in which to live in the years that lie ahead. The author happens to be neither a "country man" nor a "city man." If he has any partisanship he does not reveal it. An earlier book of his, *American Oasis,* represents an extraordinarily comprehensive review of the agricultural development of this country, written with full consciousness of the historical, cultural and geographical influences that have brought American agriculture to its present state. Yet as an agronomist and geographer, he disputes neither the desirability nor the inevitability of cities. His challenge is that if they, together with their suburbs, continue their present course of development, the values of American life, whether from the point of view of the "city man" or the "country man," will disappear.

Any book that attempts to convey a message of such importance can fail in its mission if it is not supported by a full measure of factual material. The power of this book is that it is both conceptual and literal. The criticisms that it contains of the "powers that be" or, alternately, the "business as usual" attitude, are the more effective because they are not expressed in generalities but represent reasonable deductions from factual data. The book ranges in scope, as it should, in such diverse yet related subjects as taxes and welfare, the amenities of the landscape, land speculation, Federal highway programs, why the railroads want to quit, population pressures, and the many other conditions, practices and influences that together will be the determinants as to whether or not the United States will prove to be a good or an undesirable place in which to live.

Fairfield Osborn

August 1960

Acknowledgments

By the very nature of their business universities employ professors to teach the little they know rather than to learn about the much of which they are ignorant. Under such circumstances there is a tendency in the classroom to elaborate more and more about less and less until a little bit of information is blown up into a full-sized course of instruction. If a professor of geography is kept in campus captivity for very long, he is apt to forget that the world rather than the textbook is the real object of his student's curiosity. To the Old Dominion Foundation and the Conservation Foundation I am deeply grateful for funds which enabled me to take leave of normal duties long enough to become reacquainted with what is happening to the landscape of the United States. This account is the product of their generous support.

Many private persons have also been most helpful, particularly Monroe Bush and John Willey, whose fine editorial honing ground down the roughest edges of my manuscript. To staff members of the United States Soil Conservation Service I am especially appreciative for assistance in field studies of land use. I also wish to thank the farmers who told me their personal stories, as recorded in Chapter VI. Their privacy is assured by fictitious names.

E.H.

Introduction

Metropolitan America is in a squeeze. The space it uses for living and to make a living has become cluttered to the point of frustration. Efforts to relieve congestion are feeble by comparison with the forces that make it worse. Urban decay, suburban sprawl, rising taxes, clogged highways, distressed railroads, poor public schools, higher prices to food consumers, lower prices to food producers, disappearing recreational space—these and other penalties of living in our time are not isolated ills. They are symptoms of the same deadly disease. This illness lowers the standard of living while wages rise, and it threatens to make a corpse of a once-vibrant social organism. What is this malady? How did we contract it? Why does it provoke so many forms of weakness which seem unrelated at first glance? Finally, is there a cure?

The disease is an environmental leukemia that saps the vitality of the American metropolis and its agricultural fringe. The landscape of this nation, which once offered unparalleled natural beauty, economic resources, and sites for proud cities, has been polluted through a mismanagement of space that has created expensive and ugly chaos. Instead of constructing a habitat in metropolitan areas that preserves the beautiful and functional, we have ripped our natural living space to shreds and replaced it with a tawdry, disorganized maze that is neither pleasant to look at nor economical to use. To conduct our lives and operate our businesses in the congestion we have created in the city, in the suburb, and on the highway afflicts us all with such debt and difficulty that a dangerous social reaction has set in. Discouragement with public affairs has reached the point where it is now fashionable for those with private means to "go it alone."

The better-paid urbanite deserts the city for the suburb. The suburban commuter abandons public transportation. The affluent hunter buys his own preserve or joins a private sports club. The parent who is able to sends his child to a private school. The farmer on the edge of the city sells his farm to the real-estate developer and retires. Obviously those who pull out have the wealth or credit to save themselves. A rising burden of taxation without compensating amenities drives them to their private decisions, but it is rougher than ever on the majority who must rely upon public services that no longer serve satisfactorily. Unless the American metropolis is ready to take drastic steps the ability of the landscape to function as a suitable habitat for human beings will be dangerously impaired forever.

The usual bureaucratic mind is not in condition to help very much. It is not particularly guided by cultural values or a sense of efficiency—public education and political indifference see to that. Yet the mind of the civil servant and the schools which orient it have the responsibility and the power to mold the environment we live in. We are ill-prepared to think in any other terms than those which have landed us in trouble. A better organization of space for residence, for pleasure, and for business is absolutely imperative if the rising tides of population are not to make a complete shambles of the metropolitan habitat. Within the next hundred years the United States will breed a population that will surpass that in China today. How will our children fare during the years of transition as the horde increases?

A solution is not impossible but it would require such a drastic reversal of past practice that it seems highly improbable except in the most enlightened local communities. It would be an intellectual and cultural miracle if the proper remedy were inspired at the national level. The immediate hope is that a better environment will emerge from the engineering of those who dream of space for life right in our own communities rather than of shipping life into space beyond the earth's gravitational pull. Engineers must prepare now to accommodate the vastly greater populations that are clearly coming or it will not be long before there is standing room only in the cluttered heart of Metropolis.

Contents

THE SQUEEZE

CHAPTER 1

Competitions for Space

MAN AND HABITAT

Duffy Square is hardly more than an oversized safety island, the cement surface of which rises curb-high above the traffic tides that swirl through Manhattan's theatrical district. Surmounting a similar concrete slab a few blocks to the south is the thin, ornately pedimented Times Building still girdled after several decades by a revolving belt of news announcements. In between these two landmarks is a gaudy neon world of block-long billboards, the theater marquees, jewelry auctions, souvenir shops, night clubs, and "one-flight-up-to-beautiful-girls" dance halls.

Amid this triumph of human ingenuity the Department of Parks had the temerity during a recent springtime to transplant onto Duffy Square some small but well-formed London plane trees, thereby creating a leafy oasis for the public and a roost for the pigeons which frequent this and similar guano islands in New York. A year later only a few trees remained in a rather questionable condition while the majority had succumbed.

To begin with, the park effects were not appreciated by everyone, least of all by advertising agencies, which complained to Manhattan Borough President Hulan E. Jack that

1

leaves and twigs obscured the pedestrian's view of their art. Through the intercession of Mr. Jack the arboreal obstruction of public viewing space was lessened by lopping back the treetops to a maximum height of sixteen feet so that the towering billboards could be seen in their four-story splendor. The plane trees, apparently debilitated by these amputations, collapsed under other environmental stresses. Soot, vibration from subways, poor drainage through the concrete, and heat from subsurface steam tubes—all these proved to be more than the trees could take although they had been tenderly trussed with guy wires and rubber tubing to help them withstand their ordeal.

The trees of Duffy Square are but a symbol of what happens to living things in a hostile environment different from their natural habitat. In the half-billion years of organic evolution upon the earth's stone crust, there has been a long and varied succession of environmental changes accompanied by an equally long procession of diverse living forms. Specific environments and certain species peculiar to them have evolved and vanished together through time. Most susceptible to extinction seem to have been those organisms which achieved the highest degree of adaptation to a particular set of conditions. Then, as the world about them changed, their peculiar advantages in one surrounding became handicaps in the next. Primitive unicellular Protozoa of the kind seen in any drop of pond water under a microscope have survived into our own time probably because they have remained primitive and unicellular without unusual attributes or demands, except that there continue to be drops of pond water.

The complex dinosaur, a reptile without internal thermostatic controls and apparently adjusted to a low-oxygen atmosphere in the age of gymnosperms, proved a pushover for warm-blooded mammals in the age of flowering plants and a high-oxygen atmosphere. The natural environment in which man evolved, and to which he was so well adapted that he eventually became the dominant species among living things, is now rapidly changing, chiefly through his own actions. What the future consequences of this environmental tinkering may be for the survival of the species one cannot know. But, if a specialized organism is the most vulnerable to a change in habitat, the Protozoa would still seem to merit favorable odds. Possibly the brain which has made man dominant in present zoologic time will prove to be the very instrument of his extinction. Perhaps that brain may construct an environment so different from the natural habitat that Man, like the trees of Duffy Square, may prove obsolete within it.

Space is one of the vital attributes of habitat, for its quality is a major influence upon the welfare and survival of any organism. The growth of America's population creates an extraordinary competition for space, particularly in those counties or townships with big cities which the Bureau of the Census calls standard metropolitan areas. Each of these contains at least one urban center of more than 50,000 people; several of them harbor over a million inhabitants. Between 1950 and 1959 the nation's population grew by twenty-four millions. Of this increase, sixteen million were in the 168 standard metropolitan areas which contain the largest cities and their environs. Villages and rural areas play but a minimum role in today's population explosion. In fact the rural population has declined 14 per cent in the past decade. Not only is human multiplication typical of metropolitan counties and townships, but most new residences are going up in their suburban districts rather than in their central cities.

In the same 1950-1959 period during which central cities gained 1.5 per cent in population, the suburbs spurted ahead by 44.0 per cent. Because suburban growth is horizontal and eccentric, rather than vertical and central, it consumes more land per capita than city growth. Consequently at the very time we are multiplying most rapidly, we have hit upon the most space-clogging form of community growth. Farms are disappearing at an accelerated rate to accommodate this horizontal sprawl, and the shrinkage of open space in metropolitan counties now has become a conspicuous associate of population increase.

Human increase combined with a replacement of farms by suburbia promises to solve the problem of food surpluses by substituting for it the gnawing question of food supply. An official of the Department of Agriculture has estimated that though we shall need 40 per cent more food in 1975 than we had in 1955, we are losing productive agricultural land to suburbanization and other developmental pressures at the rate of one million acres annually. Thus food supply, which is another element of habitat, and which definitely is related to adequate space, may eventually become a concern in America.

Surpluses cannot very well persist indefinitely under the twin assault of human multiplication and farm subtraction. This seems elementary when it is considered that present surpluses, while they clog the domestic market, do not reflect substantial overproduction so much as a lack of consumer purchasing power. The enormous quantities of grain now in storage under government loans could be quickly eliminated by a sensible conversion to meat, dairy, and poultry products if all families could afford to buy more of these wholesome but costlier types of food. The appetite already exists. Very likely, however, as the population grows and productive land becomes scarcer, diets will become more vegetarian than they are now. America could sustain perhaps ten times as many persons at present levels of crop production if animal products were eliminated from the diet. But this, from the nutritional standpoint, would be unwise since man is omnivorous. To cut down drastically on animal foods may not be to man's physical advantage, even if he should reconcile himself psychologically to the shift. In controlled nutritional studies with experimental animals, it has been indicated that longevity, vitality, and resistance to such afflictions as cancer, arthritis, impotency, and cataract are more closely related to the quality of food than to its quantity.

Of comparable importance, and of immediate concern to most taxpayers, is the probability that as farm shrinkage continues on the peripheries of major cities, little open land will eventually remain between the suburban outposts of abutting metropolitan areas. Unless precautions are taken, whole regions such as that between Boston and Washington are destined to become built-up complexes of fused cities and suburbs without protective "expansion joints" of undeveloped open space between them, particularly along the main arteries of contact. Environmental patterns are being frozen by misplaced buildings and streets at the very time the accent should be on flexibility. Construction itself is vital to any growing community, but it should be located on the land in a way that does not jam the routes of communication or fill up areas of recreational value. At present there is no truly rational control over the organization of metropolitan space, because it is assumed that all land is suitable for construction of some sort. Zoning limits the type of building but seldom does it prohibit building entirely and therein lies the prospect of ultimate congestion. The concept that practically all space may be developed as building sites results in unco-ordinated location of construction and in fierce jockeying for what are the most strategic trade positions at the moment. Service stations, for instance, may be erected at the four corners of major highway intersections, even though widening the arterial crossing at some future date may saddle the public with a phenomenal condemnation charge.

Never has any people had to contend with such a complex space problem as this, and there seems to be precious little awareness of its gravity or inclination to forestall it. Once environmental *rigor mortis* has set in, the expenses for demolition and renewal that eventually will be necessary to recapture spatial flexibility will wreck the budgets of states and municipalities, as we now know them. Type examples in the form of expressways blasted through cities are already familiar to everyone, and someday only wholesale demolition by the Federal Government will do the job of restoring some of the breathing space that now is vanishing both around and between industrial centers. Cities are no more able to function efficiently with each other's suburbs poking them in the ribs than are people with their elbows in one another's faces. Examples of such a condition are already clearly visible on the rim of almost every great city. Philadelphia and Boston are so like mummies, encased in five to fifteen miles of tight suburban wrappings, that not even the new expressways can free them from their frustrating strait jackets of misplaced development in areas where the land should never have been used for buildings.

The blame for this growing environmental ossification is often attributed to the inanimate automobile which takes people back and forth, rather than to the community's mental block against genuine civic planning for a skyrocketing population. Since, for the moment at least, birth control seems to be a good idea only for the other fellow's family, the most sensible alternative would be to control the use of space, although that too seems just about as unpopular. America is no longer a pioneer country in which the settlement of space should be a national goal. That will come about without trying. It is now time to guard some spaces against settlement, particularly those open lands which still lie between the suburban outposts of cities that are relatively close to one another, and between the suburbs themselves, which too often flow together like wet cement and set just as hard. In the Northeast the physical fusion of large metropolitan complexes has already begun. The suburbs of Washington tangle with those of Baltimore. Baltimore is advancing upon Wilmington. Although Wilmington and Philadelphia are separated by state lines, they are physically in each other's arms. New Jersey complains that it is but a rendez-vous between the offspring of Philadelphia and New York. Boston, while isolated in mind, is becoming linked to New York via Providence, Worcester, Hartford, New Haven, and Bridgeport. Here is the beginning of a regional city hundreds of miles in length which could become such a tangle of haphazard development as to defy dissection. That nine states and thousands of local government units, each with its own prerogatives for taxing, spending, and licensing, should jell into one contiguous built-up lump is intellectually frightening and fiscally mad.

For the future the basic problem is to devise principles of land use and rules to go with them, so that growth may continue without further congestion. This is technically possible if somewhat unpalatable to the individualist who has enjoyed freewheeling in the past. The alternative is chaos and the bankruptcy of some communities. Instead of planning a solvent future for our progeny, it has been our habit to borrow their money for our own ephemeral conveniences. In their more congested world not only will they have to contend with the outmoded, inefficient arrangement of space we shall leave behind; but also they will have to pay the bonded debts that we have hung on them for projects not so brilliantly conceived as we have smugly thought.

For a modern people who live by mortgage credit and time payments, it is not feasible to junk a city and move out when it becomes obsolete. We are not free to pile our personal baggage, machine tools, and our public leaders into some kind of caravan headed for a fresh, clean spot and a new start. That is a luxury which only the pioneer of yesterday or a contemporary tribesman in the Ecuadorian rain forest might enjoy. It is still the custom of some Indian communities along the upper reaches of the Amazon to abandon old villages and build new ones when exhausted soil, pestilence, or just a whim makes it desirable to move. The complex communities we erect in our part of the world will probably remain inhabited as long as our species persists on earth. Either we shall use our vaunted ingenuity to organize space for orderly growth in the future, or someday the habitat will become so polluted that it will menace the organism which created it.

Apart from the engineering aspects of space design there are human considerations that have to do with man as a living organism. The desecration of the natural landscape and the growing tendency to bury living things under asphalt and concrete are fraught with unknown consequences. There are neighborhoods in large cities where a child cannot walk upon sod or the bare earth. It is possible that metropolitan man may destroy the natural habitat before he has discovered a pattern for a synthetic environment that offers equal opportunity for survival of life and sanity. Dr. Herbert L. Ratcliffe of the Philadelphia Zoological Society has made observations of zoo animals which may throw light on the human animal's environmental needs. After a forty-year study of 11,000 birds and mammals which had died in captivity, Dr. Ratcliffe concluded that neither aging nor diet seems to bring on arteriosclerosis as much as either the "social pressure" of too much company or the inactivity of being caged alone. Obviously something in between the extremes is preferable, or at least the individual should be allowed the choice of crowds or privacy according to his need. Confinement in public without means of escape may develop into an unbearable stress. Sociologists who have questioned juvenile gangs in the large cities find that most youths belong because they have no alternative. As members themselves say, the pack does not permit lone wolves. Zoo keepers have also observed that animals become morose when they are isolated.

Dr. Heini Hediger, a European animal behaviorist, has observed that "in captivity the inability to run away and the greater density of animals create pressures that increase social quarrels, fighting and hypersexuality." "Social rivals," he has said, "cannot get far away from one another. After a fight, the victor and his defeated partner can still see each other and this sometimes leads to quarrels that are never settled except by death."[1] The modern man who must daily face a hostile boss or housemate is in a tighter trap than any primitive tribesman, for he cannot just pick up and go off on a hunting expedition to work off his frustrations. Whether man is innately civilized or savage is an old debate, but it seems clear that an environment that does not condition him by constant encouragements to be co-operative may in turn find him so competitive as to be hostile. More than likely the seeds of juvenile delinquency may lie in the daily neglect of children in what is too much an adult world, rather than in any temptations set out to snare them deliberately.

A Wisconsin conservationist, while stocking streams with trout, noted that a fish taken from its home becomes unhappy and that, like an unhappy person in similar circumstances, it may behave in a suicidal way. The first act of a trout upon being released into strange waters is to look for an unoccupied home. If it cannot find one quickly, the fish may actually swim itself to death in the search. Biologists have found that the stress of a new environment may cause the lactic acid level of the blood to rise to the point where death results. If the human desire to create life is matched with a desire to live agreeably, then the quality of the environment cannot be ignored.

Dr. Thomas S. Langner recently reported to the American Psychopathological Association on a study of 1660 residents of Yorkville, which is one of the better middle-class neighborhoods in New York City. The subjects, twenty to fifty years of age and selected at random, were examined as to their mental health. Of the entire group, 18.5 per cent were found to be well; 36.3 per cent, mildly disturbed; 21.8 per

[1] For sources of quoted material not identified in the text or resulting from personal interviews with the author, please see correspondingly numbered notes, gathered chapter by chapter, in the Appendix.

cent, moderately disturbed; and 23.4 per cent, impaired. Examining their backgrounds the researchers determined that the more stress to which a person was subjected, the more he was inclined toward mental disorder. Dr. Langner described the situation as "the more the unmerrier." It is an accepted fact that neuroses develop when an environment makes it impossible for a person to achieve the ambitions and goals that he has been taught in youth to believe are within his grasp if only he sincerely strives. To the man who is committed to the metropolitan environment, the city has the obligation to put within his grasp the good life that it claims it can offer, or ultimately it may have to provide him with quarters in a psychiatric ward. However, there is also the cheerful school of thought which believes that most urban miseries exist only in the minds of those who are possessed of an incurable rural nostalgia.

Man did not evolve in an urban-industrial world, and the sketchy knowledge he possesses of his own physiology and psyche scarcely enables him to know whether the environment he is creating is good or bad for the organism. To some extent he must go by hunches. But the more his manufactured habitat departs from the natural surroundings in which he evolved over eons of time, the more carefully he will have to watch his step for self-constructed snares.

Just how complicated and uncertain the search for a suitable environmental formula may be is suggested by man's own perversity, since he is that social animal which likes his privacy. Not so long ago two jolly, white-robed Camaldolese hermit monks arrived in New York City from Italy. Father Augustine, with the assent of his companion, Father Aliprando, said they were impressed with the opportunity for solitude and meditation amidst the throngs and bustle of the Empire City. Italy, they agreed, is too convivial for a determined hermit unless he sticks to his cell. "An Italian who gets on a train introduces himself to his fellow passengers and states his business. The others do the same. Then follows a general discussion of each one's affairs. But in America, what do we see? Each traveler minds his own business. He sits alone, free and silent, reading and contemplating—if not Holy Scripture, then at least the New York *Times*. You are hermits at heart." However, Father Augustine detected a flaw. "You don't have time to pray," he added, "so we hermits pray for you."

The Long Island Railway, which hauls about 80,000 commuters daily to and from the canyons of New York, is as public as the subway and often just as overstuffed. Some of its antique coaches, which date back to the days of cane seats, sway as if they were playground swings whenever they roll downgrade. Yet there is at least one rider who would agree with Father Augustine for he regards his hour-long journeys morning and evening as the most relaxed moments of his life. "At home every time I sit down the wife and kids are at me for something. All day at the office I'm either dictating, on the phone, or in conference. I'd be dead if it weren't for peace aboard the Long Island." This gentleman has a kindred spirit in the concert pianist-composer who finds the subway a suitable place to practice and create. He declares his work is basically imagination and interpretation. Since these are mental processes, he finds he can do them while he commutes. He has not divulged what his listeners think of the idea.

The phenomenon of isolation in crowds which appealed to all these gentlemen is not so good for young people, according to Lincoln Daniels of the United States Children's Bureau. Mr. Daniels believes city-type living in growing metropolitan areas imposes an anonymity and impersonality which undermines family and neighborhood control. The notion that no solitude is so impenetrable as one's aloneness in a great city is old hat. Whether this detachment is vice or virtue very likely depends upon the individual and how he feels at the moment, for there is obviously something of the hermit and the gregarious in every man.

Yet the wide open spaces, too, may have their drawbacks. In preparing men for duty in Antarctica during the International Geophysical Year, it was commonly feared that isolation at such a remote and forbidding station would be the chief psychological hazard. Yet, after it was over, Dr. Charles S. Mullin, Jr., Chief of the Neuropsychiatric Service in Philadelphia's Naval Hospital, reported to the American Medical Association that it was human beings that got on men's nerves rather than the physical environment. According to Dr. Mullin, men living in close quarters for a year realize that they must control feelings of aggression and mutual hostility. The result at Little America was inhibition, tension, and frequent pains in the head.

Whether one finds solitude in a subway or too much society at a polar outpost depends upon human behavior and upon how space is used and arranged, rather than upon the total amount of room or people. Freedom to move away from irritations even if it is by a commuter's coach seems to be a prerequisite. The old topic of quality vs. quantity is still pertinent for no one questions that America has sufficient total space for a long time to come. But if we use it badly in the cities and suburbs where people are bunched together, we may someday find we do not have enough in the right places. We shall be a combination of both the polar adventurer and the Long Island commuter—packed together and finding privacy only in the most public places. We shall be lucky if the consequences are nothing more serious than pains in the head.

POPULATION PRESSURE

Less than two hundred years ago, at the time of the American Revolution, the population of the original thirteen colonies was less than three million. Today we grow by more than three million annually. Were it possible to continue accumulating as we do, like money at compound interest,

America could top a three billion total in another two hundred-year interval. Within four hundred years, unless some external restraint countered the biological urge, this nation could anticipate a population increase of one billion every twelve months. Another five hundred years after that, or just nine centuries from now, we could delight the Internal Revenue Service by adding three trillion names annually to the tax rolls. This ought to create a good market demand for almost any useful product and the Dow-Jones index should be all bull. What China, with its head start, would have done, meanwhile, is a calculation that should intrigue Madison Avenue.

Calculations have been made which indicate that if the whole world were to multiply at this healthy pace for just seven centuries, there would be only one square yard of dry ground for each human being. If one thinks historically, seven hundred years is really not so long. Seven centuries ago, European crusaders were embarked upon their mission of population control in the Holy Land. How to limit the multiplication of people, especially those we do not like, has been a preoccupation of mankind since ancient times.

Obviously our own particular segment of the human race is realizing the expectations of the good Reverend Thomas Malthus, who theorized that man, like bacteria or any other organism, will multiply to the full extent of favorable conditions. Contrary to the popular notion Malthus did not emphasize unduly a future of mass hunger in the world; that was not his prime concept. His accent was on the positive if one may judge by what he wrote rather than by some things written about him. He said actually that man would take advantage of favorable conditions to multiply until checked. That is quite different from crying havoc. It is another way of saying that if things are very good, humanity will "live it up."

For the moment there is no need to panic about human storage room. Considering all fifty states in our union, there is lots of it. The whole 180 million of us could assemble in New York's Bronx and Central Parks, if we would carefully avoid standing on one another's feet. On a room-size photo-mosaic of the United States, these parks would be only two small specks. Nevertheless, when life goes on unchecked, miracles do happen as anyone knows who has ever inoculated nutrient agar in a Petri dish with a compatible strain of bacteria. A few days and X generations later the previously empty surface is overrun with a mass of cells, each one capable of further reproduction if only there were more space, more food, and less pollution.

The Regional Planning Commission of the County of Los Angeles has prepared a graph which illustrates how human beings have spread over the farm land of that county. In 1941 the local population was 2,650,000 and there were 300,000 acres of agricultural soils—a ratio of nine to one. By 1954 there were nearly 5,000,000 people and 225,000 acres. When the population again doubles, which is entirely possible by 1975, the farm base should be down to 75,000 acres. The ratio of nine to one in 1941 should be about 133 to one in 1975. While Los Angeles is just a pilot project in land cannibalism, it shows how the man-land squeeze play can be made to work under the most favorable stimuli.

However, the U. S. Department of Agriculture takes a dim view of using tillable soils for house sites. It would rather that people play their numbers game on steep hillsides, on sandy ground, on rock piles—in fact almost anywhere but on good farm dirt which is strictly limited. To make its point the Department tells us that to feed the new boarders who take 100,000 new seats at the nation's dining table every two weeks, farmers have to plant another 241 acres of oranges, 450 acres of potatoes, 283 acres of tomatoes, and 77 acres of grapes. They also have to supply hay, grain, and pasture for another 12,130 head of beef and 7600 dairy cows. To maintain only present dietary standards, poultrymen have to provide 296,000 additional egg-laying hens, and there must be 23,000 more Thanksgiving turkeys to celebrate gastronomic bounty in traditional style.

In stating a thesis that all living things have a vigorous propensity to propagate until checked, Malthus anticipated a biological twist to what was to become chemistry's "Law of the Minimum." This law, stated by Justus Von Liebig, father of modern chemistry, notes that under ideal circumstances a reaction will continue until restrained by exhaustion of whatever essential ingredient is present in least quantity. Malthus simply supposed that food is the particular ingredient essential to human life that someday would be available in "least quantity" and its depletion would then check multiplication. In this he probably was right but it is still a little early to tell. His guess is more likely to be correct than it was when he made it considering the remarkable advances in medicine and public health which have so greatly reduced the probability of catastrophic epidemics. Only wholesale atomic radiation—a possibility unknown to Malthus—seems a likely contender for the job of halting mankind's proliferation.

When limitations of space are considered, it is obvious that sometime between now and the year 2700, a Malthusian check of one sort or other will stop humanity's hectic climb toward stratospheric numbers. Of this we can be pretty certain since one square yard of ground is considerably less than the minimum required by each member of the species, unless our descendants go in for taller multiple-story tenements and a kind of hanging-garden agriculture by which food crops would be grown like English ivy on the walls of a Baltimore apartment house. There are a few blocks of residential apartments in Manhattan which demonstrate some interesting possibilities by harboring 1300 persons per acre of ground space. This is one and one-half square yards per capita. During a busy day when there are 30,000 people in the Empire State Building each one utilizes only one and one-half square feet of the earth's surface.

Behind every land boom is the stimulating promise of population growth, for land has no economic value without people to use it. The very substance of a speculator's dream is a blissful faith in human fertility. A fast-multiplying citizenry, an abundance of land rich in resources, and a benign economic climate were the essential ingredients in America's phenomenal accumulation of wealth. Some unhappy landlords in the Amazon Valley own tens of thousands of acres, yet their annual incomes from all this space is less than that of an American pensioner on social security. There are neither Indians nor anyone else who will live and work on the premises to make them productive.

Probably no other influence upon American economic history has been so persistent as the continuously rising value of space because of population increase. That an acre in Chicago's Loop might be valued at a million dollars while an acre in backwoods Maine would sell for ten is a circumstance that applies to human densities and business opportunities since, if anything, the Maine woods are more attractive. But offsetting the rosy future for all private lands lying in the fecund lap of growth is the dismal prospect of the burgeoning communities themselves. The very crowding that enhances the value of private land seems to cripple the efficiency and unbalance the budgets of cities, suburbs, and states. Even the Federal Government has begun to feel the backwash of distress in the local communities as frantic appeals for aid increase. To match underdevelopment programs abroad there are now overdevelopment programs at home that demand Washington's sympathy. No less a person than Mayor Robert F. Wagner of the nation's largest and wealthiest city has sounded a rallying cry to other bewildered mayors and city managers. Under the catchy slogan of "What's good for the city is good for the country," the harassed New York executive has told Congress quite frankly that local governments have neither the facilities nor the power to solve many of the new problems caused by population growth.[2]

What lies behind this curious circumstance of rising land values and community bankruptcy? Why should human growth create private wealth and public poverty simultaneously in the same localities? Why should Park Avenue real estate rise at the same time New York itself, the parent organism, sinks into debt? It is a common fact, observable in all sections of the nation, that while some private fortunes pyramid in the course of urban renewal, industrial expansion, and suburban sprawl, the public's debts and taxes climb and the efficient use of community real estate, in the form of roads, streets, schools, and parks, deterioriates. Some of the keenest minds in America plan the development and direct the use of private real-estate projects, but the more complex public job of integrating these separate developments into a functional community is left chiefly to politicians and bureaucrats who, too often, are amateur hacks in the serious business of managing property and organizing space. If they were professionals at community organization, they would not make the obvious mistakes that cost the taxpayer dearly.

Engineers who delight in the intricacies of complex construction have a ball solving traffic riddles with skyways at fifteen million dollars a mile. But what city has thought of hiring and then following the advice of an engineer who would plan the use of its land so that congestion and such colossal surgery could be avoided? There is vast opportunity on the public payroll for a brand-new profession of preventive engineering which would do for the sick community what preventive medicine can do to safeguard human health. A state highway department that builds a four-lane, divided highway at a million dollars a mile, and then allows it to degenerate into a common street by granting unlimited access to roadside homes and shops, has defrauded the public which employs it. Within a few years the same highway department will have the gall to reappear at the public trough begging new funds for a new road to parallel the one it failed to protect. Private interests which have built commercial toll turnpikes are not so negligent with their capital.

Preventive engineering lies at the heart of efficient private real-estate developments. Rockefeller Center will not be overcrowded in a hundred years because it is planned for so many buildings, so many people and so much traffic. However, under present zoning, officials admit there is nothing to prevent New York from swelling into a monstro-city of fifty-five million people, although the City Planning Commission says eleven million should be the limit. The metropolis now has eight million and the New York *Times* says one million of these already live in slums which increase faster than they can be demolished.[3]

In recent years under an urban-renewal program, 227 acres of New York City slums have been torn down and replaced with decent living quarters. There are plans for the next decade to restore 905 more acres to respectability. But in all there are already 7000 acres of shamefully degraded housing space in the city. Worst of all, while the City Council luxuriates in the spectacular surgery of urban renewal, it neglects to employ and empower an engineer whose job it would be to administer the city's space so that the causes of such extravagant squandering of public funds would not again occur. At present displaced slum dwellers and slum landlords are allowed to shift to other blocks and other neighborhoods to continue their practice of partitioning multiple-room apartments and homes into beehives of one-room units—a space-splitting trick that in the past decade alone has converted hundreds of acres of the finest West Side real estate into a second Harlem. Albert M. Cole, former Federal Housing Administrator, says that any American city without a definite plan to stop the growth of blight is facing bankruptcy, and he makes the blanket statement,

"No city in America is doing enough."[4] Here is a real job for preventive engineers who would design the future use of urban space so as to prevent the worst forms of environmental pollution.

POLLUTION OF SPACE

During the early years of this century, South America held a virtual monopoly of the world's rubber supply, which then was tapped from wild trees growing in Amazon rain forests. Later, when efforts were made to establish rubber plantations in this hemisphere, a virulent fungus known as "South American leaf disease" appeared and destroyed them. This parasite, found only in the Americas, has existed in Brazil for perhaps as long as there have been rubber trees, for they are its natural hosts. But in the rain forests the deadly microorganism does little damage because there the wild rubber trees are widely dispersed among hundreds of other kinds of trees on which the fungus cannot propagate. By being so scattered wild rubber trees are well protected; but susceptible plantation trees, growing close together in massive stands, fall easy victims. Should one of them become infected, the contamination may spread in epidemic fashion among the remainder.

The case of the native Brazilian rubber trees is a rather exotic example of a common ecological fact—pure stands of any species, plant or animal, are most likely to suffer from predators or just plain self-competition unless they are especially selected and cared for. In Nature the susceptible individual, mixed among many different types, is buffered or camouflaged. A cultured type in concentrated stands or herds is conspicuous and vulnerable. Since things that are alike make similar demands upon the environment, they tend to compete with one another if there are shortages of any kind. When corn is planted too thickly, no single plant can thrive because each receives too little sunlight. Basic to the art of successful herding and agriculture are techniques of proper spacing and rotation which help to provide better nutrition, sanitation, and escape from epidemic diseases. Urban man, like plantation rubber trees, cannot be rotated or widely dispersed. Like them he is part of a fixed, dense, homogeneous population. The difficulty of defending the city dweller against competitions for space and of protecting him from stresses, irritations, diseases, and poisonous wastes becomes increasingly acute the more closely he is packed.

In the urban-suburban society of our time the dictates of human biology and economics often conflict. Centralization may promote commercial and industrial efficiency, while the concentration of too many people and too much activity aggravates various sorts of pollution that are organically dangerous. Are there ways to use space so that health, sanity, and other desirable qualities of human life need not be sacrificed to economic expediency? Of Berlin's overcrowded housing district of Wedding, Heinrich Zille once wrote, "You can kill a man with an apartment as with an axe—it takes only a little longer." The psychiatric distress that comes of living a cubical life in a human honeycomb is overlooked by municipal authorities who content themselves with such obvious precautionary formalities as fire inspection, plumbing permits, electrical certification, police approval, and a hatful of codes about materials. However, no one seems to mind if the resulting apartment house reverberates like an African drum to every household beat so that no one literally knows a moment of silence or true privacy. Doctors responsible for a community's mental health are not asked what they think of contemporary apartment buildings that are built without soundproofing—much less are they given a chance to condemn them. Bellevue Hospital will have to grow to take care of the victims of some of New York's latest housing construction which ignores the biological requirements of tenants. Are there ways to engineer the spatial arrangements of people and affairs so that the build-up of a community does not result in the breakdown of the citizen?

Pollution of the habitat, while a common consequence of population growth, need not occur if effective measures are taken to avoid the obvious pitfalls of people-packing. Just as it costs a farmer more per bushel to raise corn yields above a natural optimum because of fertilizers, pesticides, and special care, so, too, it costs a community more per capita to increase population density beyond a certain point. New and more expensive techniques must be applied. A community that is prepared and willing to use these techniques is not in peril. The real danger is that the community may not be willing or able to pay the very expensive bill that must be paid to avoid the pollution that otherwise is an inevitable consequence of high population densities.

Careful studies have shown that each new family which establishes residence in a community may add several thousand dollars to the long-time public debt for schools, roads, sewers, water, and protection services. This subsidy for services to each new family is beyond whatever taxes and assessments will be paid by the family on its own particular residence either directly or as part of rent. It is a well-known fact that growing communities have difficulty supporting themselves and that it is almost impossible without the sale of bonds, which are means of handing down the unpaid bills of one generation to the next. The common hope is that "clean" industry may be enticed to join the community and share the added burden. The fact is that the astronomical costs of increasingly complex municipal services are now far beyond the weak tax base available to them. They are also beyond the prospect that new industry will do the job except in the most unusual locations. Only the states and Federal Government tap sources of revenue commensurate with the job of supporting schools, welfare, and roads that weighs so heavily on the growing local community.

The forms of pollution that come with increasing urbanization and suburbanization include the old reliables of smoke, smog, noise, and filthy water; but they may appear in more sophisticated garb. Ordinary smoke may be enriched with acid fumes to a lethal concentration. Detergents, those households wonders of modern chemistry, have become so prevalent in the ground waters of some communities that wells supplying drinking water now bubble and froth with a synthetic sea foam. Mr. S. C. Martin, regional engineer of the United States Health Service, has commented on the millions of pounds of miracle soaps and insecticides used annually. "We know they kill a lot of insects," he says, "but we have no idea what the long-range effect on human beings will be. For example, what is the effect of ingesting detergents on human beings over a long period of time?"[5] Unlike old-fashioned soaps, the modern suds-makers cannot be removed by municipal water works.

To increase meat supplies for more people with less grain, livestock are treated with female hormones. It makes them docile and they gain weight faster at lower cost. What consequences these powerful biochemicals may have on the human male's behavior is for him to worry about if he cares to. When General Curtis E. LeMay, former Air Force Vice Chief of Staff, announced that certain new military jet planes produce sonic booms a hundred miles wide he asked the afflicted public to consider the matter stoically. "These advances," said the General, "are bound to bring a certain amount of annoyance or discomfort with them. So far as we know today, there are no technical or scientific solutions to counter this phenomenon."[6] Not everyone is dismayed by such impressive sonic progress, however, for when a military airport was recently dismantled in northern Delaware one sentimental neighbor, an eighty-year-old lady, wrote to the commanding general with regret. "With the noise of the jets I felt someone near. I want you to know how much I will miss you."

Death rays, of course, are already with us in the form of

high-frequency radio waves capable of killing at short range and of causing serious damage to living tissues at a distance of several miles. Though these wonderful facilities are already in action, investigations have only recently commenced in ten universities and research institutes to determine how we may live safely with increasingly powerful radar and microwave generators. The multiplication and wider dispersion of mankind raises the problem of how we are going to use these devices without someone's getting hurt.

Overcrowded and understaffed hospitals have become virtual disease exchange centers, where there is too good a chance that a patient may pick up something more annoying or lethal than he may have been admitted with. Under the auspices of a committee of the World Medical Association, a colloquium was held recently to consider hospital outbreaks of respiratory, intestinal, urinary, and skin infections that have been caused largely by several strains of bacteria called staphylococci. These germs are spread through the air by means of contaminated bedding and other objects as well as by direct contact between patient and hospital personnel. When the cleaning lady in a Washington hospital was asked by a nursing mother why she did not wear a gauze mask like everyone else she replied, "Them's for the doctors and the nurses. I ain't got no contaminating breath." Research scientists reported this year that remarkable strains of drug-resistant staphyloccoci have evolved by mutation right in hospitals where their human targets are dosed with antibiotics and where poor housekeeping allows the germs to survive and escape into the community.

Even the sky overhead is no longer just the wide blue yonder according to the Public Health Service, which expressed bewilderment when it discovered that high-flying air transports accumulate ice around waste-water discharge pipes. One such ice block which broke loose on a stratospheric flight crashed through the roof of a Pennsylvania home. Other heavenly cubes weighing from twenty-five to one hundred pounds have been found upon laboratory analysis to contain "domestic water," traces of soap, and paper fiber. The Civil Aeronautics Administration has thoughtfully sought to tighten regulations so that commercial planes will not discharge water in such a way as to freeze. Nothing was said publicly about what the C.A.A. thinks of discharging just plain "domestic water" into the atmosphere.

Perhaps thinking of Cape Cod and the thriving oceanside tourist business of his constituents, Senator John F. Kennedy some time ago spoke with concern before the student body of Purdue University on the subject of atomic waste disposal. It is out of Boston Harbor that drums of hot isotopes go regularly for burial at sea. "The benign and peaceful uses of atomic energy," said Senator Kennedy, "will assume a growing magnitude with an estimated fifty million gallons a year of high level waste by the time our civilian nuclear power program is well under way. . . No issue has more meaning for our daily lives . . . for the health of our children, our life expectancy, the food we eat and the very air we breath than the threat of radioactivity and strontium contamination."[7] Going halfway to meet the danger of poisoning the sea with radioactive elements, the Atomic Energy Commission recently awarded a contract calling for radioactive waste disposal in water 12,000 feet deep off the California coast—"the material to be in drums that will sink to a minimum depth of 6000 feet." After radioactive dust escaped from an English plutonium factory near Carlisle, the British Atomic Energy Authority was obliged to order farms in a 200-square-mile area around the factory to discontinue milk deliveries because soil, grass, cattle, and milk had all become polluted.

Such are a few of the consequences of mid-twentieth century living. However, the human mind remains resourceful, offering hope that there will always be compensations come what may. Mr. Anthony Montesano is engaged in one of civilization's oldest forms of pollution control. He collects garbage from eight hundred customers in the Town of Hempstead, Long Island. Recently he flabbergasted his clients by fitting fifteen trucks with special tanks and nozzles which spray a lavender scent into their freshly emptied garbage cans. The new gadgets cost $75 per truck and the aromatic chemicals cost $1000 a year but Mr. Montesano is undaunted. "We don't mind going to the extra expense," he has explained, "as long as it makes people happier with our service . . . Maybe we'll vary the smell to keep people from getting bored. Lilies today, gladioli tomorrow."[8] In addition to its floral qualities, the perfume treatment kills bacteria that produce less wholesome odors and it also repels flies.

With all the dangers that humanity is heir to, it is usually reassuring to encounter a centenarian and to learn his opinions about how he has managed to hurdle life's obstacles for so long. When Mrs. Julia Delgado Otero of Puerto Rico, aged 120, visited Jersey City with her brother Isaias Delgado, aged 110, they were subjected to the usual quiz. Replied Mrs. Otero engagingly, "Our father left us with plenty of money and we've never had to work a day in our lives."[9] Certainly that is a form of pollution which very few would object to.

CHAPTER 2

Urban Space

A CITY'S JOB

The city is the supreme expression of a people's cultural level. It is the most imaginative, costly, and substantial demonstration of what men can do together to enrich and ennoble the environment where they pass the brief years of their existence. In its organization of space and social development the city is the difference between civilized man and the cave dweller. The degree to which any society has removed itself from the race's neolithic past is reflected in the quality of the cities it has built. Art in all its other forms is the work of individuals, but a city represents the assembled insights of a whole community which has tried to construct a more sophisticated habitat than nature could provide by blind chance. An appraisal of the kinds of cities people build is an appraisal of themselves, for a city is what they do rather than a pious statement of convictions. It is the achievement of families rather than the vow of lovers. Whatever sense of greatness, regard for beauty, or zest for life a people possess in common is reflected in the ways they have arranged their immediate habitat to match their enthusiasms. Our cities—the full cross section of them—show what we are as a people.

Perhaps Chicago is the city most worthy to represent America. At least it embodies in substantial form the ample landscape and social imagination of the nation. It suffers the confusion and irritations of spatial congestion but, in the cornfields at its back door, it still has room for expansion. It has demonstrated the power to burst the stranglehold of urban decay and to look out upon its lake and prairie frontiers as another chance to do better. Chicago has the ugliness and poverty of the slums that exist in every large city, but it has also a respect for natural and civic beauty that is extraordinary. If there is anything in the tradition of American culture which its cities have almost annihilated in recent decades, it is a taste for quality in landscape. Chicago in the preserved open spaces of its parks and by reclamation of the Lake Michigan water front strongly dissents from the indifference and opportunism that have befouled the finest natural features of most urban topography.

Chicago is a factory city. It is a commercial city. In parts it is a dirty, repulsive, and corrupt city. It is also a city of good taste and refinement. It is not a city supported by government for it is not a capital. Rather, it is a city that helps mightily to support the Federal and state governments, yet retains enough vitality to survive the bleeding process and carry on. Moreover, Chicago is one of the few cities in America with a perceptive plan for the development of its space. This plan, to which the city adheres with more respect than Washington has tendered L'Enfant, was conceived a half century ago by Daniel H. Burnham, the foremost urban designer of his time. Far from being a blueprint of ephemeral stunts in steel and concrete drawn by highway engineers or a public housing authority, this plan provides ample locations for beauty and cultural activities, as well as for the mechanics of housing, working, and moving about.

Grant Park, which lies between the commercial skyline of the metropolis and the clean, wind-swept shore of Lake Michigan, is an imaginative tribute to civilized man. A generous use of both paved and green open space accents the dignity and purpose of civic architecture. Grant Park is appropriate in a city that represents a nation rich in area but which, too often, in the building of its cities has acted as though cheated in its dimensions. The Art Institute, planetarium, aquarium, Field Museum, Buckingham Fountain, and Soldiers Field are assembled as well as separated from one another in such a way that none is cramped, yet each enhances the dignity and purpose of the other. There is grandeur in the scale of any great city's architecture, much as one might quarrel with its individual form and detail. In Grant Park one sees, from almost any place he walks, the skill and magnitude of man's constructive abilities. This is because there is sufficient space for the eye to gain perspective. Along Chicago's lake front it is not necessary to go out in a boat in order to glimpse the wonder of the urban skyline. Chicago's generous use of space in Grant Park as an accent to architecture has none of the obvious overtones of a thrifty real-estate promotion that characterize New York's costly, cramped, and spatially undignified Lincoln Center, which should have been built facing the broad expanses of Central Park, had it not been conceived as a roundabout way to upgrade the value of real estate in a run-down neighborhood.

On a hot summer day when southwesterly winds blow across Chicago from the stockyards, or southerly winds carry the scent of oil refineries, the people are aware that they have neglected their back yards while attending to the front. When Queen Elizabeth, after dedication of the St. Lawrence Seaway, paid a visit to the Windy City in 1959, she complimented the people for having linked the world's oceans to the vast fertile prairies of the Middle West. The good citizens, in turn, complimented the Queen by sending in advance of her entourage a squad of perfumers who took no chance with variable winds, but sprayed all the air with the aroma of pines. This demonstration of mingled shame and attentiveness reflects a civic conscience that one day may curb pollution, the bane of all cities. Chicago is, perhaps, the American city that will best compensate a man for having abandoned the rural homestead and the plow by giving him more than he could provide for himself in isolation. From the human standpoint, if not the economic, that is the real business of any city.

The conflict between city man and rural man is as old as civilization itself. Basically it is a struggle between elements of the hermit and of the gregarious that are in each of us. The individualist holds forth more securely on his own well-fenced and independent acres. Whatever we have of social qualities, however, are more fully developed and refined by the complexities and nuances of the urban scene, where circulation is not considered trespassing. It is the nature of cities to be cosmopolitan. Whether it is better for the whole man to "go it alone" in the country or to "pull together" in the city is an unsettled argument, but, considering the trend of the times toward bigger cities and fewer farms, the days of choice are over for most of us. Whether we like it or not, we are in fact an urban-suburban society and becoming more so. It is too late to indulge in memories of an agrarian past of free range and ample open space. Rather it is time to come to grips with the only world that most of us will ever know from now on—the complex, too often disorganized world of the city and its appended suburbs. What we make of its artificially restricted area while adding more people will have much to do with making us; for man, with his remarkable capabilities for adjustment, is largely conditioned by the environment which he in turn creates.

The average American city of our time is a working city. Economically its main job is jobs. It is the people's major source of livelihood and provisioner. It is a dispenser of welfare rather than the recipient of outside assistance. States and Federal Government draw most of their revenues from cities, yet they treat their benefactors stingily. The present character and status of the city mark a distinct departure from what they were in the past. Since the dawn of history until recently, cities have been net receivers of imported wealth and beneficiaries of employment beyond their bounds. Their citizens have been privileged minorities supported by country people and foreigners. They have been the indulged child rather than the bill-paying father. The new role of major citizen and chief taxpayer makes cities poor although previously it was their tradition to be rich.

TAXES AND WELFARE

Temple cities of the ancient Nile and Indus; the monument cities of Athens and Rome; the cathedral cities of Medieval Europe; merchant cities such as Genoa, Amsterdam, New York, and Philadelphia—all these in their golden age were the recipients of revenues poured into them from the hinterlands and from abroad. They lived on fat accumulated elsewhere by others. With this surplus wealth, more often donated by men of means than collected by popular subscription, there were built the imposing public edifices, the boulevards, the parks, museums, churches, libraries, stadia, universities, and other shrines that gave those who lived in cities a sense of privilege. Then it was that a country hick dreamed of urban splendor rather than, as now, a city drone dreams of getting away from it all around a barbecue pit in a suburban development. The degrading change in the quality of the city and public taste has come with the city's change in function and, particularly, with its new underprivileged financial status as payer of tribute rather than recipient. Instead of being the ceremonial, administrative, mercantile, and cultural center of a broad region, the city has too often deteriorated to little more than a taxpaying workshop.

About 1920 America ceased to be a nation primarily of farmers and small townsmen. It was then that the city people came into the majority for the first time. Only a few years previously the Federal Government had discovered the income tax, which at first it treated gingerly. These two events are related in their influence upon the city as a place to live. Increasing populations filled in the vacant lots where children, and at times their parents, played. Urban congestion was accompanied by new welfare responsibilities. A declining rural population, which resulted from technological advancements in agriculture, meant that the farm would no longer support the city. Instead, by soil bank and parity payments, the city eventually would support the farm. The urban underprivileged, who formerly took to rural homesteading or migrant labor in agricultural areas, could no longer look to the countryside in extremity. The hinterlands themselves were sending their castoffs to the city. While the city lost its point of vantage on the economic seesaw, it also forfeited to the states and Federal Government the future's richest source of tax revenue.

In 1932 cities collected more taxes than the states or Federal Government. Even more significantly, the cities spent that money to provide services and to create a better physical environment for their inhabitants. Now, only a few decades later, cities are low man on the fiscal totem pole. Though poorest paid at the tax till they have the same obligations and more, but they cannot meet them as well. In 1932, incredible as it seems, all cities lumped together collected 2.6 billions in taxes. All states as a group collected 2.3 billions. The Federal Government, with beginner's modesty, assessed its citizens for only 2.0 billions. By 1955, only twenty-three years later, the order had been reversed. Inflation had set in, and the cost of government at all levels indicated that people no longer had to worry about how to dispose of their incomes. The bureaucrats, without much solicitude, were doing the job for them. Cities taxed them 11 billions. States collected 20 billions, and the Federal Government skimped along on 73 billions, while entertaining dreams of more. The sum of these taxes, collected in that one year, would have bought all the farm land and farm buildings in the United States, which the Bureau of the Census then appraised at 98.8 billion dollars.

The numbers of dollars collected by all levels of government are important, but even more so is the new order of priority. While city people pay most of the state and Federal taxes, the city itself no longer is master of its own fiscal destiny. Nevertheless, the habit of expectations has outlived the habit of income and the city is still relied upon to provide the most in education, charity, transportation facilities, police and fire protection, water supply, sewage disposal, cultural development, parks, and recreation. No wonder the city, which has the poorest resources, has recently failed to do its job as well as it did when it was chief tax collector. It is not surprising that the social quality of urban life has sunk to an all-time low, driving millions into suburbs where they hope to get something respectable for their money.

At the heart of the city's plight is the fact that most of its income is traditionally derived from property taxes, and many states will not grant permission to switch to a less abusive practice. Essentially the overworked real-estate tax is a levy against the city's own physical body. Every time the tax rate is raised the city further penalizes the very space and substance of its own existence. Boston now levies an annual tax against real estate which is over ten per cent of its appraised value. If a Bostonian were to own a house for fifty years, he would pay the city more than five times its appraised worth for the privilege of having built within the city limits. It is no wonder that new buildings erected by private enterprise without special tax concessions are a rarity in the hub of New England, and that old structures wear a shabbier face than they might otherwise, were they not fearful of attracting the assessor's wandering eye.

High property taxes encourage owners to neglect the appearance of their buildings in order to reduce appraised values. To assure reasonable returns on investments, the builders of new structures approve only the most utilitarian construction. The reservation of space for recreation, landscaping, and car storage is discouraged. Embellishments and architectural finesse that would enhance are eliminated, for these desirable qualities add nothing to function but they increase assessed valuations. The age of elegance in American architecture for all but tax-exempt properties is almost extinct, except when style serves some advertising purpose. Old dwelling units are allowed to deteriorate more rapidly than necessary. Painting may be deliberately postponed. A hang-dog look is a safe look. As long as tenements remain habitable the poor, who cannot afford the luxury of good appearances, will crowd into small quarters if it means paying less rent per capita. Thus by closer packing of more tenants into the same old space, total income from a property may be maintained even while the tax rate climbs. This is sound business as dictated by the rules of assessment, but it is ruinous to the city which would like to provide public services and still look as though it were the home of cultured human beings.

Landowners are blamed for slum conditions, but in reality the city sets the stage and writes the script by placing the main burden of its own expenses upon property. Assessments against property accounted for 73 per cent of all tax revenues collected by cities in 1955. Another unpleasant consequence of loading the major burden of city expenses upon real estate is overbuilding on private land. Open space, which costs the city nothing in services but which would add much to the charm of any structure, becomes a conspicuous waste to the eye of an investor when the tax assessor penalizes it as heavily as though it supported a building and demanded services. Good architecture is enhanced by good landscaping, but cities discourage the idea by their short-sighted onslaught against open space. An investor who would contribute to the charm of his city by embellishing his buildings with landscaped gardens, lawns, and playgrounds does so at his own peril, for his thanks are a tax bill without compensating income. The unimaginative, congested ugliness of many neighborhoods may be attributed directly to the city's own tax policies. To discourage congestion, the practice of tax abatement on new developments should be reserved solely for non-remunerative space, such as parks and playgrounds that are dedicated in a binding way to the use of the tenants.

Twenty-seven per cent of Manhattan's inhabitants do not live in apartments, private homes or fashionable hotels, but rather hole up in stuffy, often squalid rooming houses. Usually these structures are dilapidated single-family homes or outmoded apartments, no longer in suitable neighborhoods or in fit condition to attract the kind of tenant for which they were first designed. The temporary State Commission on Rent and Rental Conditions estimates that ten to twelve times as many persons pack themselves into these places as they were built to accommodate. Yet New York, as well as the majority of other large cities, can do relatively nothing to stop crowding. While this is a social disgrace it is also fiscal lunacy. The simple arithmetic of space and populations should convince any controller or board of estimate that a city that relies on property taxes cannot collect enough from overloaded buildings to pay for the services required by their inhabitants. This, in part, is the crux of big-city financial chaos. The benefits a city derives from taxes on industrial and commercial properties are more than absorbed by services to the tenants of overcrowded residential buildings.

On an inspection trip to Manhattan's upper West Side a couple of years ago, Mrs. Bernice P. Rogers, former Deputy Commissioner of the Department of Buildings, visited what had been an elegant nine-story edifice containing 72 apartments. Only two decades earlier this beautiful structure, located on Riverside Drive and embellished with a marble-floored lobby, had been part of one of the most exclusive neighborhoods in America. Opened up to slum dwellers under the pressures of rent control, it had been converted legally to 301 separately rented rooms and 58 apartments. Inspectors estimated that perhaps 1500 people lived there, most of them Negroes and Puerto Ricans, who paid from $7 to $17.50 weekly for a single room. A six-year resident said that fights, marijuana smoking, dope needling and prostitution were rampant on Saturday nights. Occupying one seven-room apartment were seventeen persons who shared a single bath and kitchen. One room was occupied by a pregnant Negro mother and her four small children. For this she paid $15 weekly out of a $68 biweekly welfare check.

Upon observing these details, Mrs. Rogers expressed shock, noting that, however legal this type of living might be, it was wrong ethically, socially, and morally. She indicated that she might recommend a plan to eliminate family occupancy of single rooms within three years, but there were statistics to show that the trend is increasing faster than any measures to the contrary. The plain fact is that this is the only kind of shelter that most slum tenants can afford. It is a matter of population pressure and economics rather than city ordinances.

In February, 1960, Mayor Robert Wagner signed into law several bills that prohibit families with children under sixteen from moving into single rooms if they do not have separate bathroom and kitchen facilities. After 1965 it will be illegal for such families to remain in rooms that do not meet the minimum specifications. To help promote better living conditions, Mayor Wagner has announced that the City of New York through its Housing Authority will, if necessary, buy the single-room tenements and restore them to their original use as apartment buildings. Limitations in the budget, however, will permit this reclamation work to be of a token nature only. At the time of the Mayor's announcement there were 755 such buildings occupied by an estimated 47,000 families. In addition there were 14,000 former one- and two-family houses in which single rooms were now rented out separately to an unknown number of families. Even if the program envisaged by the Mayor proceeds without a hitch and no further deterioration is permitted, the up-hill job of reclamation of slum structures will take a long time. Spokesmen have guessed that the city could restore two dozen buildings and rehabilitate 1300 families each year. At that rate, if the city has to do the job alone, it could take fifty to one hundred years just to wipe out the present backlog.

Added to the budget-wrecking squeeze of more people into restricted space in the expanding slums is the tendency for persons of moderate and even higher incomes to adjust to smaller quarters in better neighborhoods. From the windows of Gracie Mansion, the home of New York's chief executive, it is possible for the Mayor, and those who come to consult with him, to look down the side streets off fashionable East End Avenue and see what is happening in a choice location. Apartment buildings only forty to sixty years old are having their insides ripped out and their faces lifted. Every interior partition is removed while more numerous new ones are put back in. The old plumbing, sufficient for a few families, is replaced with truckloads of glistening new porcelain and chrome fixtures. Fire escapes are hung on outside walls over the sidewalks to eliminate interior stairways and thus save space. The object is to break up the former large apartments into what are euphemistically called "modern efficiencies." These middle-class hutches consist of one all-purpose room which serves as living, sleeping, and kitchen quarters. The undersized bathroom is the only nook of privacy. Because the location is a "good" address the rents for these cubicles average $125 per month. Buildings which once had sixteen rental units now have two to three times as many. A builder could offer more space for this money but tax policy discourages it. Most of the made-over apartments are constructed for fast depreciation and the capital-gains tax route.

It should long ago have been obvious to city officials, but apparently it was not, that when citizens of all income brackets tend to squeeze into smaller and smaller quarters, the per capita revenue base shrinks while service obligations increase. When less and less building room is used to house more people, the property tax itself is defeated as a means of supporting cities. In suburbs the use of house trailers, which are not-so-mobile homes, tends to depress community finances in the same way. The circumvention of the property levy by overcrowding is, of course, the underlying cause of the proliferation of new taxes on retail sales, restaurant meals, hotel bills, electric bills, water bills, taxi rides, amusements, business permits, and of all the other assessments that make living more expensive in cities, and hastens the departure to the suburbs of those who still want space and the privilege of spending their own money.

No city that is not subsidized in some unique way can eliminate slum living if it allows people to double up without sensible restrictions. Moreover, from the viewpoint of the community as a whole, the main problem is not the plight of the slum dwellers, pitiful as that may be. What could cripple a city beyond recuperation would be too many indigent people who could not afford serious taxation and who would therefore seek to escape proportional assessment by huddling in human sties. Others who can afford to pay their share could be expected to grow weary of added burdens and to become suburbanites. The city not only fails to collect a proper service charge from its submarginal inhabitants, but it uses funds collected from other citizens to defray the welfare expenses that slums demand if their inhabitants are not to revert to a jungle code. The rising costs of welfare prevent a city from giving to its more able taxpayers the high quality of services, recreational facilities, and cultural amenities that they have a right to expect. When a city does not reserve and develop public space to give quality and dignity to its public life as a compensation for the congested nature of private living, then it further loses appeal as a place to live, even though it retains its importance as a place to work. This is, of course, the reason many in the upper brackets move out of town. They become fed up with subsidizing others while being shortchanged themselves. This leaves the city in an even worse predicament.

One raw gray day toward the end of winter in 1959, three hundred outraged homeowners from Queens and Brooklyn descended upon the New York City Hall to complain about increased assessments upon their spacious one- and two-family houses. One of the protestants, an attractive young woman, relied upon anger to warm her, for she was attired only in a bathing suit. She declared she would be forced to live in a barrel if the "tax squeeze" should strip her of her home. Another member of the distraught company exclaimed, "I can't pay taxes on such a high boost. I'm just going to have to move out of the city."[1] There was more than a casual relationship between the plight of these rugged individualists and the rapid increase of tax-abated and tax-exempt housing, which had grown from 2.2 per cent of all New York dwelling units in 1949 to 9.2 per cent a decade later. Subsidized housing which is wholly or partially exempt from local assessments does not really help the whole community. It does not even help the average slum dweller, for usually he cannot afford to live there. As for the home-owning taxpayer, it puts another load on his already over-burdened back. New tax-abated, commercial housing nevertheless is on the increase, particularly in the largest cities. The burden of this subsidy falls upon the owners of older and more spacious housing.

There is now a billion dollars' worth of tax-exempt construction in Philadelphia alone, much of it belonging to state and Federal Governments which ought to pay the same as any other business for city services. A billion dollars is twenty-five per cent of the total property values in the City of Brotherly Love. More than half the real estate in Washington, D.C., is tax exempt, with the Federal Government accounting for the major portion of this privilege. So much of downtown Washington has degenerated that private investors and developers regard the central business district east of 14th Street as taboo, even though it is bordered on the south by Pennsylvania Avenue, the main thoroughfare between Capitol Hill and the White House. This is the "other half" of what Robert H. Levi, President of the Hecht Company, calls downtown Washington's "split personality." Only the prestige and beauty of the White House and its immediate environs have saved the area west of 14th Street from a similar fate.

The Greater Boston Economic Study Committee concluded, after a recent $200,000 analysis of business conditions, that a significant number of merchants preferred the central area of the city to outlying areas. But countering this preference were rising taxes and the obsolescence of buildings. The study found that the return from private real-estate investment in Boston was less than in any other major city in the eastern United States. Except for privately financed River House and tax-abated housing projects, no new apartment building of impressive size had been constructed in Boston proper in the past thirty years. Considering the heavy levies against private property, it is no wonder that individuals and corporations are afraid to invest in conventional new construction without tax concessions. It is their cautious custom to convert old single-family houses into apartments. In this way they get by with low assessments on the old shells. The result is that the able-to-pay renter with a respectable income, who cannot qualify for public housing, takes the warmed-over quarters with nineteenth-century exteriors, while subsidized tenants move into the newest accommodations.

The whole concept of urban welfare services and of which level of government should assume the major responsibility needs overhauling, if the American city is not to become a combination hovel and tax-abated housing project with all the institutionalized drabness that distinguishes such construction. A few decades ago, when cities were the nation's major collectors of revenue, it was proper for them to carry the heavier welfare load. In those days, before high Federal taxes and easy-credit mortgages, it was not unreasonable for private homeowners, who were then truly affluent, to assume a certain social obligation. Today, thanks to G.I. and F.H.A. insured mortgages, "ownership" of a home or commercial rental property is but a thin veil of modesty hiding an all too naked long-term loan. Sometimes it reflects no more than a reasonable credit rating earned by meeting payments on the family car and hi-fi. Today's "parties-of-the-second-part" are but temporary custodians who for twenty to forty years escape foreclosure by keeping one month ahead on payments of principal, interest, and taxes. It is a common jest among realtors that they no longer deal in properties, but rather in the transfers of legal paper. The nominal buyers of private homes seldom expect to pay off the mortgages or they would read the fine print. Being financially unable really to buy their own dwellings, modern householders are scarcely in a position to carry the welfare burden of others.

THE FEDERAL POSITION

The costs of schools, welfare, and public hospitalization dominate city budgets. Any upgrading of other services or amenities which would make the city more attractive to persons of all ages and interests would have to begin with a sizable cut in the city's share of these "big three." In view of the now well-recognized mobility of the American people—one out of five of whom changes his residence every year—it is apparent that cities, out of sheer habit and old custom, are floundering with problems of national scope and Federal responsibility. For instance New York City spends $50,000,000 annually on "mainly remedial" programs for its Puerto Rican newcomers. That is more than the city spent on all its parks, libraries, zoos, and museums in 1959. This is an example of how a growing welfare obligation has undermined a city's cultural functions. The City Administration anticipates that at least one of every two babies born in Puerto Rico during the next generation will settle on the mainland during its lifetime. The majority seem destined for the New York metropolitan area, which already has 650,000 islanders. While by far the majority of these newcomers make their own way without assistance, their welfare rate is two and one half times that of the city as a whole. School costs for Spanish-speaking students are two to three times the average because of necessary special services that are not simply linguistic.

Whereas 85 per cent of the Puerto Ricans who transferred to mainland areas in 1950 went to New York, now only about 65 per cent go there; so that other cities are beginning to share the experience. Negroes, too, are shifting to cities in great numbers from southern farms where they have been displaced by technological advancements in agriculture. Since 1930 a half-million persons from Puerto Rico and the South have migrated to Philadelphia, where Judge Adrian Bonnelly of the Municipal Court identifies this influx with the city's notorious juvenile-delinquency problem. Judge Bonnelly has noted that between 1930 and 1953 the number of white children seven to fifteen years of age has increased 2.9 per cent, while the number of non-white children of equal ages has increased 89 per cent.[2] Seventy per cent of New York City's welfare budget is expended on non-whites, who make up 12 per cent of its total population. While the cities are gaining more Negro D.P.'s who need a higher rate of welfare assistance, self-sufficient whites in larger numbers are moving to the suburbs. Newark, New Jersey, after a recent study of its population changes, discovered that though there was almost no difference in the total number of its inhabitants, Negroes had increased 109 per cent while the proportion of Whites had been reduced 27 per cent in eight years. The increased financial burdens which fall upon cities as a result of these national adjustments are more properly a Federal responsibility, for they are manifestations of change throughout the whole economy and social order rather than the consequence of any city's independent internal policy.

In older, more crowded cities which have been abandoned in substantial numbers by persons with higher incomes and better educations, the trend is toward greater expenses for welfare and less for education. The misfortune of today's city is that the burden of caring for adult misfortune undermines preparation of the young for a better tomorrow. The 1960 budget for Washington, D.C., allotted 26 per cent of all funds to public health and welfare as compared with 24 per cent for education. New York City, in its 1959-60 budget, assigned 23 per cent to public hospitalization, health, and welfare but only 20 per cent to education. The average expenditure for education by all local governments in the United States was 44 per cent of their total budgets in 1955. This was approximately twice the rate that could be spared by the nation's capital and its largest metropolis. Obviously the more important cities are losing ground as desirable training grounds for the young, unless their parents can afford the tuition of private schools.

On the other hand it would seem that the big city has become well established as the nation's favorite charitable institution. In 1955 the average expenditures for public hospitalization, health, and welfare by all municipalities, both small and large, were only 17 per cent of their total budgets, while Washington and New York carried loads that were approximately 50 per cent higher. In 1955, when the Bureau of the Census compared Federal with state and local contributions to civilian welfare and hospitalization, it was found that the Federal Government bravely shouldered 18 per cent of the total burden and most of that was spent on military and veterans' care. In that same year the Federal Government paid 6 per cent of all public-education expenses while local governments paid 79 per cent and states contributed 15 per cent. In 1960, the entire proposed outlay for aid to the nation's education in the Federal budget was 50 millions less than that voted by the single city of New York.

Unless it soon receives a larger share of Federal revenues to ease the crush of education and welfare costs, the city is doomed to continued mediocrity in its other public services. Speaking before the House Ways and Means Committee, economist Wilbur J. Cohen of the University of Michigan noted that, even including its generous military and veterans' hospitalization programs, the Federal Government pays but 14 per cent of the nation's six-billion-dollar annual hospital bill, while 30 per cent is paid by cities and states. Twenty-eight per cent is paid by insurance and the balance by cash customers, charities, and others. As Mr. Cohen emphasized, 44 per cent of the nation's hospital bill is now publicly assumed although it is commonly thought that people are paying their own way. Actually it would seem that about half the citizens take care of themselves and the other half as well, particularly in cities. In Worcester, Massachusetts, eight per cent of the city's 1958 budget was allocated to defray the costs of charity hospitalization at its City Hospital. Worcester has a tax rate of over $70 per thousand and cannot afford a municipal trash-collection service.

There is no need for and no desire that the Federal Government involve itself in the actual supervision and management of urban affairs beyond reasonable financial assistance.

Carried to its extreme Federal welfare can be a bore, according to the 23,000 residents of Richland, Washington, who for fifteen years lived a sheltered existence in government houses on government land under the benevolent patronage of a Federal cost-plus contract between General Electric and the Atomic Energy Commission. The Richland community, eleventh largest in the state, paid no taxes and was untroubled by slums or parking meters. It had 9 schools, 28 churches, a hospital, a library, and a shopping center. Its municipal employees were the envy of all city clerks because they were paid according to Federal scales at rates 30 to 40 per cent higher than in nearby towns. Richland was bond free because its full set of public buildings had been generously paid for out of Federal coffers. Sewers, streets, and water works cost the people nothing. Apartments with three bedrooms could be rented for $35 monthly and detached homes, equally large, for $65. But it was all too soft and the people were unhappy. They dreamed of normal tensions, stresses, and uncertainties and wished they could share them. They were determined to get out from under the protective wing and fly on their own. They bought 4800 of the 5400 government houses as soon as they were offered for sale. Then the inhabitants incorporated themselves as a normal town with the privilege of taxation, knowing that even the first year's assessments would fall short of a drafted $2,500,000 budget. As one resident exclaimed on their day of freedom, "We always looked forward to self-government. We thought American citizens had a right to make their own mistakes."[3] The Richlanders were tired of having them made for them.

United States Senator Styles Bridges of New Hampshire knows what it means to a state when people leave the farm to settle in the city. This is a trend that started in his home territory a century ago with the coming of big industry to Manchester and other cities on the Merrimack. In the Granite State in 1850 more than half the people were farmers. A century later only about one sixth made a living at agriculture. Now the rural exodus is nationwide and there is no place for a surplus plowman but the city. It is not the progressive farmer with the most land and best machinery who is abandoning agriculture, but rather the technological casualty whose small homestead and obsolete equipment have put him behind the economic eight ball.

Representing a state with a dwindling farm population, it is understandable that Senator Bridges supports the urban viewpoint. While reviewing a recent Federal budget request for the Department of Agriculture's program, he noticed that the decline in number of farms was curiously paralleled by a substantial increase in public funds spent to support the remainder. He was shocked to discover that, on the average, every surviving farm in the United States got a $1000 Federal subsidy in cash and services during the fiscal year that began July 1, 1957. Thomas R. Reid, civic affairs director of the Ford Motor Company and vice president of the American Council to Improve our Neighborhoods, informed the 1959 National Assembly of Mayors, "While we have a million more slum dwellers than we have farm dwellers, the allocation of Federal expenditures is $3000 per farm family and only $84 per urban slum family."[4]

There are some farms which have received more in Federal aid over the years than their operators paid for them in the first place. There are others, recently acquired, whose new owners have ten-year soil-bank contracts that will cover their purchase price provided they do *not* use them for agriculture during that time. According to the 1954 census, all farms in the United States were worth 98.8 billion dollars. Agriculture Department programs for the six years 1955-60 totaled nearly 31 billion dollars. At that rate, using only its agricultural budget for nineteen years, the Federal Government could buy outright every farm in the United States.

The implications for urban man are obvious. Not only has he helped to finance the extinction of the small farmer by subsidizing those who froze him out of business with their new equipment, but small farmers, particularly former Negro tenants and Puerto Ricans, have piled into the cities, where they gravitate to old slums or create new ones. The agricultural economy, by startling modernization of methods in postwar years, has eliminated most of its former unskilled deadwood. Former tenant houses have been torn down or turned into hay sheds. Their inmates, in search of living space and not blessed with factory skills, have doubled up with urban friends and relatives or just doubled up. Approximately sixty per cent of the 600 Negroes who move into Philadelphia every month are unskilled D.P.'s from southern farms. It may seem a trifle incongruous to the old-time city resident that the Federal Government should spend liberally for the benefit of successful farmers, while his own city has to assume the burden of servicing the technologically displaced rural refugee who obviously cannot be turned out to pasture like an old mule.

It is apparent that either the Federal Government must shoulder a major share of the city's welfare expenses or the city must be allowed to dip directly into the deeper wells from which flow the copious Federal revenues. The property tax and the sales tax, which are penalties against the very structure and business of cities, have been overplayed. The assorted clip and chisel taxes, that take annoying bites out of commercial activities and put the city entrepreneur at a competitive disadvantage with his suburban counterpart, must be eased or the city will lose some of the businesses that help to defray the deficits of residential neighborhoods. Not only have the taxes of cities continued to proliferate and increase, but in the ten years 1950-59, during which the Federal debt increased 12 per cent, the debts of cities and states made a wild leap of 200 per cent. While the Federal budget rose 13 per cent since 1954, city budgets climbed four times faster. There can be no really effective organization of urban space or sensible city planning for the future until the city is relieved of its welfare load and can offer the kinds of tax inducements that would stimulate sound land use.

SPACE FOR LIFE

The flight of the better-paid middle class and its dependents to homes in suburbia has created a whole series of human and economic complications that cities dread to face. Until they do, there is little hope that they can regain either their status or function as the finest form of social organization and the best environment for people of all ages and economic status. The very key to satisfactory city organization is concentration without congestion. Despite popular belief, the two are not naturally wedded. Dense populations and cluttered space only seem to go together because of the ineptitude of the usual management of urban space. The concentration of many people within a restricted area calls for a superior arrangement of that space, but it is fully possible. Given a high degree of order and wise allocation of land to proper uses, it is theoretically possible to service large numbers of people more economically and more pleasantly in cities than in any other type of community. On the homely level of garbage collection, it is easier to get on with the job at a tall apartment building, where one stop may fill a truck, than in a suburb where a crew might have to start and stop over a two-mile route to pick up an equal load.

The same principle applies to public transportation. Buses, subways, and taxis that are well patronized at all hours can offer more frequent and economical service than if there were fewer riders scattered over a wider area. Mass pressure is the essence of a city's commercial vigor and the most vital force in its cultural alertness. In theory the greater the demand the better the service should be. But the thesis that many patrons make a better product, which works so well in private business, seems to collapse in the public administration of city services. Thousands of persons within a single skyscraper may be moved by high-speed elevators from upper stories to ground level in a matter of minutes, but public streets become a chaos when subjected to rush-hour traffic. There are no crosscurrents in an elevator system. It is an express, limited-access proposition.

As a community, we seem unwilling to solve the space puzzle of horizontal communication as neatly as private enterprise solves vertical communication in a department store or office building. Yet, from the standpoint of space design, one problem is not more difficult than the other. Railroads with their single-purpose rights-of-way illustrate the basic simplicity of the solution, which street and highway departments persistently ignore in their compromises. What railroad, for instance, would think of parking freight cars on even a little-used right-of-way? Within a skyscraper there is no compromise with efficiency in the organization of space. Within the city compromise is the rule so that inefficiency predominates. Urban space is seldom allocated with the needs of people guiding the minds of engineers and bureaucrats. Instead a few obvious issues such as the accommodation of automobiles and the zoning of land according to the influence of self-interested groups take precedence. The basic purpose of the city as an environment gets lost in the shuffle.

Most cities are not well arranged for the daily needs of their inhabitants. The jobs of working adults are usually performed at a considerable distance from the home because neighborhoods near places of employment are either so blighted or expensive that families choose to live elsewhere. The wage earners of a family must often spend an unreasonable amount of time, money, and nervous energy just going to and from work, although they might prefer to devote these assets to more pleasant pursuits. As the employment trend is toward more working mothers, the cohesion of family groups is unnecessarily strained due to this space gap between work and home. The extra motion lost in travel not only reduces the individual's purse and leisure but it forces the community to spend more on streets and accommodations for vehicles than would otherwise be necessary. The public and private extravagance which results where residential districts are widely separated from places of mass employment is appalling in view of the fact that neither cities nor the majority of citizens are so rich that they do not feel pinched.

Children and the aged seem out of place in cities or at least there do not seem to be places suitable to the needs of these members of society. In the allocation of public space and in the construction of public buildings, the needs of youth and the retired are slighted in favor of streets, bridges, tunnels, or parking lots. To be sure, schools are built but often with too much money and too little imagination. It would seem as though it were urban gospel that books and academic lessons are the only educational ingredients essential to the growth of a child's mind, body, and spirit; and that school buildings could serve no other function than those decreed by teachers. No institution has been given more money with less intelligent understanding of its inherent limitations than the public school, which is not worthy of a monopoly in the field of youth development. Most urbanites have yet to learn what farmers have always known—that even a well-schooled child may be an underprivileged, even delinquent child. Formal instruction and athletic events, in which few are players and most are watchers, are only parts of a child's needs in growing up. The Greek adage of a sound mind in a healthy body seems to have been half forgotten.

The young and old, for whom the city is poorly designed, are opposite ends of the human spectrum, but in some ways they are complementary to one another. They live in forced dependency, tied to the middle-aged breadwinners by economic necessity, inexperience, or infirmity. This "benched" status has not always been the fate of grandparents or their grandchildren. Even now in rural communities, and particularly in more primitive parts of the world, the closest bond is between the oldest and youngest members of the family who have their own responsibilities and active functions which frequently are shared. This relationship is both practical and emotionally sound, for it is the venerable ancients who instruct the young in the knowledge and techniques that come from experience. It is the job of grandparents who have leisure to train their grandchildren in the rich lore of nature and the hearth so that the young may become early apprentices to their working parents. Such an arrangement develops insight and ability in youth while it fosters dignity and self-respect in the aged. In our fast changing urban world, which honors none but the wage-spending employed, there is little of value that an old man can teach a fledgling about how to live or make a living, when it is all too apparent that he himself is outmoded and superfluous. Far from being valued for his wisdom, he is commonly despised for being out-of-date and "in the way." While workmen have their unions, employers their clubs, parents and teachers their associations, and animals their humane societies, all of which plead their causes effectively, the organizations for the prevention of neglect and cruelty to children and the aged are not as influential as they should be. The cruelty most often suffered by the young and old is the cruelty of civic oversight which slights their simple but fundamental needs for recreation, activity, and respect. The proportion of children and the aged in the population is growing and it behooves the city, in planning the organization of its space, to take cognizance of these human needs. Otherwise, the able aged will leave the city with their savings and pensions while the indigent aged will stay on. Families who can afford cultural opportunities for their children will locate in the suburbs, while the underprivileged will give the city the job of rehabilitating the youth it should have accommodated before it got into trouble.

Roughly one fourth to one third of the area of residential districts is devoted to streets, while children and old folks may have no recreation grounds near their dwellings which are suited to their separate needs. These persons seldom have cars. They are not wage earners and they may be disqualified on the basis of youth or infirmity. If they cannot walk to a recreation area, many may not go at all. A place to play and exercise or just to congregate and talk must be close at hand, preferably within the block, if it is to be of genuine daily value to either young or old. Anyone familiar with the elementary psychology of neighborhoods knows that people living near a recreation area are possessive about it and strangers are cold-shouldered. Among juveniles the invasion of another's "turf," even if it is no more than a paved street, may be cause for fighting or worse. Old people are clannish and seldom enjoy the association of strangers as much as gossip with old acquaintances. The retired gentleman who occupies a park bench outside his own bailiwick senses that he is a stranger among the local crowd. The allotment of so much space to the automobile and so little to human beings in the places where people live is civic folly and quite unnecessary even from the standpoint of traffic engineering.

There is no more valid excuse for leaving an idle car parked in a public street than for setting up one's living-room furniture on the public sidewalk. There is no justification for making cross-town traffic lanes out of streets in residential neighborhoods when their principal purpose is purely to provide access for local services. The very idea of an all-purpose street in the residential districts of a modern city is a violation of human dignity and need. If parking were banned except for pickup and delivery and if traffic in residential areas were limited to local services, the streets could be made half their present widths. All other street space could be devoted to recreation areas and walks. Parking of private cars should be allowed only in private, public, or commercial off-street facilities. No new or renovated apartment building should be licensed without the provision of recreational space which in turn should be tax exempt, since such space performs a public service.

West Bagdad is a fringe settlement twenty minutes from the center of Iraq's capital city. There a housing authority, financed by the oil royalties of foreign companies, is constructing a new type of residential district based on respect for those close relationships which the Arab herdsman knew in his ancestral desert home. The central idea behind the arrangement of the new community is as old as human society, but its translation into a design for urban housing is the product of a Greek engineering company, Doxiadis Associates, which noted that the Arab often mourns for his traditional way of life when he moves to the city. He misses evening talk in the square of his former village or around the tribal campfire. In the new residential districts planned by Doxiadis Associates, this gregarious habit is respected by assembling groups of ten to fifteen small attached houses along private pedestrian pathways. At the end of these walks are small sheltered "gossip squares" with benches and simple ornamental shrubbery. Neighboring adults congregate in these social oases for casual conversation, shielded from noises of traffic and the play of children. The whole concept has met with enthusiastic response, there being 30,000 applicants for the first 2000 houses.

Considerable thought has been given to public parks in cities, but the neighborhood play yard for children which would need no paid police has been almost forgotten. There is a time when neighborhoods are new that vacant lots offer this facility, but vacant lots are taxed private investments and do not remain undeveloped forever. Every residential block in apartment-house neighborhoods should have a public lot set aside for athletic and social activities, which are as essential to child development as any academic assignment. Girls should be given as much consideration as boys in the allocation of space for their activities. Much over-organized, adult-directed juvenile recreation activity, often confined to indoor quarters, could be dispensed with if only children were given places where they could freely behave like children rather than be subjects for professional case-workers on city and charity payrolls. When such an idea for the use of a particular open space was proposed to one sidewalk philosopher his comment was, "To hell with more free ground. Let's get development and revenue out of it!" Perhaps most of the taxpaying public believes that reservations of open space for recreation are a waste of revenue-paying ground. The opposite concept is not quickly grasped: that if more homes or apartments were built on that same land there would automatically be more people to demand services. High as they are, taxes do not keep up with the costs of service to the taxpayer; otherwise cities would not increase their bonded debts so alarmingly. Open space used for recreation does not demand city services. Instead it renders service to the city.

City streets and a few remaining vacant lots figure conspicuously in the summer recreation program for children in New York and other metropolises, where not every family vacations at the beach or a mountain lake. For thousands of tenement youngsters fire hydrants, turned to throw a brisk spray, substitute for pools and surf on the hottest days. That children will respond to even the grimiest opportunity was demonstrated by a group of Harlem youngsters who eagerly cleared a narrow twenty-foot vacant lot of accumulated rubbish and planted it with petunias, spiderworts, pansies, and morning glories. When finished they set it off with a makeshift fence to protect their proud effort. The project evoked so much enthusiasm that the children formed an association of a hundred members nine to fourteen years of age just to keep the whole block clean and in harmony with their garden. During a recent summer two hundred children, working in eight "miracle gardens" that were once litter-strewn vacant lots, raised enough vegetables to hold a "farmers' market" on the steps of City Hall. There Mayor Wagner stimulated the day's trading and lent his prestige to the enterprise by making the first purchase of a handsome pumpkin.

So crucial has the issue of play space become in New York that, when the Department of Parks proposed to spend $1,300,000 to restore an ornate Civil War monument, one irate veteran of World War II raised a howl. State Assembly-man Bentley Kassal proposed that, instead of patching up that crumbling heap of stone, a living monument in the form of a public playground should be established on the same site. In an appeal that city fathers eyed skeptically, Veteran Kassal observed, "This section of the West Side is ideal for a playground and band shell. The need of the community for such facilities is obvious. The shortages of playgrounds in New York is appalling."[5] He might have added that the money saved could have revived a whole series of recrea-tional benefits to children which the city formerly supported, but now has abandoned.

After a span of nearly seventy years, during which it was open every day of the week, the Metropolitan Museum of Art went on a six-day week in 1959 for lack of $63,000 to hire guards. Now the New York Botanical Gardens and Bronx Zoo are considering the same drastic step. The Brook-lyn Museum has closed its fourth floor to all patrons at all times for lack of custodial funds, and the Museum of the City of New York has closed its fifth floor for the same reason. The Museum of Natural History, which among children is one of the most popular institutions in the city, received in one half-year period 5000 requests from schools for classes to be guided through the building. Because of shortages in the museum's budget only 1300 of the requests were honored. City libraries, which during the depression of the Thirties were open from nine to nine, now close before supper. A letter from a third-grade pupil to Mayor Wagner indicated how the younger generation feels about having its amenities curtailed. "Dear Mayor Wagner," he wrote, "I know yore busy with problems far bigger than this one, but I am writing anyway. I love to read and I love to go to the library. I get home from school at 4:15 and if I want to go to the library, they are always closed . . . Could you please have the hours changed?"[6] The total appropriations requested of New York City for parks, libraries, museums, zoos, aquarium, and allied cultural facilities were 2.4 per cent of the 1960–61 budget, while welfare demands were 21.4 per cent. It is apparent that by assuming a Federal responsibility in caring for the indigent the city has run itself into the ground as far as its legitimate obligations to all its citizens are concerned.

The outlook of some adults in a position to guide civic policy is at times wondrous to behold. During a recent surge of juvenile crime in New York, one figure, prominent in the city's school affairs, was asked what might be done to curb delinquency. The thoughtful conclusion of this custodian of the youthful mind was that there would be improvement if parking lots were provided for the cars of teachers. While more penetrating suggestions were hung up in committee hearings, that incredible solution of an eminent scholar received positive action by the Board of Education, which some months later announced it would consider teacher car parking on school playgrounds. Public School 113, in a slum neighborhood already short of recreational space, was chosen as a pilot project. It was decided that the play yard used by 1150 pupils from kindergarten through sixth grade should be reduced by more than twenty-five per cent with a fence and gate in order to accommodate the cars of ten teachers.

When the New York *Times* editorialized, "There is something wrong with our sense of values when a school playground, especially in a congested area, is to have a space 80 feet by 45 chopped out of it for parking,"[7] the chairman of the incongruously entitled "Education Section, Citizens' Committee for Children of New York City, Inc.," hastily rebutted. She contended that it was essential to use playgrounds for parking in order to recruit and hold capable teachers. Evidently the good lady detected no touch of irony in her plea that school yards in overbuilt slums should be converted to parking lots for commuting teachers, whose own children lived in more spacious suburbs or more privileged neighborhoods. She declared, "Most teachers are in the middle-income group, for which there is a severe housing shortage in New York City. Many for their families' sake live in suburban communities or in outlying sections of the city."[3] According to this lady's insights, it is evidently more important to accommodate the suburban car than to give the space-deprived urban child a place to play.

Without a society to voice their own vested interests, the children wrote nothing to the *Times*, although in their delinquent way they may have questioned the "capabilities" of teachers, administrators, and civic well-wishers who would blithely appropriate their little play space in the name of a better education.

CHAPTER 3

City Planning

THE AMENITIES OF LANDSCAPE

The corner of 90th Street and Lexington Avenue is an ordinary busy intersection in uptown Manhattan. At street level it is a mixture of shop fronts and traffic. Above, forming the flat faces of an urban canyon are the drab walls of offices and apartments. At that spot there is little to charm the eye unless it might be an attractive girl passing by on her way elsewhere. But if a person is expected and enters the right building and pushes the right buttons, an elevator will lift him to a high penthouse situated in an open garden that has a loveliness at once so intimate and delightful that any thought of flight from the city to a week end in the Catskills is immediately dismissed.

The alchemist responsible for this transmutation of common tile and asphalt into a thing of beauty was Hal Lee, recently deceased, who occasionally wrote a technical piece about roof gardening for the New York *Times*. Mr. Lee, who obviously had a wonderful way with plants, claimed he was too lazy to fight his way through traffic to get out of the city regularly. Instead, at odd moments, he managed to drag a fair piece of country into town in the form of several tons of topsoil which, over the years, were taken up on the elevator in bags and buckets. Instead of Scotch some of his best friends sent him holiday gift-wrapped packages of dried cow dung from Toujours Manure and Bovung. By combining horticultural skill with a special flair for urban living, Mr. Lee converted a piece of the most neglected wasteland in America into ivy-covered walls, an arboretum of evergreens and bearing fruit trees, as well as a profusion of bulb flowers and potted plants that bloom in succession from spring into late autumn. The illusion of country air on this city terrace is disturbed only by "snow falls" of apartment-house incinerator ashes or, when the wind is east, by breezes from a nearby brewery.

Why roof tops are ordinarily the most despised space on the urban landscape is the most baffling mystery in the annals of city planning since, by all odds, they offer the most diverse opportunities for relaxation, fun, and privacy. Uses to which the open roof can be converted are almost infinite, as anyone can easily discover for himself if he cares to explore the little known world on top of the city. In between some pigeon coops above the tenements of the lower East Side and the formal terrace gardens which crown the heights of Rockefeller Center, there are hundreds of acres of pebbled asphalt and tile which do nothing but keep rain from filtering into ceilings underneath. Yet, spotted here and there, is a surprising assortment of ingenious roofscapes: tennis courts, swimming pools, putting greens, solaria, children's play yards, car parking lots, gardens, gymnasia, restaurants, dance patios, cocktail nooks, pet shelters. The list goes on and on, but an interesting thing about it is that most of the uses are recreational, aesthetic, or social; only a few are utilitarian. Some wise persons have found that the roof is their answer to playroom and privacy—a quick get-away from the pressures of the busy city underneath. But the public in general still looks at its feet instead of the clouds. There is one section of the fashionable East Sixties where there are so many lovely penthouse gardens that one resourceful student of nature who took to beekeeping has been able to maintain an apiary of five thriving hives from which he draws a goodly supply of honey for his family and friends.

The flooding of roof tops as a cooling device in hot weather is commonly resorted to by factories and other institutions, but the result is not always salubrious when bugs fall in the water and clog the circulation system. In Dover, New Jersey, at General Hospital this bug nuisance was licked by stocking the roof lake with goldfish. Not only were the bugs disposed of and the drains kept free of debris but the finny tribe prospered and fishwatching became a favorite pastime of the patients. The modern flat roof has not begun to have the pleasant influence upon daily metropolitan living of which it is capable. In this respect the twentieth century has yet to catch up with ancient Babylon. A persistent preference in many cities for gable roofs and other steep-sloped types in residential neighborhoods are architectural anachronisms that linger on for fashion's sake. But considering the water-proof nature of modern materials, steep pitch is no longer necessary as it was back in the days of straw thatch and hand-hewn shingles. With the shrinkage of private yards below, it would seem that roof space above is the logical alternative. It is a natural for the developers of garden-apartment projects where tenants are willing to pay for the pleasure. A roof in the city, by ingenious arrangement, can be more private than most suburban yards. In cities, where play areas are restricted, no school or apartment house should be built which is not designed for full utilization of its roof for outdoor recreation throughout the year. Office buildings and factories which overlook the noontime social and recreational value of roof gardens and open-air snack bars miss an inexpensive but pleasant way to stimulate good fellowship.

The area of roof tops is two to four times the area of streets below and entirely free of traffic although, with more sensible co-ordination of building heights and specifications, even some of the most important arterial traffic could be carried on roof tops more economically than over the unsightly and scandalously expensive skyways now coming into vogue. These steel and concrete trestles, which are in the same category of ugliness as the old-time elevated railways, gratify the ego of engineers and move cars without delay, but they are wasteful of space, materials, and the taxpayers' money. With more technical imagination and aesthetic sense the same ingredients could be assembled so as to store more cars, carry traffic, and, at the same time, house important urban enterprises. A fine arterial route through one of the most congested sections of Tokyo is the roof of an elegantly modernistic serpentine building nearly a mile long which is otherwise devoted to shops and offices. A bit of Japanese thrift and art would do no harm to either the budget or appearance of the American metropolis. With the planning power and financial assistance of Title I of the 1949 National Housing Act, this kind of civic construction would be entirely feasible in American cities. With imagination the problems of arterial traffic and automobile parking alike could be solved by dual-purpose structures.

The streamlined Tokyo building, which is two stories high, has been dubbed "The Long Castle of Profits." It is remarkable not only in its imaginative engineering but in its clever financing as well. It is a corporate venture floated entirely by private investment and contains fifteen acres of rentable floor space beneath its roof-top highway. Total construction costs are estimated at seven million dollars, whereas the average cost of single-purpose elevated skyways in the United States is between ten and fifteen million dollars per mile. Land on which the building stands is rented from the City of Tokyo at a nominal fee with the understanding that when the building debt itself is amortized in thirty-five years, the highway will be dedicated to the city without charge. Already some eighty fashionable tea parlors, coffee bars, restaurants, retail stores, and specialty shops are doing business in the sleek edifice, which began with an original paid capital of only $33,000 and a brilliant idea. City planners now conceive of the "castle" as only the first link in a larger five-road network of similar construction which will be built for an estimated 200 million dollars during the next decade. When all the arteries are finally linked, they will form the heart of Tokyo's arterial traffic system.

In an urban world rural beauty must be forsaken, but that does not mean that the human spirit should be deprived in any way of its natural affinity for the aesthetic. What is lovely is a matter of taste but taste itself can be acquired or it may change with age, place, and society. The natural beauty of an unspoiled physical landscape, whether it be the sea-shore, a prairie, a mountain forest, or shaded glen, is something of almost universal appeal. However, in an era of dense population pressure and almost no government control of the fundamental pattern of land use, these forms of loveliness generally give way, particularly around cities. To be sure, unguided human invasion of the natural landscape means a loss of primeval beauty and a senseless abuse of the environment; yet that does not preclude automatically the possibility of a man-made substitute which may be appealing in its own way.

The ugliness of the physical environment remains one of the most objectionable aspects of city life, but such offense to man's innate appreciation of beauty is totally unwarranted since the human eye and hand are fully capable of creating loveliness instead of filth. It is more a matter of culture, taste, and tax policy than any special worship of crude utility, for what is useful and efficient need not be repulsive in the least and often ought to be as pleasing to the senses as to the purse. The professions of architecture, landscaping, and interior decoration are traditionally founded upon concepts of good taste. The metropolitan scene is now the home of seventy per cent of the American people and if that environment is not attractive it can scarcely arouse those deep sentiments of attachment to the homeland which are essential to the nourishment of patriotism. In rural Mexico economic poverty is as deep as that in the more depressed sections of American cities but the magnificent, if unproductive, natural landscape is an emotional tonic to all who live with it. Even the poorest of the poor will greet the stranger with a few words which almost inevitably fall into this sequence as they pass. "Good day; where are you from? That is far away, but do you like Mexico? It is a beautiful country, is it not? God be with you until we meet again." Today America the beautiful must include the city if it is to strike deep emotional roots in most of us. A life deprived of environmental loveliness is needlessly impoverished in spirit, and that is the most intolerable poverty of all. If genuine love of habitat disappears from the American psyche, no amount of synthetic schmaltz will revive it.

On the almost featureless coastal plain of Delaware, the people of that state have taken an ordinary piece of land which perhaps never had any special qualities to recommend it even in its natural state. Yet by design and good taste they have created a campus for their state university in the City of Newark that, in the blend of its landscaping and architecture, is a composition of exquisite charm. Surely the students of the University of Delaware, having lived with beauty, will never lose the sense of it, and that is a very desirable awareness which many universities are unable to cultivate by example. While they may expound in their classrooms the basic principles of land use and aesthetics, they fail to follow their own instruction on their own campuses. Too often universities, which deride the commercial world, themselves play a tighter unaesthetic game with the business dollar in their own real-estate manipulations than many so-called impersonal corporations.

The charm of the natural world is a gift. A pleasant neighborhood is a work of art, labor, and expense very difficult to achieve. However, some city people are strikingly successful in creating pleasing effects. What person in New York would trade the half-acre Lower Plaza skating rink in Rockefeller Center for any other plot? Could the Cloisters have been more appreciated as unhewn rock and timber than as a museum of medieval art in a twentieth-century metropolis? On a smaller scale than Nature operates, but nonetheless with respect for living things, some people in cities have gained effects as appealing as anything in the great outdoors. The patio of a Spanish home with its hanging plants, formal gardens, fountains, and birds has the privacy of a hacienda in the midst of a pueblo. The patio idea, thanks to Californian example, is growing remarkably. It is a way of achieving open-air beauty and a setting of social intimacy in the midst of a city.

Behind the masonry walls and iron-grill gates of New Orleans are horticultural sanctuaries fully as attractive as a moss-laden cypress forest on the banks of a bayou. Back of the red brick walls and white marble steps of Baltimore's plain-looking row houses are some of the most scrupulously tended rose gardens to be found anywhere. One has no inkling from the street of what charm lies in the vine-partitioned handkerchiefs of land screened by solemn stone faces in the residential areas of midtown Manhattan. These are the little things which people cherish and which cause them to protest madly when the big housing authorities, armed with the powers of eminent domain, decide to level dozens of acres of cityscapes in a single sterilizing operation because they have spotted some slum buildings in an area they would like to develop to their own institutional tastes and profits. Space in itself is an asset only in proportion to the skill with which it is used. None handle it better than some little landholders in cities, perhaps because they have such small pieces. Other urbanites, if they had the insights and desire, could do as well with the countless nooks which lie neglected.

Too often there is something provisional about the public organization of space in American cities which makes them look like way stations for travelers passing through on business rather than the homes of people with a civic pride in their public places as well as in their private quarters. The plazas, boulevards, squares, parks, esplanades, greens, church yards, malls, and promenades which relieve the routine aspect of commerce and housekeeping in European towns are too often slighted in our preoccupation with utility —although we know better and sometimes do better. From local experience with our own cities, which are old enough now to teach us, the parts of town that wear best with age are those that have accents of distinction and quality in the midst of ordinary activity. Manhattan's Fifth Avenue is the envy of all our cities. Yet the secret of its commercial vitality and cultural grace is seldom copied even though the formula is quite decipherable.

Fifth Avenue would scarcely be America's most fashionable address if it were only multiples of Bergdorf Goodman, Bonwit Teller, Tiffany, and the Pierre. Nor would it be particularly appealing if Central Park continued uninterrupted to Washington Square. It is the intermingling of work space, leisure space, commerce, and contemplation all along the way which makes The Avenue chic and alive. Such an assembly is the consequence of long decades of change—of decay and reconstruction—by many people of many interests who have tried a host of ideas to find by the process of elimination what it takes to win the approval of people. Fifth Avenue is wide sidewalks where people can meet, talk, and gaze in the windows without being shoved by those on the move. It is a Saint Patrick's Cathedral and a Rockefeller Center across the street—neighboring complements which enhance each other's antipodean purposes. Fifth Avenue is history and the boarded-up hole in the ground where a new skyscraper is being born. It is the Metropolitan Museum and the elegant apartments which face it across the street, each giving prestige to the other. The Public Library in its interior function and exterior antiquity is a perfect counterpoise to contemporary business hustle all around it. At its lower end

Fifth Avenue is a sidewalk café that invites lazy conversation while offering a backdrop kaleidoscope of metropolitan traffic. At its upper end it is a hospital and convalescing patients in wheelchairs who perhaps hope someday to walk the long blocks downtown again. Fifth Avenue is Harlem and it is the Solomon Guggenheim Museum—the end of one era and the beginning of another.

A city which does not reserve spaces in its commercial districts for the human interests of people must expect to be visited only when necessity dictates, and then only as briefly as business requires. The magnetic lines of force that draw customers into downtown Philadelphia and tempt them to remain are polarized about the green spaces of its charming old-fashioned squares—a fact at first recognized, then later dismissed in the mercenary redevelopment of Penn Center, which originally was designed for fewer glass towers and more landscaped park. In the beginning it was desired to draw people in their leisure time as well as in their working hours. Despite its millions, Penn Center, around the Pennsylvania Railroad terminal, seems to be emerging as a glorified workshop and asphalt parking lot, destined to be as dead as Wall Street after six o'clock. The Quaker City's urbanites with cosmopolitan instincts and spending money probably will continue to congregate in the comfortable cafés and old shops about Rittenhouse Square, which fortunately have not faced the blighted touch of renewal. Mayor Dilworth wanted Penn Center to be different, but the City Council bogged down in a hassle over the purchase of land for a $2,100,000 park with flower-bordered walks and a fountain that would have graced the $150,000,000 redevelopment. Meanwhile the Pennsylvania Railroad sold the land to an investment company so that another ordinary office tower might rise.

Over a century ago, Samuel Ruggles, who learned something about earth moving as a contractor on the Erie Canal, turned his head and hand to real-estate development of a swamp and a hill on the east side of Manhattan Island. By shoving the hill into the swamp, Mr. Ruggles leveled one, filled the other, and finished with a dry, even piece of ground which he then carved into lots with an eye to profit and the future. Near the center of his fabricated domain, an entire block was set aside as a perpetual park named Gramercy. This open space, pledged Mr. Ruggles, was to be owned in common by all who bought lots in his subdivision. He claimed no particular altruism for this since the value of the donation was recovered in the higher prices he charged for lots which bordered on or were very near the park. Some years later, while walking about the still young city at the lower end of the island, Samuel Ruggles and a friend, the Reverend Dr. Hawks, exchanged thoughts about planning the arrangement of a growing city, and the importance, for all time, of parks and gardened squares.

"Come what will," commented Mr. Ruggles, "our open squares will remain forever imperishable. Buildings, towers, palaces, may moulder and crumble beneath the touch of time; but space—free, glorious, open space—will remain to bless the City forever." "And do you not perceive the reason?" was the prompt return of Dr. Hawks. "Man makes buildings but God makes space."[1]

A twentieth-century sequel to this conversation was a transparent scheme devised a few years ago by some influential investors who wanted a good site for a large redevelopment project. With eyes on the Gramercy district, they sought to bring about the condemnation of dwellings several blocks from Gramercy Park under the powerful eminent-domain privileges of Title I of the 1949 National Housing Act. The reaction of little landowners was indignant and explosive. Their neighborhood, they were able to prove to the satisfaction of arbitrators, far from being a slum was one of the truly charming vestiges of nineteenth-century elegance still extant in the city. They were dilapidated buildings, to be sure, and some of them were in very poor repair, but the neighborhood as a whole was proud and certainly not a rooming-house district. From the standpoint of prestige and land values the heart of the Gramercy Park vicinity at the southern terminus of Lexington Avenue is one of the best in Manhattan, and it is the consensus of all who live there that the beauty of their private preserve is what has saved them from the blight that has hurt so many other districts.

Today Gramercy Park is surrounded by a tall wrought-iron fence and locked by four handsome gates of the same material and antique workmanship. It continues to be maintained by the annual subscriptions of landowners, each of whom has a key to the gates. Inside this little reserve, in full view of passersby, are simple gardens, gravel paths, fine trees, some old-fashioned statuary, and benches on which to rest and enjoy the surrounding loveliness. Gramercy Park is an island of charm surrounded by tastefully maintained brownstones, apartment buildings, and hotels—a far cry indeed from the kind of monotonous, tightly built-up neighborhoods that were developed elsewhere at later dates and have long since died of the blight that comes of slum crowding on sites of no particular quality.

Although Samuel Ruggles demonstrated a valid and successful principle in city planning over a century ago by the establishment of a protected private garden in the midst of what was designed to become a densely settled neighborhood, his example is only rarely followed. A conventional state of mind discourages copying by developers and buyers and, curiously enough, by city administrators, who almost universally penalize the reservation of private open space by their tax policies. In the early twentieth century even Gramercy Park itself was threatened by the City of New York, which tried to force it into sale and development by an extreme tax assessment. However, the Gramercy attorneys were able to prove that the private lots of the neighborhood were more valuable, and therefore already taxed higher, because of the park. They contended successfully that the park was a common extension of all the private properties in the subdivision and that to tax it separately would, in effect, tax the owners twice for the same land.

It is almost a universal truth that private property values, and consequently tax assessments, are higher on parkside real estate than on the ordinary. Far from being a burden on the public, such space, even when it is publicly owned, tends to uphold the values of old buildings and their sites while structures of the same vintage often deteriorate into slums where there are no parks, either private or public. A city which would encourage pride in the owners of real estate, just to reap dividends in higher taxes, would do well to encourage the establishment of many small parks, squares, circles, greens, and boulevards. Neighborhoods which have a generous interspersion of such amenities retain prestige even when buildings wear out. They seldom require government subsidies for urban renewal as the people of Gramercy effectively demonstrated; thus they do not encourage the growth of tax-abated public housing which is an ever-growing menace to the owner of a small private property. Just as some of the Department of Agriculture's farm subsidy programs have been perverted to squeeze out the small family farmer in favor of the corporate and large family-operated models, so too are the little property holders in the largest cities being mowed down by the big-acreage renewal syndicates. When a building wears out on a parkside location, the chances are that someone will think highly enough of the lot to build again without an appeal for public assistance and an abatement of taxes.

In darkest Boston, where it has been discovered that the automobile does very little shopping, there is a feeble light of hope that the prosperity of suburbia can be brought back to the city by turning narrow side streets into pedestrian retail malls. The city's fathers, in a radical departure from their customary conservatism, have barred all vehicles for almost three hours on three days weekly from two of Boston's thinnest downtown lanes: Temple Place and West Street between Tremont and Washington. This cautious innovation was greeted expectantly by desperate merchants who, on the day of its inception, filled curb boxes with branches of maple and hemlock and set out pots of chrysanthemums and trailing ivy. Decorators' palms were rolled onto the sidewalks and benches were placed beneath their fronds. Using the technique of the Lorelei, soft music was broadcast to relax the weary and to entice them into tarrying until a 2:15 P.M. deadline let down the floodgates and vehicular traffic resumed as usual, flushing the pedestrians like a flock of blackbirds before a shotgun.

Less hampered by tradition, and not yet so deeply in the rut, the upstart community of Kalamazoo, Michigan, population 80,000, has gone a step farther to accommodate the pedestrian. In the heart of its central business district, Kalamazoo has ripped up completely two blocks of paving and replaced the asphalt with lawns, walks, and flower gardens to give human beings a sense of leisure and relief from the mechanical jostling that makes most city shoppers wish they were home. The new look in Kalamazoo, one of truly commendable charm, was achieved under the direction of the city's Park Department whose unconventional superintendent announced, "We want people to feel free to walk on the soft grass." The downtown-for-people idea has been a long time gaining recognition, but it is here and promises before long to be the most important innovation since suburbs were invented. The technique is strictly "soft-sell" but it works. In Kansas City the KC-80 program hopes to seal off the retail core of the prairie metropolis to all vehicular traffic and to convert it into a landscaped shopping plaza. Planner-architect Victor Gruen has thrown the middle South and particularly the old fogies of Fort Worth, Texas, into a tizzy with his spectacular plans to encircle the downtown business district with an expressway and multilevel parking garages. Inside this concrete rim streets would be reserved for pedestrians only and sidewalks would be lined with trees and open-air cafés. Some places would be glass enclosed and air-conditioned in the summer. In a town so long ruled by cattle barons with oil wells, they say that tomorrow the pedestrian will be king.

Now grass is growing in the streets of downtown Toledo, but not because the place is defunct. To the delight of almost everyone the automobile is taboo in the city's four-block center. For only $15,000 eight inches of top soil were spread over former streets and planted to grass and flowers. Patio blocks form attractive walkways. There is a penguin pool, and a playground for children almost a block long. A wading pool for the kids is just the thing to keep them from nagging their mothers to go home. Downtown can come back, for trade inevitably follows people, and people will go where they can have a little pleasure for their money. The old downtown core of any city has the variety in entertainment and merchandise and in architectural surroundings which cannot help appealing after the newness of the sleek, but too often monotonous, efficiency of the suburban shopping center has worn thin.

The central problem in city planning is to accommodate as many people as possible in a restricted area without fostering claustrophobia or pollution. Unless a city is compactly organized, yet free of congestion, it cannot serve its citizens properly. It will waste too much money fighting clogged traffic and other forms of pollution while it neglects the services which add to the enjoyment of city living. The way a city uses space inevitably affects its function and the quality of life its people lead. A metropolis should not ape the suburbs as Los Angeles has done by sprawling over the landscape. With only one quarter as many people as New York, Los Angeles covers forty per cent more area. No wonder it has neither a subway nor an effective surface transportation system. It is too thinly spread and loosely organized for efficient, self-supporting public transit service. Consequently eight out of ten people in Los Angeles drive their own cars rather than patronize the city's 1700 buses and trolleys which wander on slow schedules over 450 square miles of territory. In contrast, New York has nearly 9000 subway cars and buses which operate on fast schedules within a much smaller area of 320 square miles. Buses of New York's Fifth Avenue Coach Lines alone carry as many passengers as the whole public transportation system in Los Angeles, which in places looks as though it had been bombed out to make room for open-air parking lots.

A novice in Los Angeles might easily sympathize with the Army captain and his family who found that maneuvering on the city's interlocking freeways could be even more intricate than coming down out of a stack of planes circling above La Guardia Field. The captain, driving one car, was followed by his wife and children in another, but as they neared their destination they became bewildered and were separated in the traffic. Several hours later a police car rescued the distressed mother and gave her an escort. The captain, not quite so lucky, eventually reported in by phone when he discovered to his chagrin that he had been lured twenty-five miles out of the way.

Cities and suburbs have two contrary purposes that cannot be blended harmoniously. Attempts to mate them result in monstrosities that lack the saving graces of either. A city assembles people—a suburb scatters them. These purposes are unalterably opposed to one another. They are separate systems of social geometry which cannot be blended without chaos. A city should house its people and its businesses vertically and leave the horizontal approach to the suburbs. As has been remarked so often, Los Angeles is an overgrown suburb. For proper urban design less ground area and more sky space should be given to housing than is customary. As a city's population grows, the city itself should grow taller faster than it grows wider. Well-designed apartments with playgrounds and parks around them should become more prominent than single-family dwellings. A very high proportion of urban ground space should be devoted to the avenues of major circulation and to the social and recreational activities of people. City people who live in tight housing quarters must have the antidote of parks, promenades, playing fields, museums, ball grounds, amusement parks, water fronts, theaters, and other types of public breathing space in which to stretch out and unwind.

Good city living is a distinctly different routine from good suburban living, but it may be every bit as satisfying or more so. A suburb is designed to get people away from all but a select handful of other people, and to give each person plenty of room for private living and playing. Generally it is a safe place for the kids and a pretty dull spot for adults. The anemia of suburbia is monotony and isolation. A city is everybody. This is the foundation of cultural diversity and intellectual stimulation, but it can have its drawbacks if living conditions are too cramped, too hideous, and if physical exercise is limited to a bout with the supermarket. Diversity of people and things to do is the compensation of cities. Space should be arranged so that circulation can be convenient and rapid at all times. This is possible only if all places are relatively near to one another and if the routes of communication are open, swift, and direct. The city is for people who want to be with people and to enjoy the great variety of opportunities in business employment, recreation, society, and culture which only a city can offer. For those who lack such appetites, or whose child-rearing obligations keep them tied down, the suburb or the country is a better place to live. If the city itself is a failure, there is no place to go but the suburb because the country has too many farmers as it is.

Traffic congestion is basically bad housekeeping and bad land management. It is totally unnecessary and to avoid it should be cheaper than to cope with it. Perhaps the reason for treating the automobile as master rather than as slave is a fear that the driver will go elsewhere. The fact is that the driver has little choice. If a city is a genuine city the suburbanite will not find its assets anywhere else. To give idle cars priority over active people can only destroy the city as a decent environment.

A solution to the city's internal traffic movement would not be expensive or difficult if drastic decisions were taken to keep parked cars off the public streets at all time in all places, and if commuting suburban job holders were obliged to check their vehicles at the urban fringe every morning or else pay the bill for parking in a multilevel, high-density garage in town. It is something of a mystery why a city should be so solicitous of the suburban commuter whose object is to take a salary check out of the city, while it has become so negligent in cultural and recreational services to its full-time residents that many, who would rather remain, finally give up in disgust and move to the suburbs. It would seem that the city has such an inferiority complex that it seeks to curry favor with opportunists while it beats its own children. No cheap or reasonable solution can be expected to urban traffic congestion as long as cities think they must be open-air parking lots and throughways for commuters. The potential supply of cars ready to take up space mathematically exceeds the city's capacity to provide it. The parking meter is an extravagant pretense at thrift and traffic management for, in fact, it licenses the embezzlement of a city's most valuable public space. It is ridiculous that a few automobiles worth no more than a few thousand dollars each should occupy as much ground space as a multimillion-dollar skyscraper. The city that feels it can devote curb space to the parked automobile should broaden its sidewalks instead and give people who are on their feet a break since, after all, it is they who keep business alive.

Toronto is the only major city in the Western Hemisphere which has clamped down hard. In Canada's second largest metropolis, there is an absolute ban against street parking downtown at any hour of the day or night. Commuters are encouraged by cheap rates to park their automobiles at subway stations on the edges of the city. For out-of-town shoppers, businessmen, and commuters willing to pay, there are multistory and underground parking garages conveniently placed in the city's central commercial areas. To compensate for putting people back on their shoe leather, Toronto has developed a highly efficient transportation system of subways, streetcars, and buses which have fast, clear sailing above and beneath the streets. This intra-urban transportation system is growing in local popularity, as judged by a steady increase in patronage. The system itself is being improved and extended without raising fares because more people use it and it operates at a profit. Many cities would be better off if they offered subsidized public transportation rather than rip themselves apart to make room for idle private cars. In some congested districts even free public transportation would be justified.

More and cheaper taxi service should be encouraged in every city rather than penalized by license fees and passenger taxes such as the City of New York has imposed. Any policy that raises the tolls of cabs and other public transit facilities to obtain revenue will ultimately cost the city more in traffic pollution by private cars than it collects. Measures like these are but local variations of the taxes on railroad passenger service which are helping to kill that vital public utility. To keep private automobiles off the street when they are not in use, there should be a plentiful supply of parking space, but no city can well afford to allow single-level surface parking because of limited space. Such use of valuable urban real estate is but a slick dodge for land speculators who thus manage to keep choice sites off the market while they build up capital value at a relatively small cost in taxes. A city that allows itself to be punched full of surface parking holes sells itself short and defrauds those who pay taxes on developed property. The ultimate folly is to finance public facilities of the street-level, open-lot type which Wilmington is thinking of doing with thirteen blocks of its best downtown real estate. This is a suburban brand of commercial land use that is uneconomical in a vertical city, particularly at its core. However, facilities that provide underground storage for cars and offer park and playground space at the surface for people can be wonderful assets.

In a dramatic split with its past, Pittsburgh approached the parking problem constructively some years ago when it ripped out a filthy industrial slum at the junction of the Monongahela and Allegheny rivers to create its "golden triangle." The golden triangle is not just an ordinary touch-up job, yet, for all its publicity, the unique features of this project are seldom copied. To be sure gleaming new commercial towers are the financial heart of the enterprise, and without their taxes nothing else would have been feasible, but they are not what made the ugly duckling beautiful.

Pittsburgh did on a smaller scale what Chicago had originated earlier. It created a water front of extraordinary quality out of an eyesore. Thirty-six acres of landscaped park with broad boulevards were opened up to lend a sweeping, ground-level accent to an impressive skyline arranged behind it. This sophisticated use of land gave the city an air of urbanity that the nation's major steel center should rightfully possess. A one-acre detail of this project is perhaps its most important feature. It is a six-level parking garage for 1000 automobiles which is part subterranean, part elevated. The whole is surmounted by a terraced park with an ornamental fountain, trees, and formal gardens. Mellon Square Park is both a functional building and an island of landscaped beauty. It is a solution to congestion and a delight to the eye which any city would do well to copy. People who wish to park an automobile in the heart of a great metropolis must expect to pay a premium for the privilege, and cities should use this potential source of income to create facilities that are utilitarian beneath yet landscaped above. Subterranean garages with garden roofs could be embellished with profitable sidewalk cafés where people could relax or assemble leisurely for the trip home. Such integrated planning could make the commercial core of any metropolis more exciting to the civilized taste, and it should improve retail trade since all people are fascinated by a touch of elegance after they have seen too much of the ordinary.

Cities will never worm their way out of their dark labyrinth of confusion as long as they are under the hypnotic spell of public road officials, bridge and tunnel authorities, or street and traffic departments which are top-heavy with designers who relish multimillion-dollar solutions to vehicular congestion that should not be allowed to develop in the first place. It is the joy and everlasting pride of project authority bureaucrats to solve the impossible, even though the impossible could be avoided entirely with ordinary horse sense. Weird plans for enticing the bottomless supply of suburban automobiles ready to enter the city are but fiscal sponges that could absorb all a city's assets, yet add nothing to its intrinsic worth as a habitat. In tropical America there is a saying that if Brazil does not control the ant, the ant will control Brazil. The automobile is the American ant. The city which does not rule the automobile will itself be subjugated by engineers who, as a profession, seem averse to simple regulations that would put them out of the spectacular cloverleaf, underpass, and elevated skyway business. It seems that their reputations are made by the dramatic and traumatic, not by honoring simple preventive precautions. Immunization is dull compared with the excitement of civic surgery. No true bureaucrat was ever promoted for dreaming of a way to avoid project spending. Yet only by refusing to cater to the private automobile, except to store it off the street at a fee, can the city hope to be relieved of its pollution.

It has become a fad to level wide swaths of urban real estate to make way for expressways into and out of the hearts of cities without much consideration for what is to become of the tidal waves of traffic after they hit the streets. When a public hearing was held on a proposal to run an elevated expressway through Worcester, Massachusetts, it received a hostile reception at the hands of citizens, one of whom complained, "Each year they rip down more property, and pretty soon there'll be no homes for the people who are to ride these roads. Why should we pay for our own destruction?" Another objector told the hearing examiner that he was "firmly opposed to your placing a Chinese Wall in our community, separating one from the other." A businessman who examined the plans remarked that the proposed route "appears laid out for as much destruction as the tornado of '53." He contended that Worcester residents "don't need a 50-mile-an-hour expressway to go from one square to another" and suggested instead a belt artery circling the city.[2]

Cities do desperately need express routes to carry vehicular traffic around them, as Baltimore discovered recently when it opened its Bay Tunnel by-pass. That device alone cut Baltimore's midtown traffic thirty per cent and internal congestion was greatly relieved. However, many cities, without considering their entire circulation problem and the various solutions which there could be, seem inclined to jump at the big spectacular elevated expressways, even though by doing so they may further penalize subways and railroads which already have established rights-of-way into the metropolitan core. In its passion to help surface vehicles capture the job of underground trains, Boston has built so many bridges and tunnels to give them access that now it is fairly paralyzed in the evening when it is time for the vehicles to get out again. Near expressway ramps the movement, whether up or down, is stifled for blocks and the city's canyons fill with the blue exhaust fumes of idling motors. Meanwhile the Metropolitan Transit Authority, which already charges higher fares than most cities, is on the rocks and must be subsidized by a stiff levy on real estate to heal its annual deficit. Thirty per cent of the gross rental income of all commercial properties in Boston now goes to pay the local property tax. The average for all cities is twelve per cent.

The public expressway, in contrast to Tokyo's privately financed "Long Castle of Profits," is fighting a losing game but few admit it. One of the most spectacular is the new Cross-Bronx and Trans-Manhattan Expressway in New York, which extends for 5.4 miles from the George Washington Bridge on the west to the Bronx-Whitestone Bridge on the east. It includes a new bridge over the Harlem River which will have such a glorious maze of interlaced and spiraling interchanges with local streets that delighted engineers refer to their offspring as a mixture of "chicken guts and spaghetti." Construction costs on the Cross-Trans are running at a record clip of $13,000,000 per mile, plus land and demolition costs of $5,000,000 per mile. Work began in 1948. It will be 1964 before it is finished. Possibly the day is not too distant when five miles of city highway may be made so complicated that such a project could be a man's lifetime career. Construction engineers could sign on when they graduate from college and retire with old-age pensions the day the ribbon is cut.

To make way for the Cross-Trans, 3000 tenants have been displaced and their buildings razed. Fifty-four bridges and three tunnels are being built since every cross street must have one or the other. Even a section of Bronx River was shifted two hundred feet to the side to clear the route. The city's major aqueduct had to be relocated, and a new pumping station built to replace one that was in the path of progress. There has been wholesale relocation of sewer mains, water lines, gas tubes, telephone and electric cables. Even police signal and fire-alarm systems were rerouted. Had the ninety-million-dollar cost of this dream road been spent to improve the city's own internal transportation facilities or to link together a circumferential route to by-pass the city, it might have brought permanent relief. As it is the new expressway will add additional flow to lateral pipes that are already clogged.

Ninety million dollars would have built the multistory municipal garages that Traffic Commissioner Wiley needs to keep parked automobiles off the downtown streets so they can be devoted to the movement of traffic for which they were originally constructed. New York has a plan, already far advanced, to close off a 103-block area in midtown to all parked vehicles. By its compactness the Empire City is in an ideal position to develop a model congestion-free internal transportation system based on public conveyances and open streets. To succeed it must restrict the suburban commuter's automobile, encourage rail commutation, forbid all parking in streets except by active service vehicles, and aid, rather than penalize, its remarkable taxi fleets. It could do this and still devote more street space in residential districts to recreation which is desperately needed by the city's children and aged.

Off-street multilevel parking facilities have opponents in high circles. Herbert Askwith, a member of Governor Rockefeller's Committee on Transit Problems, takes a dim view of multistory municipal garages in the heart of Manhattan although he is enthusiastic about parking lots at subway terminals. Recently he appealed for bouquets for the Transit Authority, which opened the first of ten subway parking lots which eventually will accommodate 10,000 cars. He lauded "the admirable way in which this plan combines increased revenue for the subway system with a substantial public service in reducing traffic congestion . . ." But Mr. Askwith appealed to the city's Board of Estimate to condemn proposals for midtown garages, ". . . by giving the death blow to one of the most wasteful and dangerous schemes ever wished upon us. He was referring to what he called ". . . Traffic Commissioner Wiley's stubborn effort to get the city to squander over $90,000,000 on multistory municipal garages, chiefly in the heart of the city, on the plea that these will bring more shoppers to New York."[3] What New York wants is more shoppers, but it must be prepared to store their cars off the streets.

Among the bigger American cities, Chicago has made the strongest effort to swing commuter service to the railroad and to put local traffic into the downtown Loop on a public-transit basis. It has not spurned attention to the automobile but neither does it defer to the private car, for Chicago has discovered by actual count that most automobiles which enter the downtown sections are only passing through or looking around. Suburban rail passengers who enter the Loop come to work or shop, and the same is true of local citizens who ride the subways, buses, and cabs. The Windy City has been successful in stimulating the use of public transport, for it discovered in a recent survey that 86 per cent of the people who enter the Loop arrive by public conveyance and only 14 per cent by private car. In Los Angeles, 45 per cent of the people who go downtown use private cars. In New York, 39 per cent of the morning rush-hour mob arrives in automobiles.

It is natural that, as the hub of the nation's railroads, Chicago should be partial to that type of transport, and it has the help of the world's best talent in that sphere of public service. In a recent decade the commuter traffic by suburban railroads at the rush hour increased 8.4 per cent while passengers of automotive vehicles declined 4 per cent. When the city built its massive in-and-out-of-town Congress Street Expressway, it included rapid-transit tracks in the center of the right-of-way and integrated this service with automobile parking plazas on the urban fringe so that suburbanites of their own volition would switch from cars to trains for a faster round trip into the city. On the Congress Street Expressway the two lines of the rapid transit can accommodate fifty per cent more patrons than the eight lanes open to automobiles.

A fact which guided Chicago toward reliance upon rapid

transit in preference to the automobile was an earlier discovery that as automobile traffic increased, and public transit declined, retail sales in downtown stores also sagged. Apparently there is good evidence that the public-transit patron is a buying patron, and Chicago frankly is out to invite him in by the most persuasive means.

In addition to cluttering the routes of travel, the parked automobile at times is a blight on the landscape and an exhibition of bad taste comparable to hanging the family wash in a public park. Dover, Delaware, is one of the most beautiful capital cities in America. Its Green, laid out in 1717 on orders from William Penn, is a living museum of the colonial era. On the east side of the Green is Old State House, built in 1722 and still in daily use thanks to careful restoration. Around the Green are a number of handsome, well-preserved homes dating back to before America's independence. The entire neighborhood is an historic architectural shrine that ranks with Williamsburg and parts of Annapolis, but instead of being treated with respect its streets have become linear public parking lots. The entire government district in Dover is one of expert architecture and landscaping but the pleasing effect, as well as the nobility of the whole assembly, is demolished by parked automobiles which line the main thoroughfares and byways of the capital district. The same, of course, is true around the Federal Government buildings in Washington, D.C. The untidy consequence reflects an attitude of disrespect for government on the part of government itself. Certainly such slovenly housekeeping is a discourtesy to the citizen who makes a pilgrimage to his capital and would like to see it treated with dignity. The city that would wish to be respected must first respect itself.

URBAN RENEWAL

In Tokyo, as in any other city, there are those unlucky but industrious ones who grub a livelihood out of dump heaps.

They are the human buzzards or, as Tokyo calls them, the "Ants," who salvage something from their more fortunate brothers' trash. They are ragpickers, tin-can collectors, bottle gatherers, and waste-paper bundlers who glean, sort, and then sell the stuff to junk yards. The work is hard, demeaning, and filthy but it returns a subsistence and the city is cleaner because the job is done. Over a decade ago Tokyo's Ants and their families began to assemble their own version of a hobo jungle in a neglected riverside park. Since then this do-it-yourself slum, constructed of whatever cast-off materials the Ants could scrounge, has grown into a settlement of three hundred people who have developed a remarkable social-security system to care for themselves as well as for their dependent children and aged. Their welfare plan, to which all active Ants contribute a daily pittance, provides free: a modest wedding, medical care, and a funeral when the time comes.

Living quarters in the Ants community, while they look like hovels, are kept as neat as possible, and there is a common bathhouse in daily operation so that all who return from their dirty tasks may enjoy the pleasure and cleanliness it offers. Now the Ants have had enough of mean surroundings and they are engaged in an urban-renewal program financed by themselves. They have saved money and have won respect for their thrift and efforts to live decently. The City of Tokyo has given them permission to buy five acres of waterfront land where they will build a new community with modest apartments, a dining hall, a nursery, a bathhouse and a church. Their master plan reserves space for recreation areas and for a community livestock project of a thousand chickens and twenty pigs. The Ants, who have lived long enough in the lower depths, intend to become people.

As the Ants have demonstrated, slums are a matter of culture as well as of economics. If people possess a taste for decency, no matter how mean their circumstances may be, they will improve their environment. If they lack culture they will defile and degrade whatever place they occupy, even though it be a suite at the Waldorf. However, much as the Ants may have wanted a better life, that would have been impossible for them until they had saved the where-withal to buy it. The surge toward civic betterment which is now growing in urban America indicates that the city, far from being moribund, has within it a remarkable desire to improve. It has the culture. But to succeed the city also needs a means by which people can rehabilitate themselves, and that is a far more complex problem than urban renewal. It is wishful thinking to believe that the current wave of slum clearance, which is strictly a real-estate construction program, will in any way solve the far more difficult social task which is raised by the slum dwellers themselves. The two objectives should not be confused; otherwise the real, but distinctly limited, possibilities for improvement of the city's physical plant may be dissipated by presuming that it has welfare objectives that the program cannot possibly achieve.

In the long run it would probably be better for any city to undertake fewer urban-renewal projects and to concentrate on doing those so tastefully that they would bring the middle class back to town. This is not to deny that the inhabitants of slums need better living quarters, but as the program now operates the truly indigent are not aided anyway by urban renewal, and many of them are made more miserable by being uprooted and driven from their familiar neighborhoods into other districts where they have no ties or affections. Since the rents in renewal-project buildings are far beyond the means of most slum dwellers, the people who do move into the new apartments generally are of modest but independent means who come from decent but under-privileged neighborhoods where they have been living in old but respectable buildings. On the whole they are people who cannot afford the suburbs but do not have to live in slums.

The places they vacate then may be overrun in turn by slum D.P.'s who double up to save on rents. Such is the pecking order in the urban barnyard. It results in a lot of demolition and reconstruction but is no basic solution to the problem of degraded neighborhoods.

Most of the modern city's present slums are in what once were, and still could be, privileged neighborhoods. The West Side of New York, which only in the last decade has become as crowded and filthy as Harlem, is, from the standpoint of location, the best residential district in the city. Even now a very large percentage of existing buildings would make choice residences. Many were once the homes and apartments of the well-to-do and have real charm which would be a credit in any age to any city. Almost every city with slums can point to similarly well-situated neighborhoods with good buildings which have gone to pot only through misuse. The kind of urban renewal which simply destroys the old to put up the new does not correct the cultural depravity that creates slums. It only scatters the seed.

Although New York City has undertaken a greater acreage of slum clearance with government aid than all other cities in the United States, ". . . the situation can only grow worse instead of better" according to William J. Williams, Chairman of the Metropolitan Fair Rent Committee, which is a landlord's group. Mr. Williams notes that renewal actually diminishes the supply of cheap housing for the moderately self-sufficient, and forces overcrowding by the poor. Many slum residents are some of the 300,000 individuals and families on welfare rolls whom the city cannot afford to lodge in the so-called "low-rent" projects. As Mr. Williams indicates, about the only alternative open to dispossessed slum dwellers and to new unskilled migrants from Puerto Rico and the South is to ". . . overwhelm housing that has not been overcrowded before, enlarging the slums day by day, breaking down old neighborhoods and inducing those families which can afford it to move to the suburbs."[4]

Because there is no really effective Federal program to relieve the city of its welfare load or to rehabilitate the able indigent through productive and remunerative work, the physical and social structure of the American city is being inundated by a tidal wave of psychically sick, underemployed, poor, and culturally destitute human beings who cannot be cured simply by knocking down the buildings where they huddle and forcing them to scurry for some other shelter. The modern suburb, which is mostly new private homes and high-rent apartments, is nicely buffered against encroachment by urban D.P.'s, who have nowhere to go but some other part of the city. On the other hand, the city, having lost a goodly part of its middle class to the suburb, has no alternative but to rent its vacated houses and apartments to whatever applicants will take over.

The Federal Housing and Home Finance Agency recently warned the City of New York that it would not approve more plans for pending urban-renewal projects until the city indicated how it would prevent deterioration of the remaining old housing. It was then that Mayor Wagner acknowledged that Robert Moses had the job of tearing down slums and that Robert Felt was responsible for rehabilitating old neighborhoods, but nobody had the really crucial and perhaps unsolvable job of preventing the development of new slums. This was the joker that nobody wanted to draw. Of course, the Agency's warning was chiefly for the record since the problem is not peculiar to New York alone. The whole Federal program would fold overnight if this condition were seriously enforced, because no city is financially capable of rehabilitating all its slum dwellers to the point that they could afford respectable housing. Moreover it is presumptuous of the House and Home Finance Agency even to hint that its trivial contribution to urban betterment comes anywhere close to giving the kind of economic and social aid the city needs to lift its slum dwellers to the level of Tokyo's

Ants so that they can help themselves rather than depend upon charity.

Slum clearance under present rules should be labeled properly as slum relocation or slum shifting. It is not true urban renewal. Instead of being social uplift programs as sometimes depicted, the big renewal projects in residential areas have been called land grabs aided by government subsidies and the powerful privilege of eminent domain. It is not surprising that shrewd investors are anxious to acquire large acreages in densely populated neighborhoods and find the eminent-domain lever made to order for them. As America's population continues to increase there is no space more assured of returning both annual dividends and long-term capital gains than city land. This is apparent in the growing inclination of owners to lease rather than to sell. But, under the eminent-domain privileges of Title I, small-lot owners are compelled to sell to the big project once authorities have given the official nod.

Under Title I the Federal Government supplies two thirds of the dollar difference between the cost of a slum site and its estimated value with the buildings removed. In other words, the old rooming houses and tenements, despite their condition, have definite investment value and it costs something to tear them down. Two thirds of these charges for lost value and for demolition are borne by the Federal Government; one third by the local community. But there is an added opportunity in the Federal Housing Act and this, for the city that has a real desire to enhance its physical environment, is extraordinary. It permits a city to include a new school, playground, park, or other public work as its one-third contribution. Thus, by careful integration of its own needs with the general commercial program, a city could completely revamp its land use and public facilities over the years. Conceivably within a generation the city could improve sufficiently to compete with the suburb as a desirable habitat.

The catch is that very few projects are conceived of as anything more than monolithic apartment complexes of a stark commercial nature, and with no genuine enhancement of the environment in the way of detached public parks or schools with ample recreation space. While these facilities are not ignored, neither are they provided on a scale that population density demands. They are tokens rather than the real thing. The city should learn to attract people who have the financial means to choose as well as those who have no alternative but to accept whatever is offered, no matter how shoddy. In part, the city's reluctance to provide amenities is due to the fact that they would cost more than the city's one-third commitment. Strapped financially as the city usually is, it does not have funds to spend for the things that would truly enhance its appearance and services. Probably there would be money if the Federal Government would take the really burdensome obligations of welfare and public hospitalization off the back of the city instead of offering a comparative pittance for urban renewal which does not come close to tackling a city's major difficulties and is only a smoke screen for the real job of human renewal that is swept under the rug.

Demolition and new construction is not the only formula for urban renewal and sometimes it is absolutely inappropriate. The big bulldozer projects have a way of destroying the character of neighborhoods, which is an asset more valuable than the run-down buildings that are pushed out of the way. One is appalled to think of what would have happened had the project version of Title I invaded the once tumbledown, brick row houses and livery stables in Georgetown near Washington, D.C., before piecemeal private restoration began. Georgetown's revived atmosphere of nineteenth-century charm with its wavy brick sidewalks, shade-grown alleys, and quaint homes with private gardens might have been just another utility project. A prominent section of old Greenwich Village in downtown Manhattan was spotted for the big treatment when its residents rebelled against the Housing Authority and its messianic attempt to level what they loved just because certain buildings were poor while the land was some of the choicest speculative real estate in the city.

In their own slow but independent way the villagers have since restored much of their community to the envy of all Manhattan. The rest will come in time when the people are ready—probably with the abolition of rent control, which by a weird logic forces landlords deliberately to neglect their properties against an understandable desire to conserve them. Rent control in peacetime, when capital and building materials are freely available for construction, serves to create slums. Landlords with buildings under regulation either let them deteriorate so as to pocket what otherwise would be spent upon maintenance, or partition their holdings into rooming houses and "efficiencies" so as to be eligible for decontrol. These dodges are definitely wasteful of good housing, but it is good business because legislation makes it so. In Manhattan scores of blocks of rent-controlled luxury apartments have been deliberately demolished or gutted in order to escape from the misguided holdover of wartime regulations. What might have accommodated people of means has been converted to hutches or replaced altogether by commercial buildings with no living quarters at all.

If the city were deliberately bent upon expelling its able taxpayers in order to expand its welfare activities, it could not have legislated more wisely. Because the big-project type of urban renewal cannot cure the causes of slums, a city should be leery of that approach unless it has funds to provide, as an added feature, the amenities which would make a difference in lasting human appeal. Otherwise it would perhaps be better to concentrate upon the conservation of present housing and to encourage the normal type of private investment which has built cities in the past.

CHAPTER 4

Suburbia

PARADISE GAINED

Suburbia is today's tomorrowland come true. This pastel-colored playpen world, like any other pioneer institution, is a woof of dreams woven upon a warp of desperation, but in its secret mind it is sure that, as a way of life, it approaches closer to the stars than has any system of the past. Whatever failings suburbia may have, it has the saving grace of space. Even the meanest trailer camp on the wrong side of the expressway has play room for the children that is safer than a city street. Today's ranch home in Blue Heaven Acres, be it only a no-down-payment soapbox on a slab, is as much a product of faith and hope as the wilderness cabin that inspired pioneer America to fend for itself in the forest rather than accept the social security of European servitude. The world of subdivisions and developments has put the city's rootless ones back in contact with their own pieces of the bulldozed earth. At this late date in the industrial age that is no small achievement.

Despite some variations such as mountain-top and shore-side vacation colonies or winter retreats in the sun for aged pensioners, suburbia is essentially the nation's year-around residential nursery, riding high on the boom of human multiplication and the protective instincts of parents who want to give their spawn a sporting chance. It is today's response to the age-old nesting urge which, from the beginning of time, has been the most important business of living things. Newly married parents stick to fundamentals. Instinctively discounting world-shaking threats of holocaust each young couple seeks a plot of earth on which it may rear its own. That is the essence of suburbia's popularity. It is the habitat that in our time comes closest to what the human animal requires for its basic task.

In recent years suburbs have grown in population much faster than cities. Future consumption of space promises to occur at an even faster clip. A Levittown of 21,000 single homes sprouting from nearly 5000 acres of potato fields is but a suggestion of things to come. Every great city is now swaddled in depth by a soft absorbent cushion of residential developments that expand all around it. At a recent count Los Angeles had nearly 60 suburban communities in its orbit, some more than forty miles away and each with its own planetary system of interlocking subdivisions. The concept of a city as an urban hub surrounded by a rural countryside is something out of the horse-and-buggy past that the younger generation in major metropolitan areas has never known. To them a city is a vertical core surrounded by miles of horizontal developments that in some places do not end until one is again in the vertical core of another city. The farms that previously lay between have vanished beneath an advance of human glaciation that has obliterated them as effectively as if a new ice age had been born.

From the environmental standpoint, the most remarkable feature of suburbia is this mass consumption of space and its ever accelerating conversion of open farm land to the more rigid pattern of residential use that for all human time is not likely to change again so drastically, except where demolition will open wider roads or remove homes to make way for commercial structures as the community grows. This is the inevitable consequence of locating four families on an acre of ground that in the city might have supported a hundred apartments. The children in a single-family Cape Cod cottage on an ordinary 70x120 foot suburban house lot have more room of their own to play in than is provided for youngsters from 250 apartments in New York's new public-housing projects, where between three and four square yards of playground are the official quota for each apartment. Such are the facts of life which generate enthusiasm for suburbia. In its allocation of space for living, the modern commuters' development is a triumph of parental instinct over the inhumane forces of an urban-industrial society, which too often values the job more highly than the family that the job supports.

Because suburbia is also a real-estate promotion, beginning with relatively cheap rural land and ending with a settled residential community, it has the extraordinary opportunity to become anything its designers are able to imagine and its future dwellers are able to afford. Sometimes it is a bleak collection of look-alike people-cartons, perched upon the skinned red earth of an eroding hillside without a shade tree and seemingly strung together with a web of electric cables, telephone wires, and wash lines—a sight almost as repulsive as a company coal town in the West Virginia mountains only not so dirty. Again it may be an exclusive assembly of custom-built executive mansions, each on its own five acres of woods and meadows, with a liberal sprinkling of streams, ponds, tennis courts, equestrian trails, and a community golf course with clubhouse and bar. The farm that is sold to a developer resembles a blank canvas prepared for an artist. Either a wonder or a travesty can emerge. Since the production of developments and subdivisions is a risky, competitive business, there are some pretty severe restrictions to checkrein the noble imagination and good will of the promoters if they should so happen to be endowed. None dares to be too visionary about his business unless he is dealing

with a clientele which can afford the luxury. Ordinarily suburbia is what people can afford to buy on mortgages that
government agencies will insure, but even what is cheap can
sometimes be reasonably good.

On a mass scale very few developers have been able to offer more to the average workingman than Levitt & Sons, the
creators of Levittowns, who were among the first suburban
developers to realize that people need more than houses
when they move out of the city. Into the Levitts' pioneer
spectacular on Long Island went nine community swimming
pools, twelve ball fields, a half dozen "village greens,"
twenty-five playgrounds, and several complete commercial
shopping and recreation centers. Today there are an estimated 82,000 people, more than half of them children, living
in Levittown's 21,000 individual houses.

A feature of Levittown which relieves the monotony of its
repetitious house styles is the extraordinary landscaping of
each individual lot that in design and quality of nursery
stock is conspicuously superior to the usual in low-cost developments. This aesthetic detail alone has contributed much
to the value of the properties and to the pleasure of living in
the community, which each year grows a bit more mellow.
Levittown is one of those fortunate residential districts to
which the patina of age is an asset rather than a sign of
decadence. Good lawns, shrubs, perennial ornamentals and
four fruit trees were planted about each house when it
was built, and more botanical embellishments have since
been added by the individual homeowners. On a summer
day the seemingly endless maze of almost identical streets
has a plain but comfortable thin-shaded look which reas-
sures commuting fathers that their daily journeys are not in
vain. With a human population of about eighteen per acre,
there is green living space for all, which would seem incredible to the tenement dwellers of Manhattan thirty-two
miles away where the densities in residential areas average

several hundred persons per acre and run as high as 1300 per acre.

For persons with higher incomes who seek a more sophisticated kind of suburban environment, there are opportunities on the edge of practically every large city. Hugh McDiarmid, a commercial developer in Fairfax County, Virginia, specializes in this type of subdivision for persons who can afford houses in the $25,000 to $30,000 class. Fairfax lies at the doorstep of Washington, D.C. It is one of the fastest growing bedroom counties in the United States and its slogan might very well be, "Washington Sleeps Here." The Fairfax County landscape is peppered with every conceivable type of development from the most elegant Potomac River estate project for high government brass to the tawdriest of newly built communities in the scrub pine brush, where not a single house has inside plumbing because there is no sewer within miles and the soil is too impermeable for septic tanks. The McDiarmid subdivisions near Vienna, including "Holly Hill" and "Woodside Estates," while not in the exclusive estate class are remarkable in that they have most top-drawer attributes at an economy price. Individual properties have sold for only a few thousand dollars more than mass housing on small lots in the Washington area, yet no home stands on less than an acre and most have two to five acres of grounds.

Every dwelling is individually designed by a professional architect of the buyer's choice and is custom built to avoid repetition of style and detail. The natural landscape, which in the Vienna district of the Virginia Piedmont possesses incomparable loveliness, is never violated, except to clear the building sites and to construct simple access roads leading from the public highways. The natural undulating contours of the land are left untouched except to construct a pond here and there to enhance the scene. There are homes at Holly Hill and Woodside Estates which, as long as masonry and wood shall last, will be enjoyed not only for their interior accommodations but for their settings that are a generous sample of Nature in an expansive mood.

The McDiarmid developments, like many others, have a feature which to some is a handicap. They are strictly residential with no shopping centers, schools, churches, or other public institutions. Residences are too dispersed and the inhabitants are too few to support common facilities. No public transportation is available but then most people who have settled in Holly Hill and Woodside Estates are two-car families—one for the commuting father and the other for the errand-running, child-chauffeuring mother.

Commerce and industry have found that suburbia is also their promised land. Retail trade follows the well-heeled consumer and industry locates where there are skilled labor, lower taxes, and cheaper ground. Farmland, well located for industry, sells for $500 to $3000 per acre around big cities whose own factory-district land may average $100,000 an acre or $1000 per front foot. When it is less expensive to buy a 200-acre farm located between railroad tracks and an express highway than to purchase a cramped factory site inside the city, the inducement is strong to take the farm and possibly a few more along with it just for speculation. Even if most of the land is superfluous it makes a fine long-term investment that can only rise in value once development begins. Practically every big industrial company committed to suburban expansion is potentially in the real estate business —a sound hedge first exploited by the railroads, which make money from the rent or sale of land even in years when their trains run in the red.

Today a pattern of land use that is characteristic of the city is reversed out in the country. Whereas crowded urban industry in dingy buildings generally downgrades the quality of adjoining residential zones, in suburbia it can be an advantage to live near an industrial park where streamlined buildings may be surrounded by ample acres of woods and meadow. Seldom do residential developments possess such greenbelt buffer zones as those provided by leading industrial concerns. A new suburban plant by I.B.M., nestled among a few hundred acres of tastefully manicured golf courses and picnic grounds for its employees, may be the only "open space" that prevents a few jet-propelled subdivisions from bumping into one another.

Of course, most suburban industries do not have the extra cash to put into land or landscaping and they may present as hideous an effect in the country as in the city. How to encourage "clean" industry and exclude the objectionable is a raging issue in most new communities, for it is just as easy to create a slum in suburbia as in the city. A truck trailer terminal or service station with an automobile salvage yard attached can accomplish wonders at destroying residential land values for a quarter of a mile around. Suburbia is too often splashed with this kind of irresponsible free enterprise that destroys everyone else's investment.

Sterling Forest is a grandiose scheme without present parallel in suburban planning, but it is perhaps only a forerunner of things to come. This twenty-seven-square-mile tract is forty miles up the Hudson River from Manhattan. There a real-estate concern by the incongruous name of City Investing Company is developing a country "campus" for American industry on what formerly was a wooded reserve in one of the nation's most fashionable rural districts. Sterling Forest, a fabulous holding of the Harriman family until 1952, borders Palisades State Park and the exclusive executive community of Tuxedo Park. It is served by the New York Central Railroad and the recently completed New York State Thruway. Its 17,000-acre campus—larger than the whole of Manhattan Island—will require years to create, but the master plan calls for several manicured industrial research centers, three residential suburbs, an eighty-acre regional shopping mart, and 5000 acres of private parks that are threaded with natural lakes and spring-fed brooks. To gild the lily 125 acres of landscaped gardens are being created through the co-operation of commercial growers of flower bulbs in the Netherlands. In convenience and pleasurable surroundings for work and daily living no detail is omitted which might attract a new elite—the finest minds in American industrial research. In development of the property it is intended to disturb as little as possible the natural loveliness of the beautiful Hudson River countryside.

At Sterling Forest the Union Carbide Corporation is leading off with installation of a nuclear study center, complete with a reactor similar to those in use at several universities. Other large corporations are establishing laboratories for studies in chemistry, electronics, and specialized areas of advanced technology. The landscaped gardens—the most lavish touch of all—draw their inspiration from the Kaukenhof Gardens at Lisse in Holland, where ninety acres bloom in the spring. In the almost forgotten tradition of the finest early American city parks, these gardens have been designed by some of the foremost contemporary horticulturists and architects to be embellished with sculpture, fountains, and rock gardens, as well as a winter conservatory and a terraced restaurant. William Van der Lee, Edward Stone, and Carl van Empelen are among the planners.

As if to underscore the versatility of talent now applied to suburban development, Stanford University on the Pacific Coast has demonstrated that it is just as feasible for an institution of higher learning to go commercial as for a professional realtor to don academic robes. Thanks to an astute proviso in the deed of its founder, Senator Leland Stanford, who seventy years ago may have guessed what was coming, the University is forbidden to sell any of the 9000 acres with which he endowed it. The former senator's tidy fourteen-square-mile parcel, which is approximately one third the area of San Francisco itself, has now become the choicest single piece of open land within commuting distance of that metropolis. Since the University's own needs for classroom space are modest by comparison with the extent of its manorial demesne, it has devised a plan for commercial development which ingeniously abides by the terms of its stewardship. Five thousand acres are not to be sold, but are leased in a way which would have delighted the proprietary spirit of Senator Stanford, as well as such early American realtors as William Penn or Lord Baltimore, whose fondest dreams were of just such a quit-rent system in preference to the fee simple. The Stanford plan guarantees substantial growth of both a well-planned community and the University's endowment fund.

The names of the commercial companies which have acquired long-term rights on the Stanford campus for administration buildings and laboratories read like a page out of Who's Who in American Industry. Eastman Kodak, Kaiser Motors Corporation, and General Electric are among them. An 83-acre regional shopping center began with an initial $15,000,000 project of 50 stores. Eventually a suburban "city" of 45,000 homes will be constructed; the houses themselves are being sold while the ground is conveyed as a leasehold. Inasmuch as the University is to remain lord of the land in perpetuity, it is careful to preserve the natural aesthetic qualities of the environment, not only to insure the pleasure of its tenants but to uphold forever the value of its own property.

The progress of such new departures in suburban development as Sterling Forest and the Stanford University campus will bear watching. If they succeed in truly shaping the environment of the suburban world in a way that provides such necessities of life as a home, job, and place to shop without butchering the natural beauty of the landscape at the same time, then it is possible that great quantities of private capital may be attracted to similar large-scale ventures in the future, and the day of the truly planned community may be at hand.

This kind of investment in a total community, which is such a new experiment, promises a number of attractive inducements both for prospective stockholders as well as for those who would become tenants on the corporate lands. The annual ground rents paid by leasees are similar to the land tax which any householder has to pay anyway whereever he builds. Today's fee-simple ownership is scarcely more than a license to hold as long as one pays taxes. Stock in corporations that would hold in perpetuity the land, sewers, water works, and other general assets of the complete, well-designed suburban community should approximate the ideal investment. They could pay attractive current dividends comparable to those of a public utility company, while at the same time (population increase being what it is) the capital appreciation prospects of good land holdings ought to be excellent—a kind of story-book investment hybrid. By single-management control of ten to twenty square miles of contiguous property in a metropolitan county, it would be possible for a corporation to plan the use of land in a systematic manner so that space would never become congested; so that community facilities would be neither overbuilt nor underdeveloped; and so that the natural beauty of the landscape would be preserved forever to keep the environment attractive and enhance everyone's investments —owners and tenants alike. Tremendous savings should result from such a rational approach in contrast to the waste that is inherent in the haphazard mushrooming of present suburban communities. The latter usually are nothing but fortuitous assemblages of unrelated speculations, put up for quick disposal to persons inexperienced in community-making, in which the original promoters have not the least interest beyond disposition of the last lot.

The potentialities of industry's shift to suburbia are just beginning to be recognized. While employment in manufacturing was falling off in New York City during a recent six-year period, jobs on suburban Long Island increased 94 per cent. New York's Regional Plan Association expects employment in Manhattan to drop 10 per cent from present levels by 1975, while there will be increases of 100 per cent in five suburban counties and at least 50 per cent in six others. This is some of the fuel that stokes the fires of commerce and accounts for the stupendous investments now going into shopping centers and factories on fields where cattle grazed a little while ago. Capital is convinced that suburbia is not a fad, but a proved way of life that promises to hold its popularity for the foreseeable future. R. H. Macy & Company was convinced of this when recently a day's sales in a single suburban branch ran to $200,000. When Gimbels moved into suburban Yonkers, it triumphantly announced its new middle-class status by declaring, "Boys' Bargain Basement now in the Penthouse." In suburbia nobody but nobody is somebody.

Most of the old-established department stores in downtown Minneapolis have heeded the skywriting in Minnesota's heavens by leasing suburban trading posts in the $20,000,000 Southdale shopping center which has gone up seven miles out of town. Southdale has 72 stores with 19 acres of floor space and a parking lot for 5200 cars. In northern New Jersey 75,000 people turned out on opening day of the Garden State Plaza shopping center at Paramus, just eight miles from the George Washington Bridge. Garden State started off with 60 stores, plans to expand to 120. It has everything including a branch of Merrill Lynch, Pierce, Fenner & Smith to make it easy for housewives to trade in du Pont and A. T. & T. while on their way to the supermarket—testimony to the fact that some suburbanites save more than Green Stamps. On Garden State's 150 acres, there are 5500 parking spaces and room for just as many more. To engineer its automobile traffic system took more space than all the buildings. This new retail mart had such an impact upon local trade throughout northern New Jersey that established merchants desperately tried to throttle its momentum but in vain. It has since been joined by Bergen Mall, a $40,000,000 whopper with 28 acres of merchandise space divided among 100 stores, the largest of which, Stern Brothers, hires 1000 employees. Not only the landscape but the mores of society are in transition.

The good health of suburban commerce is a reflection of the good jobs and better wages of suburban residents. When the annual family income throughout the nation averaged $4785, it was $7869 in suburban Westchester County. Families in the bedroom town of Scarsdale, which is within Westchester County, averaged an incredible $16,986. Coupled with their good wages is the low level of welfare obligations supported by suburbanites. While the poorer-paid citizens of New York City were bogged down spending nearly one quarter of their public budget on relief and public hospitalization, suburban Nassau County got by with spending less than three per cent in 1958. Apparently it was hard to find a great many who needed help in Nassau.

Occasionally a suburban community is so successful at attracting industry that, like Teterboro, New Jersey, it scarcely taxes the ordinary homeowner at all. Every place seeks radio and T.V. broadcasting stations that ask for practically no service yet ladle gravy into the local treasuries. When the Consolidated Edison Company's nuclear-fueled power plant goes into action in Westchester County, the county itself will reap an annual tax windfall of $358,000. The local Buchanan school district will pick up $420,000, and the town itself another $99,000. It is possible that the tax rate of local householders in the Buchanan district may be cut 80 per cent. Of course this is the rosiest side of the suburban scene, which unfortunately is not repeated widely enough or often enough—but perhaps it is as likely as winning the daily double. There is no doubt that suburbanization is a cream-separation process, whereby the better paid middle class is floated off by itself where it spends less on public welfare and more on its own desires. That, in turn, is nectar to the smart commercial bee intent upon making honey.

This is not the way it was back in 1898 when the Westchester Homestead and Land Improvement Company tried to establish suburban Indian Hill outside New York City by awarding a full-size building lot "entirely free of mosquitoes" for each fifty cigar coupons of the Manhattan & Bedford Cigar Company. Of the 4000 stogie smokers who eventually claimed a prize, 3576 never even bothered to pay taxes and most of the others evidently were so discouraged by the difficulty of reaching the then almost inaccessible Shangri-La that they did not build so much as a summer cabin. But time has vindicated the extinct M. & B. Cigar Co., for today Indian Hill is smack in the middle of one of the more desirable residential areas of Westchester County—yet most of its proper landlords cannot be located. Perhaps it is just as well; for even if some heirs now should come forward, they would only be told that a modern throughway is about to rip through their neighborhood and that it is a good thing no buildings were put up in the first place. Indian Hill, like so many other pioneers, was born sixty years too soon.

PARADISE LOST

Since colonial days in the sylvan lands of William Penn, the Great Valley west of Philadelphia has been thought by generations of proprietors to have the richest soil and the loveliest terrain in the Middle Atlantic States. Fields and pastures on its limestone and shale were important provisioners of the revolutionary army during the bleak years of rebellion, and right down to the present they have remained choice finishing grounds for Western cattle turned out for a final fattening on their way to abattoirs in the Quaker City. Valley Forge is part of the Great Valley region and, in the autumn when the leaves of its hardwood forests are aflame, it is a place of almost magical loveliness. Fortunately in the past very little industry has come into Great Valley, having spread instead along the banks of the Delaware River up to

Trenton and down to Wilmington. The interior in places is so comparatively undisturbed that Washington himself, were he to revisit the scenes of old campaigns, might easily find his way about.

Now Great Valley is in trouble. The suburbs of Philadelphia have finally reached it and are spilling over its rim in a tidal wave that is shoving the remnants of history off the map to make way for split-levels and supermarkets. While this might be considered progress by some, the majority of the old landholding families would rather that kind of progress should go elsewhere and leave them alone. By and large they are not tempted by the rising values of space, for most of them belong to affluent "Main Line" society, among whom the lovely acres of woods and meadows have an aesthetic and prestige value that exceeds monetary consideration. Families are known as "the 27-acre Smiths" and the "93-acre D. Jones III's." Had this not been so, then Great Valley might long ago have been desecrated in the commercial manner that has unnecessarily destroyed much rural beauty along main highways in eastern Pennsylvania. The contrast between the old-fashioned rusticity of the Main Line estate area and the congested, unsightly West Chester Pike, which lies to the southeast, is a contrast between two concepts of land use and environment which could hardly be reconciled. In Great Valley wealth is used to protect the landscape from desecration, whereas West Chester Pike, and the kind of development it represents, defiles the landcape to make a fast dollar. But West Chester Pike rides the ave of the future. Behind it is the massive swell of population pressure that demands release from the city, and it is not too particular what the suburbs offer as long as it is something—on credit.

Tredyffrin is a township of twenty square miles just outside Philadelphia that is caught up in this wider conflict between the new and the old. The northern part of Tredyffrin Township is Main Line and Great Valley struggling with its back to the wall to preserve a heritage against an advancing suburbia that constantly probes for an opening. It is a struggle for the occupation of space between those who want to keep and those who want to get. The expansion of subdivisions in Tredyffrin has been so persistent yet so scattered in recent years that it has run into a peck of troubles of its own—the kind of headaches common to most suburbs which start out as housing developments and shopping centers, only to find that it takes more than living quarters and a supermarket to make a community. The most painful discovery of all is the realization that suburban living is full of unexpected expenses that have to be met out of the tight budgets of people on fixed wages. About the first panacea that occurs to frightened householders who find themselves in this squeeze is to clamor for almost any kind of new industry to come and share the tax burden. That is what the suburbanites have asked for in Tredyffrin Township and that is what Main Line does not want, particularly in Great Valley.

There is not much doubt as to where the political power lies in Tredyffrin. Only five per cent of the population is in the estate country, which covers roughly 45 per cent of the township. Since people, not the acres they own, cast the votes, Main Line is seriously outmaneuvered. Local politicians, being particularly sensitive to 95 per cent majorities, not only are willing to invite industry but have proposed the cruelest cut of all—that this new industry should settle in the estate country where there is the most room. The local planning commission has selected 3000 acres in the heart of Great Valley, previously classified as purely residential, and redesignated them as "prime industrial land." This is more than half of the Main Line district in Tredyffrin Township. The arrogance of this high-handed tactic so incensed most of the offended landowners that they petitioned the Chester County Court for permission to secede from Tredyffrin and form their own independent Borough of Great Valley.

But the county court was no more sympathetic than the planning commission. In a decision that rejected the plea, Judge Ernest Harvey conceded that the area is "unusually beautiful, safe and healthful, serene, comfortable and suitable for so-called gracious living." But he could find no compelling reason to approve secession for he added, "We need not discuss the expediency of incorporation, when obviously the sole present objective of the petitioners is to keep free of industry and commerce the lands within the area which the Tredyffrin Township Planning Commission has designated as possible prime industrial area."[1] The judge thought the petitioners should find other means to guard their interests. There were few if any among the losers who believed that a minority of five per cent could find other means to stand off for very long a majority of ninety-five per cent and a planning commission stacked against them. The planning commission for its part tried to justify its action by noting unctuously that Tredyffrin is in the direct path of the outward expansion of Philadelphia's metropolitan area, and "one consideration which cannot be ignored is the dire need for suitable lands for the future economic well being of the four counties around Philadelphia."[2]

That this "dire need" has arisen because of negligence in proper land planning by the four counties does not seem to penetrate the consciousness of either the electorate or public officials. The Tredyffrin incident points up the fact that any group of people who are respectful of the landscape may become sitting ducks for an onslaught of irresponsible mass pressure that in any economic extremity would be willing to destroy the good qualities of the environment for a shot of revenue. Condonation of this kind of fiscal opportunism is suburbia's most serious threat to its own dreams of a pleasant habitat. It is akin to the practice of cities that allows commercial advertising to deface public property in the holy name of revenue. It is a disease that can lead to a complete breakdown of public discrimination and good taste, which, by so much bad example, is already at a shoddy level.

The push to suburbia seems a magnificent inspiration to all aspiring refugees from the city. Each downtown mugging, each outbreak of juvenile violence terrifies more parents into risking whatever credit they can muster just to get away where the whole family might feel safer; where the children could receive a better education and associate with more desirable companions. Blurbs in the Sunday papers that depict endless delights at Riverforest Heights put their minds in a giddy spin. "Excellent schools," "low taxes," "next door to open country," "short drive to town," "exclusive community of friendly neighbors"—such pabulum to the harassed is very attractive especially when it is sweetened with "low down payments" and "monthly installments just like rent" and "you own your own home." The catch, of course, is that no one gets anything for nothing even at Riverforest Heights, despite all the "savings by experienced builders."

While local taxes may have been low the year Riverforest Heights was on the drafting board, by the time 500 happy families have moved in and demanded services a rather remarkable metamorphosis has begun which never seems to end. More children arrive each year, and each September the school enrollment goes up. Taxes seem to have a way of growing up with a growing community. Meanwhile, new subdivisions rise all around Riverforest Heights. The leafy trees on the horizon are replaced with utility poles, while the river that was there for a summer is boxed up in a concrete culvert and buried by bulldozers to make room for more house lots. The short drive to town takes longer and longer as more and more commuters share the once open road and throttle it with traffic. The irrepressibly enthusiastic promoters liquidate their Riverforest Builders, Inc., hitch up their office trailer, and move on to create "Meadow-land Farms," a few miles farther out where it is again "next door to open country" and "taxes are low."

The anguish of the harassed taxpayer in the expanding suburb; the distress of the estate owner who resents encroachment by industry; the concern of the industrialist who must find room for expansion just as urgently as a ballooning population must have more jobs—all these bewildering human responses to the new changes that are taking place beyond the rims of cities are penalties that arise from the basic fact that more people need more room for everything, and they must find it where they can on their own when there is no co-ordinated regional policy or plan for the use of land. The inexperienced, politically influenced local planning board, that arbitrarily plucks several thousand acres out of a choice residential classification and plunks it into the industrial pot, is acting in panic to resolve a problem that should have been anticipated long before things got so critical. That is not planning; it is political mayhem after it is too late to plan. Far too much so-called community planning and zoning has no rational basis, but is this sort of manipulation by pressure groups and insiders with political pull.

The householder in a new subdivision who does not anticipate a rise in taxes does not understand the basic facts of suburban life, and it is doubtful if he ever found a clue to them in his high-school civics course. Every new facility and service today costs more than it did even a few years ago. As long as inflation continues (and it has been pretty steady throughout the conscious years of most young people who are candidates for suburbia), it may be anticipated that each new school will be more expensive than the last. Each street or sewer will cost more. Each new police car and every new policeman to drive it will up the tax rate of a new community. There is no way to accommodate people and serve them without more buildings and more personnel on the public payroll. Furthermore, since the suburb is the favorite type of new community, new householders cannot expect to freeload on previously existing facilities built to serve a sparse rural population. In the suburb practically everything is as new as the people. No wonder the tax rate turns out to be new too. Inflation in taxes and prices is a direct consequence of population inflation and the higher costs of creating goods and services that more people demand. Unless living standards are to decrease, higher prices and heavier taxes must be the inevitable companions of population growth. Most things that people need become more difficult to get the more people there are to supply.

It has been calculated that every new home costs the average suburban community about $1500 in public expenses beyond what would have been spent had the house not been built at all. In one California district the added burden upon the public for each new home and family is $13,000. Bond issues for schools, streets, civic buildings, sewers, water mains, recreational facilities, etc., represent expenditures beyond current income that eventually have to be paid for. Only if growth were to stop could a community catch up with its obligations, but to stop growth is the last thing most eager-beaver communities would dream of. Trade interests oppose any such heresy, and most householders are under the blissful delusion that newcomers help them pay off old debts instead of sticking the community with new ones. There is not much chance to get public support for serious land-use planning when the majority is that naïve. It should be obvious that taxes on all properties, old and new alike, have to be raised to cover surcharges for any new community investments and services. No matter how recently one may have settled in a suburb, others will come later and their arrival will eventually raise the tax rate.

The public cost of accommodation is accentuated in suburbs because the dispersed and horizontal pattern of growth covers more space per capita than city growth. Longer streets, longer water mains, more school buses, more of everything that is multiplied in any way by the vastly greater consumption of space per capita raises both capital and service costs above those in the city where people live vertically and compactly. In one suburban community in Maryland, local police prowl cars drive the equivalent of a great circle around the earth every six days. In a city the same number of patrolmen could protect as many people by walking the beat on their own shoe leather. As every suburbanite soon discovers, the old woes he leaves behind in the city are soon exchanged for new woes in the subdivision. Each is his own judge as to whether or not he struck the better bargain.

In just two years between 1956 and 1958, real-estate taxes in suburban counties outside New York City rose fantastically in response to an equally fabulous population growth. Taxes in Suffolk County, Long Island, increased 53.7 per cent. Those in Rockland registered a gain of 54 per cent; Nassau, 20.7 per cent; Putnam, 19:6 per cent; and Westchester, 14 per cent. However, the suburbanite can be consoled in that nearly all these added levies are spent on services that directly benefit him and his children. The welfare load in development communities is very low while public schools, at least so far as physical plant is concerned, are almost invariably better than in large cities. Since 1940 the population in Nassau County has increased 190 per cent while the school tax has jumped 641 per cent. This result, of course, has stung the homeowners painfully but investors in Nassau's commercial real estate are really at their wits' end. Within a recent six-year period, the annual returns from commercial rentals plummeted to three per cent from a previous nine per cent. That kind of trivial dividend today is ruinous. Several real-estate investors have sought relief through the courts, hoping to get reduced assessments. Meanwhile more and bigger schools are on order so that, even if assessments are lowered, the rate will probably climb. Suburban homeowners would be among the first to agree with Tax Foundation, Inc., that all taxes, direct and hidden, now claim about one third of the average family's income. According to Tax Foundation, Inc., a family earning $4500 annually pays $1393 to Federal, state, and local governments. A family earning $8000 pays $2726.

People in a few fortunate communities are not so much concerned with taxes as they are with preserving the way of life that enticed them to the outskirts in the first place. Greenwich, Connecticut, is an attractive suburban township of 50,000 residents, and would like to remain beautiful. Industry would like to move in, but Greenwich has let it be known that it can do very well without a new wave of industry whether it is "park" type or not. Unlike Tredyffrin, the anti-industrialists are definitely in the saddle and the Planning and Zoning Commission, with a fine instinct for self-preservation, thinks likewise. Practically the whole town is zoned residential and 75 per cent of it is zoned for house lots of one, two, and four acres or more. This has discouraged extensive spread of cheap subdivisions. But a short ride to New York City via the New Haven Railroad or the Merritt Parkway, the "back country" estate area of Greenwich enjoys living in gold-plated rusticity on a Madison Avenue income, and sees no reason to change. Dean Clark, Chairman of its Planning and Zoning Commission, says, "Intruders from any direction must be held at bay."

When an interloping, speculating newcomer recently invested $60,000 in some "back country" acreage, Mr. Clark estimated the land might sell for $300,000 if his Planning and Zoning Commission would allow it to be developed for light industry, office, or laboratory use. Knowing the sentiment of

the town's majority, the Commission was against it. "Perhaps some day such may be the case," Mr. Clark hazarded,
"but for the time being, at any rate, the people of Greenwich clearly want the character of this town protected.
. . ."³ Greenwich has taken a cold, hard look at the future
in a way that most communities refuse to do. It has detailed
plans which envisage that ultimately 15,000 more persons
will be permitted to settle within the "acreage zones" and
22,000 more in the medium or high-density areas. After that
the door will be bolted. This is the way a suburban town can
retain its country character on the edge of the city, but to
do it the citizens have to carry the tax load without aid from
industry or commerce.

THE PRICE OF SPACE

People have discovered that the other half of suburban life
is spent on the highway, and potential customers are inclined to analyze the communication angle rather thoroughly. The canny ones know by clocking it themselves
how many minutes it takes from Great Neck to Herald
Square. The logistics of transporting the wage-earning end
of the family to and from the job is discussed as seriously as
the accouterments of the electronic kitchen. Just to test the
convertibility of time and space, one enterprising developer
on Long Island recently offered the identical seven-room
ranch house in four different locations. Prospective buyers
had the choice of an expensive lot closer to New York City or
of cheaper ones farther out—the farther the cheaper. At
Hicksville, which is thirty-one miles away, the house sold
for $14,790. At Babylon, forty miles out, a duplicate sold
for $13,990. At Commack, forty-six miles distant, the price
tag on the same building was $13,790. At Captree, fifty miles
beyond, the house listed at $12,990. Of the first 121 sales,
the Hicksville home proved to be an overwhelming choice

despite the fact that it cost $800 to $1800 more than its duplicate in the other areas. Sixty-five customers bought Hicksville; 32 chose Commack; 14 picked Babylon; while 10 settled for Captree. Some close figuring was involved in these decisions, but the main point was clear—the suburban homeowner does think of the commuting problem before he buys, and he puts a price on time and space.

The effect of distance upon costs of land to subdividers and, eventually, the sizes and costs of lots are a vital matter. In Oakland County, northwest of Detroit, raw land runs from $100 per acre in remote sections, while prices are as high as $16,000 per acre in the more desirable residential districts. Around Chicago there is practically no development land left in the older suburban areas, but farther out prices of single improved lots range from $45 to $225 per front foot. It is said that land prices around Chicago have been going up at the rate of ten per cent annually. Outside Los Angeles the acceleration of land values has been just as great. There a single unimproved one-acre lot may sell for $6500—with improvements it might be over $10,000. Around the big cities where express highways are fairly well developed, the average commuter can calculate that a thirty-mile trip means an hour's travel time each way at a cost of at least thirty dollars weekly. Sometimes parking charges make the rate even higher. Car pools, when possible, cut the cost but add to travel time.

When the American Automobile Association made a traffic study in 1957 to determine the impact upon the suburbanite of commuting difficulties in the Washington metropolitan area, it found that driving time into the center of the city from points 15 miles beyond varied from 36 to 51 minutes. The average commuter must count on spending seven to eight hours a week behind the wheel—the equivalent of adding a day without pay to the work week. And this does not include the time it takes to park and get from there to the job. One Washingtonian who gave up an apartment on Connecticut Avenue, where it cost him $2 a week to go to work on the streetcar, found that it nicked him $19 a week to commute from a suburban split-level in Montgomery County 12 miles and 35 minutes away. Included in the $19 tab is a $7 weekly fee for parking close to work. This is not the end of the family transportation charges. In the city the grocer and other service stores are within walking distance. In the development a car must be used for practically everything but walking the dog.

The rate of suburban growth around Washington in the past few years has paralleled the growth of the Federal bureaus, and the prospects are for further expansion of both. Montgomery County, Maryland, spurted ahead from 165,000 to 300,000, or 81 per cent between 1950 and 1957. Fairfax County, Virginia, shot up 105 per cent from 100,000 to 205,000 in the same period. When growth of this magnitude occurs in so short a time in areas that have had no previous experience with such human inundation and are utterly without a rational philosophy of land utilization, it is no wonder that irreparable damage is done to both the appearance and utility of the landscape before people wake up. The rise of rural slums and an inadequate highway grid are inevitable. Both of these counties have their share of such grief. They will be saddled with the consequences for all time to come because the general pattern of settlement was fixed without reasonable preparation. Pioneer America was settled in this way, but on the whole the result was salutary because the settlers were farmers and the farm itself was both home and job. The separation of job from home is the fundamental weakness of suburbia. Everything the family needs, including employment, is available only at a distance.

Suburbia holds forth the promise of much, but delivers only a fraction of its potential because of its haphazard, unco-ordinated growth. The consequences of free-for-all development can be shrugged off for a while, but by the time great areas of space have been committed the community is bogged down in debts and costly mistakes that have to be corrected at even greater expense. Yet open country, which entices the settlers, retreats farther toward the horizon with each new subdivision. Since the pattern of suburban growth is horizontal, dispersed, and eccentric to the city, which is the economic center of gravity in any metropolitan area, subdivision land will never have the intrinsic worth that city land possesses. Costly renewal programs by private investors such as are justified in the hearts of cities will seldom be warranted in suburbs because it would be cheaper to by-pass them entirely and start over on fresh ground. Future renewal of suburban slums will be chiefly at public expense, if they are renewed at all. Ultimately as houses wear out, most suburban land will have little trade-in value, principally because its original cost is rather artificially inflated by liberal credit and it lacks intrinsic locational advantages.

Since open land on the suburban fringe is private property, owners cannot let it stand idle or in agriculture forever. The open spaces available one year are gone the next. Meanwhile the chance to acquire real parks and public recreational space is lost. Some cities have found that suburbanites come into town to visit parks because they have none of their own. To live horizontally and at the same time to multiply rapidly consumes an enormous amount of space for homes and highways. The abundance of private land which suburbia offers to each family is something of a modern miracle, but it is a miracle achieved at great expense and definitely it is the product of a deliberate trade of time for space.

When one stops to think of it, the modern commuters' suburb is an extraordinary phenomenon. It gives more people more space at a time when population growth is more rapid than at any other time in history, but to gain this advantage the breadwinner must travel tedious and expensive distances to his job every day. The most unbelievable part of the suburban story is that it is really possible at all. For a family to have a fifth of an acre to itself in Levittown or five acres in Greenwich at a time of accelerated industrialization and human proliferation is almost a contradiction to the logic of geometry.

If one judges this situation realistically, it is apparent that the era of the commuter suburb's explosive growth will be rather brief—in terms of human time and social institutions, comparable to the flash of a meteor against the long darkness of a winter night. We are already witnessing the suburb's heyday; and those of us who have found a niche in its promised land of split-levels and curvilinear streets should consider ourselves privileged not only in terms of present alternatives but in terms of the lesser opportunity there will be for later generations to enjoy the same escape. When the day comes that the time spent commuting cancels out the value of making the trip, then the spread of suburbia will stop and a return to vertical city living will be necessary to accommodate the growing hordes of humanity. Although this sad day cannot be averted, it can be delayed by better land-use planning for fast, cheap routes of transportation.

By whatever degree travel time can be reduced the periphery of suburbia may be extended. It is said that when subways were first built in Manhattan, they increased eight times the value of land around outlying stations because a new generation of commuters then was willing to settle so far from the heart of town because it could get to work so fast. The future limits of suburbia probably will be determined not by available land many miles from the city but by the time it takes to get from home to job. If the future use of suburban space does not make reservations for fast, easy, and cheap transportation, the surge to the outskirts will gradually peter out. Any community which wishes to strangle its future expansion need only neglect plans for limited-access express highways and rapid-transit systems. The first step in such planning is to set aside land for these facilities while it is still available. Later may be too late.

CHAPTER 5

Suburbia–Continued

THE WEB

Back in 1953 David Connor and his family moved to Green Knolls, a new development of split-level homes at Plainview on Long Island. In 1959 the Connors, among 350 other householders, were informed by the State of New York that their dwellings had been condemned to make way for the new Wantagh-Oyster Bay Expressway. Between 1953 and 1959 suburbia had grown so fast and so solidly beyond Green Knolls that the newer residents farther out needed more and better highways even if it meant putting those roads through the parlors of earlier settlers. Former open space had been so completely filled in that someone had to get out of the way. By the time the Connors had found a new home most of their dispossessed neighbors had already left, taking payments from the state as their only consolation. Neglected lawns in the evacuated no man's land turned to weeds while abandoned houses were ransacked by vandals even in broad daylight. As Mr. Connor remarked just before his own departure from Green Knolls, "It's eerie, that's the only way to describe it. When we moved here six years ago, I never expected to be the king of a ghost town."[1]

While this was an unpleasant denouement for the Connors

and for others like them, every taxpayer in practically every metropolitan area in the United States is in debt for bond issues floated to pay the frightful costs of destroying newly developed communities in order to build even newer highways. Yet not one of these metropolitan areas is ignorant of the impact that expanding populations make upon suburban growth. Despite the obvious sprawl of humanity over the countryside and every indication that more is to come, very few communities or states take precautions to buy land for future public purposes while it is still undeveloped and relatively cheap. It was clear to the State of New York in 1953 that all of Nassau County lay in the path of a tremendous surge to the suburbs, yet it did not prepare even then for the expected growth by buying raw land it knew it would have to have soon for new highways.

Just before the days of Green Knolls, the taking of land by the state for future use in that area might have cost between $2000 and $4000 per acre. Two decades ago it could have been acquired for as little as $200 to $300 per acre. Once it had been covered with split-levels, the condemnation charges had risen to perhaps $50,000 per acre—and it takes sixty acres per mile to build a modern expressway. To cut a ten-mile swath through settled communities, in order to make roads leading to other newer communities beyond, can cost as much as $30,000,000, whereas, if the land were bought two decades in advance of growth, the cost might be a comparatively trivial $15,000 to $20,000. Often landowners on the peripheries of growth will grant highway easements without any charge at all just to attract mass pressure in their direction and thereby hasten the rise in market value of their other holdings. This is the magnitude of penalties laid upon the ordinary taxpayer by politicians and highway departments which refuse to engage in preventive engineering. Then people wonder why population growth and development inevitably results in a rising tax rate.

Some time ago the Planning Board of Bucks County, Pennsylvania, which is on the edge of Philadelphia, proposed to the state's own Highway Department that it acquire a specific right-of-way with no buildings on it. Philadelphia had constructed a road that obviously would dump a lot of traffic on the county's doorstep and somehow it would have to be accommodated. But the Highway Department replied that it was without funds although it recognized the wisdom of the proposal. When, at a later date, the Planning Board was confronted by a developer who asked permission to build in the zone of the proposed right-of-way, it was helpless to prevent him. He owned the land and neither Bucks County nor the state would buy it. When the Highway Department was asked by the Planning Board what it would do when a road had to be built, it replied to the effect, "Let them build and we will condemn when it is necessary." Presumably the Highway Department expected by that time to have boodles of cash from another bond issue which it could then bulldoze away without restraint.

It is estimated that the New York-Connecticut-New Jersey metropolitan region, which at the moment contains almost 16,000,000 people spread over 1100 square miles, will increase 25 per cent in population by 1975. The increase in area, however, will be perhaps another 700 square miles if suburbanization continues its present pace. The entire state of Rhode Island covers only 1214 square miles. While the metropolitan region pivoting on Manhattan is the largest in the United States, it is only one of many from coast to coast which are all off on the same kind of land-gobbling binge. For the moment there is plenty of space in the United States. If population growth were to stabilize at the present level of increase, it would take 4000 years to suburbanize everything from coast to coast. However, since populations grow like compound interest and double every fifty years or less, it could be only 350 years before every acre of the United States is part of a housing development. If then people were fairly well distributed, there would be neither a single farm left without three or four Cape Cods to the acre nor a remote mountain top without a split-level. People would be saved the effort and expense of going on vacations, for the landscape would be crowded everywhere and it would look pretty much alike beneath all the roofs and asphalt. There would be less room for a swim at the beach than in the bathtub, provided there were enough water to fill the tub.

Obviously the dynamics of population expansion are fantastically unlimited while the area of land is so finite that sometime within the next few generations the present trend in housing will be modified, or the nation's food supply will be grown on roof tops and in window boxes rather than on farms as we now think of them. Mathematically there cannot continue to be both population multiplication and land subtraction at present rates without reaching some kind of saturation point. Perhaps the change will come when all the open land between the largest cities is filled in and the congestion will have become so impenetrable and costly to deal with that the whole idea will be scotched for economic reasons. Either horizontal suburbia with all its merits of ample space for the family will have passed on with the dodo for lack of area, or a mass approval of birth control will have swept the American mind. It is anybody's guess as to which notion will prevail, but the arithmetic of space calls for a showdown between the nation's room and its roomers unless future generations become frogmen and mermaids and take to the sea. Other mammals have done it.

While portions of today's suburbia grow up like Green Knolls as tight complexes with no reserves of open space for future roads or recreational areas, other portions are scattered like shot from a blunderbuss without the slightest umbilical tie to their maternal metropolises. These dispersed housing developments often leapfrog so far into the cornfields that all public services are left behind. Instead of sewers each house has a do-it-yourself septic tank. Instead of water mains each home has a well. Instead of public buses and trains, there is nothing but the private automobile and the obsolete art of walking to put people in contact with jobs, supplies, school, and the rest of society. No dauntless pioneer on the fringe of Indian territory was so far removed from the essentials of existence.

It is no simple trick to perform these acrobatics year after year; but it looks so easy in the color brochures of the developers who pick up $1000-per-acre land in the rural sticks and carve it into house lots that the F.H.A. and V.A. cooperatively revalue at $2000 to $3000 each as soon as houses are erected on them. This wonderful opportunity to kite the mortgage value of land eight to twelve times beyond its intrinsic worth with the blessing of government insurance lies behind the happy urge to send suburbia sprawling in all directions over the countryside. Under these easy rules any farm which a promoter can lay his hands on becomes a potential subdivision. Yet Albert M. Cole, a former Administrator of the Housing and Home Finance Agency, apparently did not recognize that this agency had any responsibility for the consequences. In an address before the Prefabricated Home Manufacturers Institute, Mr. Cole lamented the fact that spreading metropolitan areas were becoming "a maze of septic tank suburbias." With a solicitude not bestowed upon the candidate for a mortgage, Mr. Cole cautioned the same person after he had become a suburban taxpayer that within a few years he will face demands for millions of dollars to "straighten out the mess." While the F.H.A. has been insuring mortgages on homes without sewer connections, the Housing and Home Financing Agency, according to Mr. Cole, has been "flying a warning flag about the growth of the septic-tank civilization, citing the grave need for planning on a metropolitan scale, and calling for action to follow that planning."[2]

It was a myopia of this peculiar brand that recently inspired F.H.A. to drop its minimum-room requirements for a single-family home from three and a bath to two and a bath at about the same time Federal Housing Administrator Norman Mason called upon the U.S. homebuilding industry to erect better houses. If one considers the haphazard way in which subdivisions have sprouted and sprawled on the very outskirts of Washington, D.C., it is clear that the Federal housing agencies are impotent to offer the kind of leadership that might avert the appalling waste the suburban taxpayer must underwrite. In generalities their advice is good. In specific practice there is neither muscle in the arm nor vision in the head.

Henrietta Township is a suburban area outside of Rochester, New York, where a single developer sold 640 homes without a sewer system. Almost as soon as the proud but unsuspecting owners had moved in, turned on their faucets, and flushed their toilets the lawns and gardens began to ooze like a wet sponge. At that point local health officials minced no words and wasted no time. The people were ordered to install a sewer system at once and to discontinue the use of septic tanks. Already mortgaged up to their necks, the new homeowners screamed that they would be ruined. Fortunately they were able to get the developer to pay half the cost, but they were obliged to take an assessment for the balance.

At Sedgely Farms in New Castle County, Delaware, ninety distraught suburbanites with overflowing septic tanks were informed by their deputy county engineer that it would cost them as much as $5000 per home to tie into the county sewer system. They were over a mile beyond the nearest main trunk with very few habitations in between to help carry the burden of extending service to their hinterland bathrooms. While some of the residents of Sedgely Farms favored paying even this fantastic cost, others balked and asked to wait until more people should build in the area and help to carry the burden.

To wait for proper sewer service calls for some restraint according to a New Jersey resident in the same predicament.

In this particular instance the people had acquired attractive summer cottages in a newly developed seashore community in popular Atlantic County. The land was old coastal marsh which had been covered over with a thick layer of dredged sand. It all looked very beachlike and ready for the patter of bare feet. The bungalows were built on concrete slabs, and each was supplied with a septic tank with overflow tile beneath the surface. When, by chance, a surveyor probed for the ground water table after people had moved in, he found that it was less than a foot from the surface. Puzzled as to how a drowned septic tank could function, the surveyor inquired of an elderly couple if they had experienced any trouble. "We manage by being careful," was their discreet reply, "but those with children have a rule to use 'it' three times before flushing." The disposal wagons do a steady business in that community.

For those dependent upon septic tanks it is an advantage to be on flat ground. At least the houses themselves are not likely to slide away. Around Los Angeles many homes are built upon hillsides and some of these locations are underlain with sheets of shale rock tilted seaward. When the underground shale is slicked with sewage effluent or too much lawn sprinkling, the loose earth above it may be inclined to slip downhill a bit. Since this is one of Nature's ancient ways of leveling mountains, the leveling of a house is easy. The residents of Portuguese Bend, south of Los Angeles, learned this geologic truth the hard way. When the septic tanks of their new homes had saturated the shale beneath their 225-acre hillside community, everything began to respond slowly to the tug of gravity—lots, lawns, shrubbery, and 156 houses, each costing $25,000 to $50,000, gently slumped downhill as though they were so much custard pudding.

Every commercial insurance company knows people will take outlandish risks if they can hedge themselves. Now that good locations for developments near cities are getting harder to find, some operators have no compunction about building on river flood plains or in the drainage areas of creeks that usually are placid but sometimes discharge a flash of runoff water after a heavy thundershower. That is the very reason that insurance companies refuse to issue policies covering flood damage. But, even around Hartford, Connecticut, the insurance capital of the United States, where everyone should know better, there are hundreds of houses in the path of peril from springtime overflows of the Connecticut River. Most of these are in new developments that are down on an obvious flood plain; but that location did not disturb either the speculators who built them or the F.H.A. which backs the mortgages.

So many communities have suffered devastating flood damage in recent years that Congress has been under heavy pressure to let the government underwrite the losses of citizens and corporations which foolishly wander down to the water's edge. The plaintive theme song is that floods are calamities of Nature, whereas in fact wherever flood damage occurs it occurs because Man trespasses where Nature has clearly warned him to keep away. Rivers and creeks established their rights-of-way in ages past while engaged in their vast working of sculpturing the landscape. It would be well if Man, a rather recent visitor upon the terrestrial crust, would respect his elders. The greater number of floods that have destroyed residential and industrial properties in recent years are not due to increased sunspots, nuclear explosions, or a switch in ancient storm tracks, but only to the simple fact that more foolish people have built in places where Nature intended that high water should run occasionally.

It is of such strands that the web of suburbia is being woven across the open spaces between cities. The cities themselves are the anchor points to which the first threads are pinned. From there on, unlike the webs of nature, there is no supervising architect or engineer responsible for a rational design. Everyone with a yen to try his luck at catching flies, spins his own subsidiary web. The result is tight weaving in some places and in others a thin scattering of miscellaneous fibers. Once these unco-ordinated networks are thus strung up in piecemeal fashion, the opportunity to employ a master spider, who might have done a professional job, is lost forever. The only resemblance that these disorganized products of the superior human mind bear to the skillful, efficient, and beautiful work of the lowly, ignorant araneid is that they catch their prey. No wonder one is left with the impression that, after all, this is their main purpose.

THE FLIES

Salvador Dali has created the "Crisalida" as an advertising gimmick for the manufacturer of a commercial tranquilizer. It is a plastic-covered cocoon sixty feet long and high enough to walk through. Soft lighting effects and a breathing pulsation created by puffs of air are supposed to mesmerize persons who enter to the smiling welcome of its mellow-toned hostess, who is the most soothing feature of the exhibition. Within the time it takes to wander the sixty feet through the Crisalida's cushioned corridor the visitor, with a long line pushing behind him, is supposed to experience a "transition from anxiety to tranquility." Any community under tension might consider the installation of a public Crisalida as a dry variation of the ancient Roman bath to induce relaxation among the populus on an assembly-line basis. It would be cheaper than parks, less tiring than gardening, and it requires comparatively little space considering the number of people it can process in an hour.

With the acumen of an artist, Dali grasped the essential struggle of the human fly to escape the web of a routine environment and devised this easy sixty-foot tunnel to lead him to nirvana. While it may be a preview of the future, nevertheless, for the moment there are still many old-fashioned souls who prefer traditional ways to exercise their muscles and relax their nerves. So long as there are holdouts of the old vintage, there will be some agitation for open space in suburbia. Though no form of mass settlement has ever given the individual metropolitan family so much room as the modern subdivision, the community as a whole is likely to end up with less public recreation space than any other civilized people has ever known. Absorbed with their own gardens, most suburbanites give no thought to public pleasure grounds until suddenly preschool children have grown into their teens and they have no place to go for group sports and picnics. Also the parents of these young people, once they are released from playpen duty, look for recreation away from home only to discover that there are no nearby public parks, athletic fields, or beaches to go to.

For a people so long devoted to the great out-of-doors, it is a hard comedown for modern Americans to find that even in suburbia the opportunities for teenage and adult athletics are almost nil except at private country clubs where membership rolls are usually restricted to keep from being overrun. Thomas K. Cureton, Jr., Professor of Physical Education at the University of Illinois, believes that a hothouse life unvaried by outdoor activities leads to relatively early physical deterioration. He says that middle age may be defined as the point at which physical abilities begin to decline and that recent health studies show there is a marked tendency for that middle-age decline to set in prematurely after the twenty-sixth birthday.

To offset early wilting of the human organism, Professor Cureton advocates a program of adult physical activity that includes walking, running, skating, skiing, dancing, canoeing, rowing, climbing, and cross-country hiking. It is the consensus of physicians that exercise should be a matter of daily routine rather than of week-end and vacation spurts. If regular and moderate exercise is essential to human health, as the renowned heart specialist Dr. Paul Dudley White believes, then some space for sports or just plain hiking and cycling should be set aside in each new community. Dr. White is himself an ardent cyclist, but it takes a good deal of searching these days to find a safe place to ride a bike.

Dr. Paul B. Stoxen, a Chicago chiropractor, looks at the suburban scene a little differently. He finds that many of his patients get either too much exercise at the wrong time or the wrong kind of exercise altogether. He blames a whole new series of ailments upon "modern machines and the mass movement of people to the suburbs." At an annual meeting of the National Chiropractic Association, Dr. Stoxen said he had observed that too many city dwellers unaccustomed to outdoor activity suddenly take on too much when they land in suburbia. They may become afflicted with "patio posture," which comes from improperly lifting heavy objects such as flagstones for patios, or they may get "tractor back," which is a compression of the spine produced by riding power lawn mowers. "Green thumb thigh," in Dr. Stoxen's glossary, is an ailment which the neophyte gardener acquires by spading. It is possible that these unfortunate patients already have passed prematurely their middle-age peak by the time they have won their middle-class rights to a suburban existence, and the best thing for them is to go back to the city.

To go back to the city is the last thing that would appeal to the average suburbanite, at least until his children are through public school. What is desirable is that suburbia be made to live up to its bright promises to both children and adults. Basically the concept of clean, spacious residential neighborhoods on the edge of the working city is an excellent one. To maintain that residential character and enhance it with community recreation grounds that are pleasant to look at and adequate to play in is all that most taxpayers would request in the way of community environment. They want suburbia to succeed and they have put their life savings into a dream that it will. The acquisition of public open space within walking distance of the home of every school-age child is as vital in suburbia as in the city. Adults can go longer distances in a car although they, too, prefer facilities that are close at hand. In solidly built-up developments landscaped yards are no substitute for a baseball diamond; neither are the streets.

The most respected of human attitudes do not develop or flourish amid ugliness. If children grow up spiritually undernourished, the society that they create in turn will be underprivileged and anemic. A concern for the qualities of landscape can scarcely be brushed off as idle sentimentality, for the really important thing is not what is done to the inanimate environment but what that environment can do to living people. If the human organism is constantly harassed by tensions and stresses, or if the little part of the world it lives in is tawdry, disorganized, and cheap, it will surely be conditioned to react in a frantic, unbecoming manner. On the other hand, when things go well and the environment is both beautiful and functional, the citizen himself is likely to be more agreeable to others and more contented with his own existence. If it were not to live a fuller, richer, pleasanter life people scarcely would go to the expense and effort of moving to suburbia in the first place. Those who plan the suburbs of the future could not go wrong if they were guided by what is right for people rather than by what they think people will endure if there is no alternative. The good life can be lived only in a good environment. Dr. Paul B. Sears, a past president of the American Association for the Advancement of Science, remarked in an address before this eminent group, "Our future security may depend less upon priority in exploring outer space than upon our wisdom in managing the space we live in."[3]

Of course, if nothing at all is done to give people a break, they will manage somehow by themselves to find a way to rejuvenate their spirits. The growing popularity of suburban Crazy Couple Clubs is heartwarming assurance that inanity can forestall insanity. Crazy Couple Clubs are organized by suburbanites who are bored with propriety, tight budgets, and the long time it takes to become twentieth vice president. According to insurance broker Arnold Domenitz of Manhasset, Long Island, "We're getting tired of doing the same old thing. We're also tired of battling our way into theaters and then fighting the mob to get a drink afterward."[4] The Manhasset Club is composed of thirteen couples who spend a biweekly night on the town in some absurd, offbeat escapade at a ten-dollar limit per couple. For the total $130 the whole jolly gang may exercise with a yogi, visit city Night Court, or descend upon a Greenwich Village bistro. A session with Alcoholics Anonymous, followed by attendance at a bartenders' school the same night, is better than par for the course. For the tired suburbanite who would like his entertainment brought to him like milk or the daily newspaper, there is an agency in New York City which rents beatniks to house parties. For $25 to $50 an evening the hired guests will appear in beards or leotards, read their own poetry, and give their hosts and hostesses a glimpse of what it is like to be real beat in case they do not know already.

THE WISE USE OF LAND

Geographer Jean Gottmann uses the Greek word *Megalopolis* to describe the collection of large cities between Boston and Washington, D.C., which has expanded so extensively through residential and industrial suburbanization that now it is possible to distinguish the skeleton of a single gigantic conurbation several hundred miles in length. As that gargantuan growth continues the skeleton will put on flesh and, according to Dr. Gottmann, the world will see emerge for the first time the cityscape of the future—a vast assembly of many vertical centers and innumerable horizontal outskirts. Today a ride from Boston to Washington via the New

Haven and Pennsylvania Railroads is a preview of this new world in the making. Someday from the air this landscape might resemble an enormous pan of fried eggs—the yolks being the tall cities, surrounded by their flat suburban whites. More conurbations of the megalopolitan type are emerging in other parts of the United States and elsewhere in the world. This being fact and not popular-science fiction, it would be well to plan the use of limited space in these compact areas so that our particular pans of eggs will not look scrambled instead of sunny-side-up.

In 1950 the Bureau of the Census indicated that the urbanized area of the United States was about 15,000,000 acres. Because of the fast horizontal spread of modern suburbia, about 400,000 to 500,000 acres now are added annually to built-up districts. At this rate 1980 should find the total urbanized scene twice as large as it was in 1950. This kind of Jack-and-the-Beanstock growth could easily get out of control. In many places it is out of control already. The whole modern suburban experiment is so new it is not surprising that it is as full of bugs as a street light in June. These defects should be corrected before the model goes into real mass production, or the tax load on suburbia for repairs and replacements later will become so insupportable that property owners will be driven back to central cities for shelter.

Unlike living organisms, the man-made environment has no genetic guidance system for future growth. The adult clam would have a hard time if Nature did not anticipate that, as the soft living muscle grows larger, its inanimate shell must expand in the same proportions. But there are no mysterious guiding genes within the embryonic city or suburb that automatically control its expansion in such a way that it will be as viable at maturity as it was in infancy. This is where use of the human mind with its analytical abilities should come into the picture. The fact that the inanimate suburban environment cannot determine, without help, its own most efficient and beautiful shape makes it necessary for Man to do the job. Unfortunately government is trained to run things but not to create them; accordingly, the community that waits for government initiative in this complicated matter is likely to atrophy for lack of interest. Some speculative builders have only a temporary stake in the communities they design, as a rule, it is difficult to be sanguine about assistance from that source either. As liberty is the product of eternal vigilance by the total population, so, too, is the quality of its environment. Good suburban planning calls for active interest by informed citizens themselves, particularly when they are organized as civic clubs that are open to all.

Official planning personnel are often hog-tied by political pressures that prevent them from doing the competent professional work of which they are capable. After all they are salaried personnel who need their jobs to live. They cannot stick their necks out very far in opposition to influential self-interested groups. Unless citizens as a whole, with no private axes to grind, are alert as to how their community should grow, they must not be so naïve as to expect much from hired planners who understand only too well where the power lies. Most professional planners could draw marvelous patterns for the future. Almost everyone who takes pride in his talent has filing cabinets full of excellent blueprints that never will be executed because they either run counter to too many selfish interests or do not promote the ambitions of influential parties. This unfortunate circumstance would not exist if the strongest stimulus for planning came from the general electorate. Zoning maps and regulations are only as good as the people who order them drawn and supervise their use. They may be no better than snake oil for community aches and pains, or they may be just what the doctor ordered for the patient's welfare. It depends upon who puts in the call. Civic plans are human instruments, and maps easily can be made to favor one man and penalize another while having the superficial look of scientific impartiality. Not a few zoning maps have been drawn with such schemes in mind, which is why they are so often ineffective or worse. Some actually hobble a community just to steer economic growth where interested sponsors own the land. The community which thinks that because it has zoning therefore its future is secure is living in a dream world. In suburbia, where so much open land is put into new development every year, almost anything the human mind can think of in the way of habitat from the superlative to the miserable could happen—and does.

It is axiomatic in civic planning that public lands are highly vulnerable to infringement and competition among government agencies themselves. As population pressure increases and private open space disappears, this competition will become even sharper, each agency claiming a greater need. This being universally the case, steps should be taken, before it is too late and too expensive, to acquire enough public lands for all future needs so that no legitimate facility, whether road, reservoir, school site, park, beach, or airport, need be denied for lack of space at some future date. This sounds like a large order and it is. Open land is limited. When it is gone, it is gone forever. The government, which since colonial times has been a dispenser of lands, must now become a purchaser. But there is little likelihood that any governmental unit from the local to the Federal level will acquire the necessary space without being prodded to action by the electorate. A major reason is that men in office today see little reason to spend money for assets that obviously will not be essential during their own brief tenure. As they often see it, the expedient thing to do for their own political enhancement is to spend on projects of the moment rather than to accumulate reserves that would only make it easier for some future successor in office. Their attitude is comparable to that of those corporation executives who seek temporary popularity and quick profits by issuing big dividends to the detriment of capital reserves that should be set aside to assure sound future growth.

As time goes on, suburbia in the major metropolitan areas will run out of open space that is within reasonable commuting distance to the central cities. When that happens, apartment buildings will come into vogue while individual house lots that seem large today will be further subdivided in many places so that more homes can be built on them. Standards as to space eventually will change in suburbia to accommodate more people just as they change in cities when populations increase. As suburbia now is pushing farms and estates off the landscape, it, in its own turn, will be compressed into a more compact shape by population pressures of the future. Since most people must circulate daily to make a living the city-type apartment building will be built where transportation facilities are best—within easy reach of commuter trains or close to the cloverleaves of expressway interchanges. Already new apartment buildings have become conspicuous in such locations in the tight, built-up suburban rings that lie just outside the largest cities.

The Regional Plan Association has jolted complacent suburbanites of the New York area by revealing a remarkable upsurge in apartment-building construction in what were previously considered communities of single-family homes. Not everyone has the credit to buy his own residence or cares for the responsibility of operating one. Yet many of these people are fed up with environmental conditions in cities and are willing to commute to apartments on the outskirts, where rents are about half what they would be in town. They are willing to trade time for a chance to reside in better neighborhoods and to send their children to better schools. In the tristate metropolitan area of New York, New Jersey, and Connecticut, authorized apartment construction rose to 17,160 units during the first half of 1958. Sixty-six per cent of all new dwelling units in this same tristate area were located in the inner ring of suburban towns, as compared with 34 per cent in the core cities and outer suburbs. Multifamily units accounted for 46 per cent of all new dwelling units authorized in 1958, and this trend to apartments seems to be rising. In smaller metropolitan areas, this switch to apartments will not occur until time and growth have brought on the crowded conditions and higher land values that warrant them.

Commenting on the significant break-through of apartments into older suburban communities in the New York area, the Regional Plan Association warned, "Unless the patterns of streets, highways, parks, schools, and the myriad of other facilities originally structured to serve low-density one-family areas are expanded and restricted to serve the higher densities, the seeds will have been sown for a premature deterioration of these areas."[5] In other words, if the circuits of community services become overloaded, either a new wiring system will be necessary or the fuse will blow. Without a reserve of open space to draw on for all types of civic services, it will be almost impossible to bring in new facilities and at the same time maintain a suburban atmosphere. Even slums may emerge with all the attendant ills of rising costs for welfare and a decline in the quality of local services, which seem to be the inevitable accompaniment of slums.

In Nassau County, Long Island, the apartment-house trend is now gathering strong momentum. Although this county has an area of 192,000 acres, it was down to its last 23,045 acres of desirable homesites by 1959, according to the Nassau Planning Commission. More than half a million persons were added to the local population between 1950 and 1957, bringing the total to 1,178,075. As land became scarcer it rose in value until ordinary residential land sold for $7000 per acre, and that prompted builders to turn to apartments instead of houses, which became too expensive with raw land costs so elevated. Most apartments rent for $115 to $200 per month in Nassau, and builders have no trouble filling them by emphasizing to prospective tenants from the city that they can reach downtown Manhattan in less than an hour via the Long Island Railway. It could take almost as long during the rush hour to make such a trip from parts of the city itself. In Nassau County new permits for apartment units now exceed new permits for single-family residences, and in some places the old residents are alarmed. The apartments do not offer sufficient tax base per family to carry their proportionate share of school and road costs. That throws the burden of population inflation upon the established single-family homes or stimulates pressure for industry to come in to help carry the load. Since the industrial-park type of industry also requires land, a suburb that is already short of space has lost its chance for that brand. What it gets is not always desirable either in appearance or from the standpoint of polluted air and water—but people who need tax relief cannot be choosers.

Recently over three hundred residents of Mineola, a pleasant suburban community in Nassau County, packed a public hearing in the local firehouse to protest against revisions of their zoning code which would have allowed an increase of apartment construction in the community. In East Rockaway, another Long Island suburb, which is already noted for its apartments, a similar objection was successfully raised to prevent apartment construction over a wider area. Small homeowners who disapprove of apartments in their residential communities contend that they bring high-density populations, which promote traffic congestion and overcrowded schools at a time when it is difficult from the dual standpoint of space and tax revenue to expand these services economically. They raise the question of optimum densities which most planners believe should be faced by all communities before it is too late. From the ideal point of view it should be known, when land is still open country, just how it should be laid out for future residence, circulation, shopping convenience, and industry. In practice this is almost impossible except in such unique instances as Sterling Forest and Stanford University's development where all the land for a future community is controlled by a single investment corporation which intends to maintain a continuing financial interest in the finished product.

To be realistic it is obvious that someday whole villages of apartment houses must come to suburbia. There is a point in space at which horizontal sprawl becomes impractical from the transportation standpoint. Only if people were willing to be regimented and assigned to live near the offices, factories, and stores where they work, could the urgent need of easy circulation by car or rapid transit be avoided. Most homeowners certainly would resent being told that they could not live more than a certain distance from their jobs because highway facilities did not permit greater freedom. Few persons can take a job anywhere and make as good an income as in the place where their ability is particularly valued and where they are already known as reliable persons. Ordinarily an employee must stay with an appreciative employer no matter where he may buy his home. More industry in suburbia must be expected in the future, and it should be planned for by setting space aside for it. More people will require more jobs and the central cities do not have the necessary room for the truly mammoth industrial expansion that will be necessary if everyone is to have a job who needs it.

The most reasonable solution for the coming day of greater population pressure is to plan apartment suburbs just as today there are suburbs of single-family homes. How to do this is a neat problem in population density, time, and distance. When more people arrive they must either be spread out or be piled higher. If they are spread out, the density will be low and more space will be necessary. In that case travel distance must increase. If travel time is to remain constant, then the rate of speed must accelerate to compensate for that increased distance. When speed is accelerated, then highway facilities must increase not only in area but in quality. In other words, the costs of accommodating more spread-out people with better highway facilities will rise faster than the population itself. If the population increase rate is X, then the highway increase rate will be X plus Y—the Y in this case being definitely a positive number.

When people are densely packed as they are in apartment houses, then public bus and rapid-transit facilities become practical, and that is a compensating factor that may reduce routine transportation costs for individual and community alike. This is another question of population density, time, and distances. When the people of Levittown, Long Island, were interviewed by sociologist Max Wolf of New York University, they were asked to name their principal gripes and delights. Their principal delight was the "more house for the money" which they believe Levittown offers. A principal gripe was the bad and costly public transportation service within the community. What these people apparently did not understand, and which most suburbanites fail to get through their heads, is that it is impossible to provide both adequate and cheap public transportation in a horizontal community. This is not a question of bad management or political shenanigans. It is a question of time, space, and customers. A service that both pays its way and is satisfactory to its patrons is impossible.

In Levittown the population density is about eighteen persons per acre. In Manhattan in residential neighborhoods it averages between 300 and 500 per acre. A bus would have to travel between sixteen and twenty-seven miles in Levittown to pick up as many passengers as it would in one mile in Manhattan. Obviously, one way to compensate for low patronage per mile is to run fewer buses per day, hoping that passengers will pile up. However, the waiting interval becomes so long that many suburbanites abandon entirely the practice of using local public transportation. No company can afford to give cheap efficient service in the face of such handicaps. With the coming development of apartment-house suburbs, population densities in these areas may reach the point where public transportation will again become feasible. That, of course, will be a major gain for suburbia.

A consequence not so pleasant to contemplate will be the development of slums. They will come as they do in cities when dwellings age and deteriorate in the less desirable neighborhoods. When this slippage begins, the preferred occupants gradually will move out while others, who cannot afford to be choosy, will move in, especially if they are permitted to pack the living quarters with more people to help pay the rent. A suburb which does not plan the use of its land from the beginning to preserve and enhance the qualities of site by all possible devices, such as those used in the Levittowns and other superior developments, will likely go downhill with time rather than hold its own. Parks, playgrounds, adequate streets, highways, schools, shopping facilities, and protection from blight by anything that detracts from residential charm are all essential premiums that must be paid for sound insurance against slums. The community which neglects this kind of life and health protection will ultimately suffer the severe tax pains that come with an attack of slum virus.

The rise of trailer parks in suburban areas is a case in point. Three million Americans now call 1.2 million trailers their permanent homes. Every tenth house built today is of this type. Most trailers congregate in permanent parking lots where electricity, water, and sewage hookups are available. Monthly charges for parking and facilities usually run between $40 and $150. Densities average ten to fifteen units per acre. Eight per acre is considered low and twenty is high. The usual value of these houses when new runs from $5000 to $13,000, in contrast to the prices of conventional homes that average twice as much. The population density per acre in trailer camps is far higher than that of single-family residence districts, while the value per family of site and vehicles is far less. In any residential community these discrepancies oblige the conventional homeowners to subsidize through heavier taxation the low levies assessed upon families in trailers. In communities with high tax rates the tax advantages enjoyed by trailer owners encourage others to follow suit. The conventional home loses market value and the seeds of slum conditions are sown. For fiscal solvency the residential community which welcomes trailer-villes should rely more heavily upon other forms of taxation than the property tax so as to equalize the burden and to secure the revenue that adequate public services require.

CHAPTER 6

Farms on the Urban Fringe

THE PART-TIMERS

Harold Perkins has a farm of less than one hundred acres in the Baltimore-Washington-Annapolis triangle. "The cities get closer every year," Perkins said, as he surveyed a field of Maryland broadleaf tobacco which had developed beautifully under irrigation. "Now they're thinking of putting an airport in here." The prospect of being a displaced person does not sit well with Perkins. "If I do have to leave I'll buy another farm. I don't want the city. For five years during the war I worked in the Baltimore shipyards. I worked with Herman. One day Herman asked me, 'Hal, what do you do weekends?' 'I go back to the farm,' I told him. 'I take a walk in the woods, and work around the place. There's always something to do. What do you do, Herman?' 'I go down to the corner bar-saloon,' Herman said, 'and get soaked.' "

Harold Perkins' precarious situation on the edge of town is complicated by the fact that he is a member of that large class of men with small farms who have lived through a technological revolution that has made them obsolete. Despite the fact that they have adopted some of the latest methods and have purchased some of the best new machinery, their farms are too small to keep either man or machine fully employed. An investment of any kind, whether human or mechanical, which cannot be used represents so much overhead expense that its earnings are largely canceled. To keep the homestead and to preserve a rural way of life Mr. Perkins is a "part-timer." He works in town as a carpenter and runs the farm in his spare time.

During Harold Perkins' lifetime changes in technology, together with urban pressures, have altered the rural scene almost beyond recognition. As he has observed, "When I was a boy we plowed with horses. There wasn't time enough to work away from home if we had wanted to. When I worked in the fields I could hear the birds chirp and the bugs burr. When I'd go fishing on Sunday down by the Patuxent River maybe I'd see somebody; maybe I wouldn't. If I did he'd be someone I knew. Down on those flats I'd hear the frogs croak and sometimes an owl would whoo. Now I drive a tractor and I can't hear anything but the motor. At home, with the window open in the bedroom, I lie awake at night listening to tires whine on the black-top. Sometimes there's a police siren, then an ambulance. Not long ago I went down to the Patuxent to fish. There was a mob of people I didn't know with their lines all over the place. I couldn't get near the s.o.b. and when I came back through the woods, instead of hearing an owl or a frog, there were two kids with Presley haircuts carrying a radio that was blasting off. That's how it's changed around here, but I don't want to leave. I could make a living in town with my toolbox but I prefer part-time farming. There's risk but there's a kind of security, too, that a city man doesn't have. I've worked with them and I know a house and lot are no security without a steady job. I can always give myself something to do on the farm even if someone else can't use me. People have to eat. I'd rather be raising it than begging it."

One third of the farms in the United States are now operated by persons like Mr. Perkins, who work at jobs in town or have some other source of income besides the farm to keep them solvent. Most part-time or residential farms are too small or too poorly equipped to enable their owners to earn a living without outside revenue. The majority are located near cities to which their owners commute to work. Field and barn chores are done mornings, evenings, and on week ends. The city has been a boon to this breed of able but underemployed farmers, for it has salvaged a way of life which otherwise might have been abandoned. Although nearness to town means that ultimately they may be forced to sell, they will realize enough money from the transaction to buy other land. Meanwhile even the overflow of a trespassing humanity and dilution of the rural environment by suburban sprawl are bearable infringements because they come with the town job that keeps the farm itself alive.

Part-time farming has been going on for generations in sections of the country where industrialization and city building are very old. The State of Rhode Island is a key area in which to observe what happens as population increase and urban sprawl exert themselves upon the rural hinterland. Little Rhody is now more densely settled than India or China. It is almost as packed with humanity as Java and, understandably, it is a state without any local agricultural surpluses. Three quarters of the milk consumed in Rhode Island comes from outside the state. Even hay to feed local dairy cattle is imported from as far away as Canada. A cow in Rhode Island is a queen among her species, for her milk, quart for quart, is worth twice as much as that from her Wisconsin cousins. It is all a matter of supply and demand. There are more farms, more cows, and fewer cities per square mile in Wisconsin. In Rhode Island the cow must compete with people for room. Superficially one might think that Rhode Island would be the El Dorado where every American farmer would want to operate, yet agriculture constitutes less than two per cent of the state's economic activity; and if one were to drive through the local countryside, he would be impressed by the great amount of land in undeveloped woods rather than in cultivated fields. There is scarcely a place in the state which is not to some degree susceptible to urban pressures, and the woods make charming homesites.

In Rhode Island land, wherever it may be, is in demand for residence, industry, game lodges, resorts, or private recreation. So little space is devoted to agriculture, partly because city people bid up the price of land beyond the means of most professional farmers. Whatever labor a farmer hires must be at wages comparable with city pay, while taxes are at suburban rather than at rural levels. The best soil in the state lies on famous Slocum Plain, where the aristocratic Narragansett Planters once practiced Negro slavery to make butter and cheese for the West Indies trade. Today the New Haven Railroad owns the heart of Slocum Plain, where it intends to raise an industrial park rather than alfalfa or potatoes.

Mr. and Mrs. Elmer Young of Greenville, Rhode Island, have a seventy-five acre farm, yet they both work at other jobs. Mrs. Young says, "I love the farm; it's beautiful to look at but we can't make a living on it, and I wouldn't live in town for anything. Even my ten-year old son, Elmer, Junior, is very happy although he has hay fever. He takes shots the year around. Diana, my youngest, is seven. She has two cats and a collie dog. Cynthia, just turned twelve, has the pony she always dreamed of. It gives her something to do. It's the biggest thing in her life. She's trained it and rides it in shows. That's one of the reasons I work. It buys the little things that make life wonderful.

"It wasn't always this way," Mrs. Young related in her sprightly manner. "I had to wait until all the children were old enough for school. Even now I can only work in town six hours a day but I like it. My husband has an egg business. He buys eggs in the country and distributes them in Providence. We tried raising eggs ourselves but there wasn't enough in it. We tried broilers too. We were too small and it's too risky to be big. To do that you have to have money that you feel you can take a chance with. We never got that far ahead. If you don't have money for gambling you're better off out of farming. So we rented the broiler equipment and the poultry house to a turkey raiser. He started his poults on our place and things went well for a while. This year he gave up. Elmer, my husband, got his start in the commercial egg business by having this place of our own so we feel that the experience was worth it. Most of our seventy-five acres are wooded although we have a lot of apple trees. I don't know how many; quite a few acres. We tried the apples, too, but we were too small. There are so many bugs and diseases. You have to have the right kind of equipment to do the best with an orchard and we couldn't afford it. We are both better off at our other jobs."

Part-time farming is not a new thing in the lives of Mr. and Mrs. Young. "My dad was a part-time farmer; so was Elmer's," remarked Mrs. Young, who is a slim, attractive young woman, obviously enthusiastic about her busy career as mother, wife, and secretary in Greenville. "Here in Rhode Island you're not isolated in the country. You just turn out on the road and there are neighbors. We're used to being farmers and working in town. My daddy kept Ayreshires. He did the milking before he went to work and after he came home. Of course we helped him. Elmer's father raised vegetables and kept a peach orchard. We didn't inherit either place. When we were first married we rented in the country; then we bought seven years ago when Diana was born. We wanted a place of our own where the children could grow up knowing it was theirs too. It will preserve memories for them when they are older."

There are times when Mrs. Young wishes that she and her husband did not have to work away. "I'd love to farm full time; so would Elmer, but it's too hard if you don't have capital to get started. Most farmers in our area need outside jobs. It seems they can't make enough on their places. If you inherit a made-up farm you can make money keeping it going but you can't start from scratch like we did, pay for the place, and make a living too. It seems it takes one generation to get a farm going for the next. We still raise some vegetables and strawberries and a few apples—as many as my husband can sell retail on his egg route, but I don't think either of us would want to depend on the farm for our living. It's a wonderful life in the country with a little extra money." Forty-four per cent of all farmers in Rhode Island would agree with Mrs. Young for they, too, are part-timers.

The city-bred woman who stays home all day on an isolated part-time farm may not share Mrs. Young's complimentary attitude toward the rural scene. Not so long ago a salesman in Washington decided to buy a place in the backwoods of Frederick County, Maryland, because he and his wife liked "the pretty brook that runs through the place." The brook, lined with magnificent oaks, hemlocks, and tulip poplars, was indeed beautiful but not a living soul could be seen from the house, which was tucked into a ravine at the dead end of a winding road that led off from the main highway around a blind bend. It was a hermit's dream. When a visitor dropped in to greet the new owners he was informed by the lady of the house that her husband liked the place a lot but he only saw it week ends. She lived there and hated it. "The brook and that view of Catoctin Mountain wore off in a hurry as far as I am concerned," she announced positively. It was apparent that she had made up her mind to return to civilization. "It's lonely up here. It wouldn't be so bad if my husband were around and farmed the place, but I'm confined with the kids all day, all week. I get despondent. Do you suppose any woman ever liked living here? I think it must have always been like this but now a woman feels she can complain—a farmer's wife couldn't. We won't be here much longer although my husband seems to think we will."

COMMERCIAL FARMS

As a moth is drawn to candlelight that may singe its wings, the most daring farmers are those that continue full-time husbandry on the urban fringe after their neighbors have sold out or have taken city jobs. They are in danger of being singed by high costs, but there is also a chance to make a lot of money as long as they can stand the heat. The best market is where people are; so the edge of town is the choicest spot for the farmer who can hang on and produce. Milk, eggs, poultry, fresh vegetables, fruits, and ornamental plants have a ready market in any metropolitan area. The bigger the city and the fewer farmers left around it, the better the market for the lucky survivors. If any husbandman in the Corn Belt or the Wheat Belt should become discouraged over surplus production and under-consumption, he should take a trip to southern California and look at farms on the outskirts of Los Angeles. There he may preview the future when there will be more people and less agricultural space. What he will see is not a Hollywood cinerama, but the production is just as lavish and almost as incredible. The leading lady is Elsie the Cow, but she is not the kind of country gal he knows back home.

In a zone near Paramount, called "Little Netherlands," dairymen of Dutch and Italian extraction manage large herds of cattle which they have bought from stock dealers as far away as Wisconsin. The hay they feed is brought from irrigated valleys that lie beyond the mountain ranges that enclose the Los Angeles basin. Grains used may come from the Middle West via the Panama Canal, and concentrated molasses to enrich and sweeten the bovine diet is imported from Hawaiian cane fields. These dairies are more like milk factories than normal farms, and the cows go about their business as though they were contract laborers working for a Christmas bonus.

Space is expensive because all of it would have immediate value as house lots if developers could get their hands on it. Ten acres of bare land would bring between thirty and sixty thousand dollars, which is more than one would have to pay in southern Wisconsin for two hundred acres with house and barns. This land is so prized because Los Angeles and its suburbs have already urbanized more than half of the suitable space around them. After the rest is gone, which could easily happen by the year 2000, the metropolis and its satellites will have only the sea and the mountains to grow on. This land squeeze has compressed old-fashioned dairying into a new mold. Cows no longer go to pasture as a herd led by a grandam with a tinkling bell. They are organized into proletarian work shifts, numbers are stenciled on their flanks, and each has daily and seasonal production quotas to fulfill or off she goes to the sausage maker. The "pasture" is no meadow of clover, but rather a compact, hoof-tramped feed lot in which each animal has a stall and everything she eats is brought to her. Land is too expensive to use as exercising ground. In this way it is possible to keep as many as two hundred milking cows on ten acres.

The hired men live in the city or in suburban developments. They drive out to the country as though they were going to an aircraft assembly plant. They have a union, social security; they may even punch time clocks. They receive city wages, averaging over $500 monthly, for appearing twice a day to milk cows for four hours at a stretch. Every cow has a shower bath, and her udder is wiped with a clean towel from a local laundry service before each milking. The milking itself is done with machines in sanitary parlors into which the cows file according to the numbers on their flanks. As milk is taken, it is piped to a stainless-steel refrigeration tank which is emptied daily by a stainless-steel tank truck that carts it off to the bottling works. The whole operation is one more suited to UNIVAC than to the average farmer.

The Los Angeles system is unique only in that it is well

developed on a mass scale. It is a mode of milk manufacturing that is becoming more prominent in the vicinity of many large cities and, because of its efficiency, seems likely to displace old-fashioned methods wherever land is expensive but the market is attractive. Economically there are two basic classes of commercial dairy farms: (1) those which sell to dairies for direct human consumption as fresh whole milk or cream; (2) those which sell milk to manufacturers of butter, cheese, condensed milk, and other processed items. The farmer who can market milk to dairies for direct consumption rather than to manufacturers receives a handsome premium—a selling price that nationally averages 51 per cent higher.

Milk is approximately 86 per cent water and highly perishable. Costs of transportation are therefore high per unit of value. This fact limits the ability of surplus milk in one area to depress the price at some distant point. Consequently the fresh milk industry is one of the most widely dispersed types of husbandry. Every community has its own milkshed, the limits of which are often fixed by regulation. Such regulation protects producers within the restricted area from outside competition and makes possible the supervision of dairy sanitation by local authorities. The premium market price is one of the magnets that holds the dairyman on the urban fringe, but he obviously has to be a smart operator to stay there. Up until 1958 there was at least one surviving dairy farm in the New York Borough of Queens. It was started in 1900 by Austrian immigrant Isaac Balsam. At last count there were 200 cows giving over 3000 quarts of milk daily on this ten-acre plot which might be reached by taking the subway to Ozone Park—that is, if an expressway or housing development has not recently annihilated it. In the Bronx the days of the true dairy husbandman are ended, but the local zoo has a miniature farm and a few cows so that school children may see that milk is not made like Coco-Cola.

Practically every farmer on the urban fringe who can

ignore sentimental attachments to his own acres is now more excited about the rising values of land and the population surge behind the boom than about such hayseed topics as animal breeding and soil fertilizers. As enterprising dairyman, John Hauptmann, on the suburban outskirts of Hartford, Connecticut, expressed the sentiment, "We farmers raise three crops. We go onto a farm in our youth and raise a family. Over the years we produce something for the market but with very little profit. Then, when we are ready to retire, we make the harvest of a lifetime by selling our land for the capital gains that will keep us in our old age."

Mr. Hauptmann cited the example of a fellow dairyman to show what he meant by farming in itself not being the attractive part of the business. This man whom everyone respected for his ability had $44,000 invested in a farm that netted only $3100 in 1957, although he and his family worked seven days a week. "By comparison," Mr. Hauptmann commented, "the peddler who delivered that same milk for the dairy got five cents a quart and earned $5200 in the same year without any invested capital—and he worked only five days a week." Mr. Hauptmann and his two married sons have $175,000 invested in a 180-acre farm which they operate together. Their 120 milking cows produce an average of 2000 quarts daily, "for which we get 8½ cents a quart while the customer pays the dairy 27 cents." "That," says Mr. Hauptmann, "is an abuse of capital. If, eventually, we couldn't make a profit on land, we would be better off in some other business." Of course John Hauptmann, as well as other efficient and well capitalized dairymen, does make a livelihood even on 8½-cent milk by getting into high-volume production, but the little fellows who cannot keep up with the times by turning out more per man as well as more per cow must abandon commercial farming. They are technological discards—able to survive only in a museum.

The situation of the Connecticut Valley dairymen points up the basic status of full-time farmers on the urban fringe.

Their capital investments are extraordinarily high. While the prices they receive are above average for the country as a whole (because they are close to the ultimate consumer), they are not always commensurate with big investments. Farmers on the edge of the city cater to the best market, but they see middlemen making more than they do with less effort and less risk of capital. Many are quite willing to get out from under by selling to suburbia if they can make a satisfactory capital gain. Despite the fact that nearly a half-million acres annually are converted from productive farm lands to urban real estate and another half-million are turned into roads, airports, military installations, and other non-farm facilities, surpluses produced on the remaining fields continue to depress the market value of most agricultural commodities. Phenomenal overproductivity on the part of the most progressive full-time farmers acts like a tranquilizer to shut off the alarm signals that would otherwise alert the nation to the potential danger of drastically reducing its food-producing land base at a time of unprecedented human increase.

The astonishing productivity that has enabled fewer farmers on less land to boost yields over fifty-four per cent in the past twenty years is the result of putting into practice the knowledge gleaned from a long accumulation of scientific research data. Much of what is done today to increase yields per acre and per man was learned through experimentation years ago. Some aids, such as chemical weed killers, plant stimulants, and animal-growth hormones, are of more recent vintage. But no matter how much may have been learned by scientists, this knowledge would not have been put into practice by the farmer unless he had been both driven by competition and encouraged by the market. The very market which most agriculturists would say has been unfavorable has nevertheless been good enough and stable enough to enable the top 44 per cent of America's husbandmen to corner the business. The bottom 56 per cent are now farmers in name only, for they produce no more than nine per cent of all agricultural commodities. They hold land, usually in small, poorly equipped units, and most of them make their living chiefly at jobs off the farm.

As John Hauptmann, one of the successful full-time professionals, has said, "The only way to beat low prices is to increase production." In 1957 when the average Connecticut dairy cow was giving 7020 pounds of milk annually, Hauptmann's herd averaged over 11,000 pounds. A year later the average for his herd was up to almost 13,000 pounds. Obviously, an ordinary dairyman with cheaper cattle and an inferior farm could not survive such furious competition. All over the country, in every type of husbandry, the able manager who has strong capital support is compensating for low prices by increasing production. This kind of technological prosperity freezes out the incompetent or financially weak more effectively than a general economic depression, and it gives the American public a false sense of agricultural security because it is not generally aware of the strong forced draft that is blowing hard on the fire under the boiler. With all this effort, what is surplus today is only about five per cent of total national production, yet that is just enough to depress prices to government support levels. These in turn are adequate to encourage the efficient but they slowly strangle the weak.

In the past two decades the man who was afraid or unable to borrow money for modernization and expansion simply dropped by the wayside. The bold and the confident added three billions to their debts in 1958 alone and now owe close to a total of thirty billion. But it has been a good gamble because inflation and savings out of profits have more than covered the increased debt. All farm assets, including livestock and machinery, were worth 203 billions in 1958 as compared with 42 billions in 1940. Buying additional land on mortgages to expand a farm has seemed safer and surer than buying gilt-edge stock. It will always be possible to build more industry, but the fifty states will never have more space. Over the long haul the only way the price of land can go would seem to be up. Eventually human yields will catch up with crop yields and the agricultural price structure will stiffen like a starched collar.

If it had not been for past government purchase-and-surplus-disposal programs at home and abroad, there would have been a glut of agricultural produce on the home market in recent years that might have wrecked prices and slowed the present technological revolution in farming to a crawl. Any pronounced weakness in the market of basic commodities would have frightened the professionals who have had to take risks in order to grow big. As it was, the willingness of government to bear the costs of surpluses telescoped into the brief period of two decades the changes that otherwise might have taken a century. It was largely due to such assistance that the best operators were able to ease the financially weak or timid out of business. The latter did not complain too severely since either they were able to sell out at a good price or they put their land in the soil bank and took full-time or part-time jobs in town. Today there are only two thirds as many farmers as there were in 1940, and one third of these survivors are just hanging on because incomes from town jobs are more than they get from their farms.

The decline in manpower on the farm has also coincided with the disappearance of the work horse and mule. Twenty years ago draft animals were the power behind American agriculture. Today they are about as rare as the ox was at the turn of the century. By eliminating most horses and mules, nearly twenty per cent of the nation's cropland has been released from growing hay and grain for their feed. This tremendous addition of arable land to the nation's soil bank coincided precisely with the period during which spectacular advances were made in better crop yields and more efficient animal feeding. Since very few mules or work horses now remain, never again will America receive such a generous bonus of productive land at no expense except what has been invested wisely in better motorized equipment. These are some of the cold facts about American farming which Secretary of Agriculture Ezra Taft Benson had in mind when, in an address before the Friends of the 4-H, he stunned some of his listeners by predicting that only one boy in three now growing up on farms will find opportunities as an adult, "on any kind of farm." Like the horse and the mule, Man, too, is becoming obsolete in the country.

FROM CITY TO FARM

Sometimes it is not the city that pirates the farm but the farm that snares a man from the city. This sort of thing was much more frequent years ago than it is now. During the days of massive European migrations, many newcomers to America dreamed of acquiring their own farms. To reach this goal they willingly toiled for years at sweatshop jobs to save the nest egg. Even now, there are city people who occasionally quit the nine to five rat race in exchange for longer hours of labor but the more independent existence of the country. Probably the greatest rent in the social fiber of our time is the vanished opportunity in agriculture for the poor but willing. With few exceptions, there is now little chance for anyone, even with a grubstake of money, to escape from metropolitan life and almost no opportunity to set up a homestead in the wilderness on the strength of one's nerve. Whatever parts of the wilderness were fertile are now claimed. The bottom rungs of the ladder, which enabled a thrifty man with little capital to climb up from the soil to independence on Main Street, have been cut off.

Today one must achieve financial independence first before he may enjoy the luxury of the soil. As one Dean of a College of Agriculture has said, "If you have enough money to buy a farm, invest it and work at something else more profitable." Never again will there be a whole generation of poor but proud men who could just go off and establish themselves on the land if it seemed servile to take orders from a boss. With the loss of easy opportunity to acquire land there has been a loss of confidence, and men have turned from a quest for adventure in the economic world to a hunt for security. There are still on the land some of that remarkable generation who broke away from the city in large numbers and became independent by means of toil and thrift on their own farms. Some are in full or partial retirement, but the wonder of their acheivement is the delight of their old age and they like to tell their saga.

Moses Racusin, a poultryman of Farmingdale, New Jersey, came to America from Russia fifty-three years ago. "My grandfather had a farm in the old country but we were Jewish. We could see there wasn't much hope for us. The Jews were scapegoats—they were blamed for troubles at home. It was getting worse for our people; so father decided it would be better to come and make a new life in America. He had three sons. He came on ahead. After a while he got fixed and sent us tickets to follow him. America was the way we heard it was in the Old Country. Nobody got fooled who came here. In those days we weren't afraid to work either. A friend of mine who remembers how we struggled to get our start, said the other day, 'We used to have houses of straw and men of iron. Today we have men of straw and houses of iron.' When we came we didn't see any cars. There wasn't any TV. We didn't even have good roads. Today the newcomers who just arrive from the Old Country bring their own patent medicine with them. They think they should have everything right away without saving. I gave a speech to some newcomers the other night. I told them they would get everything I got if they worked for it but they shouldn't expect charity. I don't think they liked what I said. I earned $8.00 a week when I was married."

When one listens to old Moses tell his story in this day of

easy goals and casual satisfactions, the patience and persistence of his generation seem scarcely credible. "After my father had all his family here we started to dream." Incidents of the distant past were recalled by Mr. Racusin with zest and detail. "We thought of grandfather's farm: a cow, chickens, some ducks. We hoped for land of our own in New Jersey. We lived in New York City then and we all worked in the garment district. We knew you can't ride before you walk. For twenty-five years we worked in the lofts. We were getting old. I was already 46. My father had died but his sons still hoped to farm. We used to come out this way on holidays on the Jersey Central. It doesn't run any more. There was an old conductor on that train. We would listen especially for him to call out, 'Farmingdale—next stop, Farmingdale.' That was the sweetest music to our ears and we felt excited. There was never a better name or place than Farmingdale. I like to say it. Finally we had money but we knew it wasn't safe for all of us to quit our jobs. We talked together. We chose our land and decided I should go first because I was the eldest. It was like Father going to America. If I did well my brothers would follow one at a time. That was 1932.

"My wife and I worked hard. Sometimes we wonder how we did it. But we're old now. We're not so strong. You see I am over seventy. In the city we worked too, but here we loved our labor. There were no conveniences then. The buildings were poor. We carried the chicken feed by hand in buckets. I couldn't have done it alone. My wife was always with me. The place I have now is my third. Each time I could improve myself I got a new piece of land and built better buildings." Mr. Racusin's present home is a modest white stuccoed house of trim lines and in the very best repair. His poultry "sheds" are two excellent concrete-block laying houses designed for the most efficient operation. Each laying shed is composed of eight apartments and a head house. Each apartment accommodates approximately 350 laying hens. It consists of a side wall of boxes or nests into which the hens retire to lay. The back wall is a ladderlike arrangement of roosting poles on which the birds spend the night.

"I'm only working part-time now," said Mr. Racusin. "I use only one laying house. The other I rent to my son Nathan. I have three sons who are poultry farmers. They all live near me. I am not a rich man but I am very happy. I have all my children and their children near me, and, believe me, that is nice for an old couple. We like to give presents to our grandchildren. They don't cost much but I must have a little money to be a good grandfather, so I won't quit. I will work as long as I am able."

Nathan Racusin, who is following in the path worn by his father, came over to inspect the laying shed that he rents from his parents. He has his own farm as well and keeps 6000 birds altogether. He is a civil engineer, Rutgers '41. He worked for a while for T.V.A. constructing a dam. Called into service, he was sent to New Guinea. While there he made his decision and wrote to his father, "Dad, I've had enough knocking around. Don't sell the land. I'm going to be a farmer." Old Moses had bought enough land with his last place to make two poultry farms. He had been thinking of selling off half of it when Nathan wrote.

"I always hoped he would," said Moses, "but he had to make up his own mind."

"I've never regretted it," added Nathan, who is one of the fortunate few of the younger generation who have been able to renounce a promising professional career to become a successful farmer.

Mrs. Racusin, who had been grading eggs in the basement, had left to prepare coffee, which she now announced was ready. In the house the elder Racusin completed his story. "Today the young farmer must be strong and he must do things right. The weak ones will never succeed, but they still try. People from all walks of life come to Farmingdale from the city to try the chicken business. They're shopkeepers, factory workers, professional people. They come on Sundays. They see a chicken farmer like you see me now, sitting here drinking coffee. They see the crates of eggs in the basement and they figure in their heads the fortunes they could make. So they quit their jobs and invest their savings. They don't hold out enough cash for emergencies. Things go all right for a while but they can't always be good. In time the weak ones drop out. The strong ones find a way to survive. Nathan has been a hard worker." Coming from Old Moses these words had the qualities of a paternal blessing as well as praise. It is no wonder that father and mother, as they sit at their table in the basement grading eggs, count themselves fortunate. No, America had not fooled anybody—but the Racusins had not fooled America either.

Farmingdale is in Monmouth County, New Jersey, which ranks second from the top among all counties in the United States in egg production. Its remarkable reputation is founded on hundreds of tidy, efficient, one-family egg "factories" such as those operated by the Racusins. From Monmouth County comes a major share of the white "Jersey" eggs which are the pride of New York City's breakfast tables. It is no wonder that hobbyists and part-time farmers who try to compete with these professionals complain that often they do not recover the price of feed when they sell eggs. The methods of the specialists are too advanced and too costly for the amateur to copy. Sometimes they are almost too much for professionals as well. Nowhere in the country is the competition in agriculture sharper than among the farmers on the edge of the city, where only the best can survive because the overhead is great, the market competition is severe, and there are many others who would also like to become farmers if only they could find an opening.

SYMBIOSIS

Though city and farm compete with one another for space, there is an occasional case of symbiosis, wherein each is benefited by the progress of the other. It is an embellishment to most cities to have within their limits such surviving remnants of agriculture as greenhouses and nurseries of ornamental plants. Boxed, potted, or framed, these relics of a faded farm supremacy keep their place in the city because the more metropolitan it becomes the higher is the premium the city pays for these pleasant tokens of the country. The gravel floors of hothouses and the dirt paths of nursery gardens are reminiscent of the earth which lies not quite forgotten beneath so much asphalt and concrete. The aroma of plants and of freshly spaded soil is some kind of reassurance that there is still an atmosphere to be inhaled with relish rather than with a cough and a sneeze.

Among the most curious specimens of rural-urban symbiosis is the growing of mushrooms which thrives in the rapidly suburbanizing outskirts of Philadelphia and Wilmington, particularly in Chester County, Pennsylvania. Unlike flower culture, mushrooming is singularly unattractive in its imprint on the landscape and upon the atmosphere. In fact, it is so objectionable that many communities prohibit it or confine it to out-of-the-way places where it will not detract from the value of other properties. But in its curious reliance upon both city and country, mushrooming is perhaps the epitome of a togetherness that helps even if it is more than a little trying on the partners.

Commercial mushrooming began in America about 1890 when a few enterprising Quakers in Chester County decided to copy culture methods that had been practiced in England. Until then those who relished the pungent fungi were amateur connoisseurs who collected specimens in the wild and relied upon age-old methods to distinguish the edible from the poisonous. The growth of cities created a greater demand for mushrooms. At the same time it became more difficult for urbanites to scour for their own as private woodlands were enclosed. Mushrooms wilt quickly and, if they are to be eaten fresh, should go to market the day they are picked. It is to Chester County's advantage that it lies within a short haul of all the great cities on the East Coast. One half of all mushrooms served on American tables are grown within a twenty-five-mile radius of Kennett Square, which, of course, considers itself to be the mushroom capital of the world.

Also within reasonable radius of Kennett Square are the famous horse-racing tracks of Pimlico, Laurel, Bowie, Delaware Park, Atlantic City, Aqueduct, Garden State, Freehold, and Belmont. In this day of mechanized agriculture, these city institutions are the last major stronghold of the horse and the best surviving source of ample, uniform horse manure which is needed for the organic compost on which mushrooms thrive. To mushroomers the city horse has always been a little special, for compared with the country horse he is better fed. This is reflected in the superior quality of the subsequent compost. When mushrooming began in Chester County, the city livery stables of draft and carriage horses were major sources of supply, so that all through the years this peculiar form of plant propagation has been more or less intimately dependent upon urban support. Of course, as with most things, it is possible to manufacture synthetics which some claim are equal to the natural.

Today city and farm are more closely linked than ever in their curious symbiotic association with mushroom culture. Good old-fashioned top soil is needed to cover the organic compost in which the mushrooms are grown. Nearly a hundred acres in the Pennsylvania-Delaware area around Kennett Square are annually skinned of their best earth. This would be the ruination of productive agriculture but inasmuch as this is a zone of rapid suburbanization, the growing city often comes to the rescue. Some realtors who are about to create new developments may be only too willing to sell the top soil from future lots to earth-moving contractors at the going price of $600 per acre—often as much as the land itself may have cost. This is sheer gravy for the speculator, who continues to own the land. The future greenhorn home buyer is not likely to detect the difference until it is too late.

In this ingenious way the mushroomer gets the soil he needs without destroying a productive farm. By the time the homeowner in the new subdivision realizes what is wrong with the lawn that failed, the mushroomer has harvested his crop and is anxious to get rid of the old top soil. He can use it only once because it might acquire pathogenic micro-organisms that would be injurious to future crops. For as much as it cost, it is sold back to the new homeowner so that he can finally establish his cherished lawn. The same truck which hauled away the virgin top soil may possibly haul it back again, a little shopworn and mixed with spent compost. As the homeowner shells out a few hundred dollars to re-cover his peripatetic earth, the process is successfully re-peated elsewhere and thus several businesses in both town and country are continuously sustained.

THE HOLDOUTS

On the urban fringe it takes a good farmer or a rich one to hold on to his land and his equilibrium when he is assaulted with rising taxes one day and cajoled on the following by speculators with fat wallets. Since cows earn less than people, whatever the city wants it is likely to get, but the types of farms with the greatest resistance are either effi-cient commercial enterprises or subsidized estates. When one estate manager on the outskirts of Wilmington, Delaware, was asked how he kept the land wolves from the door, he replied, "I have no trouble; I farm with money not for money." His tenure and the life expectancy of the farm he manages depends more upon the Dow-Jones average than upon the prices of milk or winter wheat. When a caller dropped in to pay his respects to a dowager who owns a fine dairy farm nearby, the maid in starched apron and cap who answered the bell offered apologies for her mistress who had "just flown to London to attend a week-end party."

Since the days of first European settlement along the Atlantic seaboard, it has been fashionable for persons of wealth and social prominence to maintain country estates. To the Narragansett Planters of colonial Rhode Island and to the tidewater gentry of Maryland and Virginia, manorial properties, tended by Negro slaves, were a means of support. Other estates, equally elegant but seldom profitable, were developed on the fringes of Boston, New York, and Philadelphia. They were the country mansions of city notables whose fortunes came from trade and speculation rather than from the soil.

Seventeenth century Dutch patroons, who held sizable grants of land along the Hudson, aspired to copy medieval manors and to acquire tenant serfs, but only a few could persuade free people to settle as renters on their properties. They learned the lesson which an abundance of land in America taught all would-be aristocrats—it was not enough to possess raw real estate. There had to be some other way to get and hold the human labor force that could make it yield a return. For the most part the Hudson River estates passed on as woodland to succeeding generations; and it was not until the industrial revolution, clipper ships, and the New York Central Railroad brought wealth to Wall Street that country mansions began to rise along the river. Today, as in earlier times, the estate farm is usually a net expense to its owner rather than a source of profit. It remains as much as ever a subsidized symbol of social elegance, good taste, and prestige.

The estate farm does not appear in the census of agriculture. This is because it has an identity which, while very real, is difficult to reduce to a slot on a punch card. It is found in every economic class of farm listed by the census. It could be a 1000-acre commercial dairy grossing more than $50,000 yearly, or it could be a ten-acre residential retreat with its open fields artfully abandoned to the rustic beauty of flowering weeds. Recently a society matron in Fairfield County, Connecticut, was horrified by the suggestion of an agricultural agent that she improve a nonproductive field of goldenrod and daisies by seeding it to alfalfa. "My friends and I are sick of hay," she remarked. "It's all so green."

Isolated estate farms are found in every part of the nation and on the outskirts of every large city, but there are only a few rural communities where the estate either dominates the landscape or is sufficient in numbers to affect the character of local taste and society. In most agricultural areas the country gentleman is respected for his wealth but he is looked upon as a speculating interloper—a "fanny farmer" who embellishes his property in ways beyond the means of ordinary tillers of the soil. He is an outsider who has bought his way into the club but never quite belongs. However, along the East Coast, from Boston to Richmond and Charleston, the country squire is at home. This is his country and has been ever since the first lands were granted by the kings of England to their favorites. Though a stone-walled meadow stocked with Angus on the Island of Aquidneck is not in itself a passport to Newport's top drawer, it could be a big help. The "Main Line" of Chester County is to the fox-hunting executives of Philadelphia what Westchester County is to New York's Madison Avenue. The larger the eastern metropolis, the broader is its outlying belt of estate farms to which the men who make decisions can retire and relax in formal informality with their own kind. For the privilege of keeping expensive land in farms near the city, they must pay a premium that the ordinary agriculturist could not afford.

Precisely because the owner of an estate can do things

that the working farmer cannot afford, he makes an important contribution to the beauty of landscape which is lacking in many American communities where ownership of country land is not a tradition in the upper circles of urban society. The Middle West is particularly barren of these embellishments except in the remarkable "Bluegrass" regions on the fringes of Lexington, Kentucky, and Nashville, Tennessee. One of the redeeming features of New York City is the short distance one has to travel to get away from it into the estate country of Westchester County. There on the outskirts of the most congested real estate in America exist some of the most delightful rural landscapes because it is a social custom to keep farms that are "too valuable" out of the hands of developers. This same respect for the countryside, as a tradition rather than as a commodity, is commonly observed about the major cities of the "Old South," and it is evident in the Southwest, particularly in California and Arizona.

Doughoregan Manor, a few miles west of Baltimore, is an estate farm with a long history, for its beginning is coupled with the beginning of this nation. It was the home of Charles Carroll of Carrollton, a signer of the Declaration of Independence. Before that it was granted by Lord Baltimore to his attorney general, who was an earlier Charles Carroll. Today in a utility shed of Doughoregan one can see the brougham in which a former governor of Maryland, John Lee Carroll, made journeys from the Manor to Baltimore and Annapolis. The farm, still in the Carroll family, is a modern dairy and beef enterprise of 2500 acres. Formerly it was five times larger. In the shrinking process it has contributed lands for roads, schools, a city, and part of a Franciscan monastery. The manor house, while still an occupied residence, is considered an historic shrine by the people of Maryland. Built in the days before the American Revolution when Catholics were forbidden to practice public worship in the colony, it has a private chapel in a separate wing where Mass is still said on Sundays for the local congregation.

The way land has been used at Doughoregan Manor is the way land has been used on the Maryland Piedmont from the days of slavery and tobacco to the present. This is not exactly a coincidence, for in times past the Carroll family has taken a hand in shaping the agricultural history of Maryland. First it was a tobacco plantation; then it shifted to wheat when Charles Carroll of Carrollton brought the Ellicott brothers to his estate from Bucks County, Pennsylvania, to establish a flour mill at what became Ellicott City. While he was interested in raising wheat and milling it, Charles Carroll was even more intent upon making Baltimore a successful challenger to Philadelphia in the export of grain. To further this ambition he was instrumental in organizing the Baltimore and Ohio Railroad, which in its beginning went to Ellicott City as a train of horse-drawn cars. Later when its tracks were extended to Ohio, steam engines brought Middle-western wheat to the port of Baltimore.

During the early days of the wheat era at Doughoregan Manor its own records report that at harvest time there were "forty slaves in a row swinging cradles across the fields." As Baltimore grew, so did the number of work horses in its livery stables. Hay to feed them became a profitable crop as it did for other farmers close to large Eastern cities. This was the beginning of grassland farming, which is a marked feature of the Piedmont estate country today. Corn, too, was grown to fatten beef and hogs for the city butchers. Then, when the automobile and motor truck arrived, Doughoregan Manor turned to dairy cattle and a herd of Angus. Today, as Washington and Baltimore grow closer to one another, the rural lands in between are going into subdivisions. The great estates, which may not last much longer, are already giving way to more viable models with smaller acreage and smaller houses—some have no cultivated fields or any livestock unless it be a riding horse.

The passage of the large estate is due not so much to the temptation of profit as to a confiscatory combination of taxes that makes it almost impossible to transfer such a grand possession intact from father to son. In economic self-defense owners must gradually reduce the size and value of their possessions. Even if one generation is so fortunate as to acquire an estate, the succeeding generation may not be able to pay the penalties of income and property taxes and still have enough reserve to carry the additional inheritance tax. The result is a trend to change the style of estate farms to something smaller and cheaper. Many persons still remember the time when the Frederick W. Vanderbilt and Franklin D. Roosevelt families lived in their mansions on manorial grounds at Hyde Park on the Hudson. Today those imposing homes and abbreviated portions of their estates are national shrines—the balance has gone into the usual kind of subdivisions, roadside drive-ins, and shopping centers. One of the Vanderbilt stables is a summer theater. Trees which President Roosevelt planted as a reforestation project and of which he was particularly fond have been bulldozed away for streets and house lots.

The changes in the Hyde Park estates reflect a change in American civilization. They are relics of the archaic age of low taxation. The Roosevelt family, for instance, in the brief span of a decade released its river front on the Hudson to the Federal Government, sold off most of the backlands on the Albany Post Road to developers, and retreated to the farther interior. While these back lands have their own charm and loveliness they lack the superlative grandeur of the Hudson, which may have helped to nourish in the late President a magnificence of spirit and a boldness of mind that could not have been evoked by the quieter, subdued environment of a lily pond on Val Kill Creek. If the present generation must witness the passing of the great estates, it must also expect to lose the advantage of the occasional product which could look out upon the world with a lofty, even Olympian demeanor because it was bred in such a world. It would take a man of the best in Western culture to speak up for the poorest of it. A man from the mansions of Hyde Park could afford to be the generous advocate of better things for the ill-fed and the ill-housed whom he came to know in his sojourns amid the eroded, impoverished lands around Warm Springs.

Considering the lack of foresight which many communities have shown in failing to purchase parks or other recreation grounds as urbanization spreads, it is fortunate that in some places there have been individuals who have acquired rural property and made a private green belt of estates which preserve the natural countryside from the common types of desecration which have despoiled so much where commercialization is the primary interest of landowners. To appreciate the esthetic value of the estate farm to a community one need only to take a Sunday drive. In Connecticut let him compare the lovely woods and fields he sees along the Merritt Parkway with the billboards and roadside commerce of U.S. Highway 1. If he lives in Delaware let him take Route 52 to Winterthur and afterward follow Routes 13 and 40 into confusion.

In every state along the Atlantic Coast there is a shrinking belt of rural loveliness that in the past has been preserved by private subsidy in the form of estates. These have survived where most working farmers could not afford to resist the encroachment of cities. It is a commentary upon our times that only with wealth earned in cities are some people able to preserve green farm land where otherwise urbanization would cast its total blight. The working farmer is already priced out of the market on the city's edge except when he establishes a "factory type" enterprise that requires little land. Now the leveling nature of modern taxation has made it more difficult even for the wealthy to maintain estate farms that since colonial times have been among the delights of the American landscape. Wherever these properties still exist they represent the last reservoir of clean open space in the paths of future urbanization. If they, too, are chewed up before local communities have devised some way to control space in a rational way, then there will be obliterated forever from the environment of metropolitan counties a cultural heritage that once enriched the lives of everyone, whether they were owners or merely passers-by. This is a kind of economic vandalism which impoverishes the habitat and lowers the public standard of living of every citizen.

CHAPTER 7

The Farm as Space

HUMAN GLACIATION

The process of human glaciation, by which productive cropland is buried beneath an avalanche of shingles and concrete, is beginning to arouse some concern among professional agriculturists. In just the past fifteen years an area equal to one twentieth of all the productive cropland in the United States has been removed from the plow by advancing urbanization. This is because approximately half the acres of tillable soil in this country are located in and around growing metropolitan areas. At that rate another 150 years would find us cropping mountain sides, marshes, and other areas that for the moment are unsuitable, in order to make up for the loss of one half the present cultivated land. It will be expensive to reclaim what are now considered wastelands. We have already had a taste of this sort of thing in some of the Western states, where the Federal Government and private landowners have together invested as much as $5000 per acre to bring desert lands into irrigation.

Recently the supervisors of a soil conservation district in Charles County, Maryland, seriously asked the Federal Government to spend upwards of a half-million dollars to protect 1600 acres of land that today is mostly wooded and hardly worth more than $80,000. Government economists said this could be justified because "someday that land may be needed for crops even if it isn't needed today." Of course, this kind of reasoning is hard to fathom, but it reflects a point of view that cannot be ignored because it is already being used in Congress to get appropriations. Freezing economic assets on such a scale to bring wastelands into cultivation is comparable to the elaborate terrace building of the pre-Columbian Incas. These stone-faced agricultural monuments on the flanks of the Peruvian Andes have been estimated by anthropologists also to represent an investment of $5000 per acre by today's standards. Such lavish spending on overhead may be one reason why their civilization was threatened by internal weakness even before Pizarro deceived Atahualpa.

Dr. E. A. Norton of the U.S. Department of Agriculture says, "If both the rate of population increase and the rate of annual disappearance of cropland remain stable . . . it will likely mean the passing of the age of comparatively cheap food in America."[1] That is a polite way of saying that food will cost more and there will not be so much money left over for the other things that have created a high standard of living in the past. No country where food is expensive enjoys a rich life in other respects. Under such circumstances the market basket behaves like a blotter that soaks up the wages of the average citizen. One need only recall what happened to meat prices during wartime to realize what would occur should today's surpluses turn to a slight deficit. A little bit of privation in the stomach has a remarkable loosening effect upon the pocketbook and could provoke a dizzy inflation in food prices.

For the moment a better technology is more than making up for the shrinkage of agricultural space. Otherwise, of course, a food pinch would have developed already. Every state has examples of increased production by fewer farmers on less land. In Delaware in 1945 there were 9296 farms.

When the last census was taken in 1954, there were 6297. In 1945 there were 923,000 acres of land in farms. Recently farm economist William McDaniel estimated the total is down to 800,000 acres. However, a productivity index which stood at 100 in 1946 had increased to 159 in 1958. As long as a technological revolution can compensate for the cannibalism of farm land by metropolitan sprawl, the American city will have a full stomach, but it had better not press its luck too far. There is a point at which the farm will vanish. According to one of the best contemporary standards the limit at which a farm ceases to qualify as such is reached when it drops below three acres in size. This is the point-of-no-return established in 1959 by the Farm Bureau of Caroline County, Maryland, when it refused to qualify aspirants for its annual Farm Beauty Queen Contest if the old homestead had shrunk beyond that limit.

Economically the farmer should be the last person to give a hoot about the extinction of the farm on the urban fringe. Except for whatever sentimental ties he must sever, no happier fortune could befall the plowman than to be approached by a realtor willing to pay him more for his land than he could earn by working it a lifetime. The sudden golden shower of capital gains that attends the transmutation of cornfields into speculative real estate has caused nearly every farmer on the urban fringe to put out the welcome mat for the bulldozer. Of course the shrewdest husbandmen hold out as long as possible inasmuch as the last acreage to go into developments usually brings the fattest price. Understandably, most farmers do not want to be spared this delicious fate. When Fairfax County, Virginia, recently tried to limit suburban sprawl in outlying agricultural districts by raising the minimum area of house lots to three acres, the local farmers blew their tops. They contended that the new ordinance would force them to stay in farming whereas otherwise they might have a fling at real estate. They challenged the legality of the zoning ordinance in the courts and defeated it. They argued that most homeowners could not afford three acres of land at house-lot prices and that therefore the zoning ordinance deprived them of customers and a chance to sell their land in smaller pieces at maximum prices. The judge agreed and invalidated the county's restrictions.

THE WOLVES OF NO MAN'S LAND

Most farmers on the urban fringe, even if they had not wanted to sell their land to an advancing suburbia, are eventually persuaded by a series of events to change their minds. Slowly they are overwhelmed by an endless rise of taxes to help defray the mounting costs of new schools and roads, as well as the wages of the inevitable bureaucracy that comes with urbanization. In the country the many duties of local administration are usually carried on by senior citizens without salary or for nominal stipends. As long as a place is truly rural, the population remains relatively stable and schools built by one generation may accommodate the next with slight additions. The tax base is adequate to support simple services without much of an annual increase.

The advent of suburbia changes that. In the absence of industry there is nothing else upon which to hang the burden of heavier civic expenses; so tax assessors hit the farms on the assumption that if one of them sold for a high price to a subdivider, then they are all worth a mint of money. This sounds reasonable but the fallacy is that the expanding community, no matter how fast it grew, could not use all the land at once even if every farmer were willing to sell. But the assessors are hungry and they are often under the pressure of land speculators with political influence to put the squeeze on operating farms so that owners will sell quicker at bargain prices.

The premature expulsion of the farmer from the edge of the city via the tax-pressure route commonly creates a belt of idle land which grows into unsightly weeds and brush between advancing city construction and the outer rim of operating farms. This desolate no man's zone is composed of the slaughtered carcasses of farms which, as it were, hang on the hook in cold storage awaiting the slicers and cutters who will hack out pieces for the retail trade. No genuine farmer could afford to hold high-tax land even if he were cropping it, but the land butchers are able to hold it in complete idleness because that is their business and they have the capital to buy today for sales that may not take place until five or ten years hence. They are well-financed professionals who understand the beauties of land-value appreciation under population pressure and are prepared to invest in them. They know that space in the path of growth increases in value faster than money in the bank; and they are favored further by the fact that their profits, in contrast to ordinary income, will be taxed as capital gains. The farmer is financially unprepared to play in this big league; when he sells he makes a nice profit, but not the kind of killing that would otherwise be possible. When the stakes are really high, City Hall or the County Court House may step in to take care of its own during the final ripening period when land values make their fantastic final spurt.

Generally, it is while land between an advancing suburbia and the belt of retreating farms is ripening in the hands of professional land wolves that the future shape of a growing settlement is determined. The design they create is seldom drawn for the ultimate utility and convenience of tomorrow's community or for preservation of landscape beauty and function. During this crucial stage, when there are fortunes to be made or lost, energy is not wasted on silly byplay. That can come later with the promotion blurbs appealing to prospective homeowners after the main battle has been fought behind the scenes. In fact rational master plans are seldom possible, even if some operators wanted them, because many individual speculators are involved and each is restrained or pushed by his own clientele, associates, and political connections. It is during this interim period between liquidation of the farm and the arrival of the bulldozer that the hottest jockeying for licenses, permits, and special zoning concessions goes on. It is no small wonder that a functional design does not emerge, but rather a patchwork compromise by which the influential get the commercial sites and the multi-family dwelling permits, while the weak find themselves holding low-value single-family residential land which they may have to sell at little profit, if not a loss. In the course of this melee the mistakes are born that breed future suburban-renewal projects before even the first ranch house, supermarket, or dual-lane highway is built on what used to be a peaceful field of clover.

NEW SPACE FOR THE CITY

The disappearance of farms on the edges of growing cities is a matter to which few urbanites have given thought; yet it is more important to their welfare than to that of the agriculturists who are displaced. Land to the farmer is basically a business medium. While he may have a personal preference for one place rather than another, and it may be an inconvenience to give up a homestead so that a city may grow, the affected husbandman is not damaged irreparably. He may keep his business alive by shifting to a rural district. For the moment at least the total farm economy is not hurt by urban raids on agricultural lands. In fact the net result is to reduce surpluses slightly, stiffen prices, and enrich the individual farmer. However, land is a substance of more intrinsic significance to the growing city. It is the basic raw material of its existence. It is not soil but rather space—for which there is no substitute anywhere else. The city, unlike the farmer, cannot move. It is committed forever to its location. As it consumes space to expand, it makes commitments which, while they may be modified, may never be undone

completely. Only a Carthaginian annihilation could remove
a city and restore the land to a pastoral condition.

In his use of land the farmer harvests a crop, plows under
the useless aftermath, and starts afresh with each new seed-
ing. He repeats this cycle over and over, year after year. If
he is an intelligent man he learns from this experience and
his techniques improve as time goes by. To the agriculturist
land is a renewable resource, capable of restored fertility
and ever better crops. He does not plant for permanence
but for the season, and he expects that each new effort will
eventually be superseded by another even better. The farm
is an enormous blackboard upon which the operator continuously draws and erases patterns of use. Its function is to
be neutral—constantly subject to change and improvement
under increasingly better management.

The city uses land differently. What it plants it cannot
plow under except at a sacrifice. Buildings and streets are
not crops to be harvested but useful facilities to be preserved
with care, and utilized where they stand decade after decade. Though a city may learn from experience how to make
better use of land, only in the most exceptional circumstances can it afford to apply this knowledge by tearing
down and starting over. If it learns anything that is widely
applicable, it is how to plan the future consumption of virgin space so as to avoid the mistakes of the past. A growing
city which cannot learn from its own experience how to
utilize newly acquired farm lands more appropriately than
in the past is destined to consume this irreplaceable resource
to the ever-increasing expense and dissatisfaction of its citizens. It is difficult for the American city to adopt such an
attitude of self-criticism toward its own growth because
throughout our history the conquest of space has been glorified. Almost invariably it has been considered an obstacle
to be overcome rather than a limited asset to be handled
with thrift.

In a country of continental size it is too easy to look upon space as an obstacle to efficient organization. It means long routes of transportation, sometimes across deserts and waste-lands, to connect the really productive and inhabited centers. The American urbanite has not been conditioned to look upon space as a limited commodity because the occasion for this point of view is recent, and a rural heritage still dominates our thinking. The very flight to suburbs reflects an unwillingness to face the basic problems of city planning. The sprawl of suburbs over the landscape without a coordinated design for their expansion suggests a complacent belief that space for expansion and linkage is inexhaustible. If there were a consciousness of the actual limited supply of space where populations are concentrated, it would have provoked by now more positive civic action. As it is, the waste and misuse of space by both government and private investors is creating a situation which could destroy the fiscal solvency of communities as well as their usefulness as habitats for the human organism.

From the standpoint of the greatest good for the greatest number of American citizens at this particular moment in the nation's development, the most important function of the farm on the urban fringe is as a reservoir of space which eventually will be urbanized. Unless a growing community regards the farms on its periphery as the most important raw material out of which its future will be molded and treats them accordingly, there can be no sensible policy for the eventual allocation of their space to urban uses. If a community must first misuse land, create congestion, license inefficiency, and promote dissatisfaction before it is shocked into seeing the importance of rational space allocation, there can be no hope. We shall have to live with folly if we are not wise enough to prevent it, and this will become a permanent drag on our economy and a constant irritation to our daily living. That we have muddled through in the past will not comfort us in the future. Effective urban renewal is already far beyond the financial means of our economy; yet the speed-up in population growth and metropolitan expansion has only begun. The deluge is yet to come and we have only a sieve to bale out the boat.

It is a function of the human mind to anticipate danger and to keep the human organism out of trouble. In no matter related to the domestic environment is there more urgent need for intelligent foresight than in directing the final disposition of farm space as it is incorporated into the city and suburb. Yet, at present, this vital community matter is generally ignored and left to contending speculators as though it were an old bone to scrap over. Those who look upon the consumption of farm space by the spreading city as progress, regardless of the ultimate use and arrangement of that space, are a type of Chamber of Commerce enthusiast with little understanding of man's basic biological and psychological needs. It may be good business and good politics to think of the farm on the edge of the city as an anachronism that should be prematurely taxed into submission and sold into the hands of land jockeys who are out to snare the developer with the deepest pockets and strongest nerve. To be sure, this is growth. This is action. A city with friends of this conviction needs no enemies to create a troubled future.

It is not surprising that the average metropolitan citizen has given no thought as to how open farm space should be converted into cities and suburbs. Even professional planners must be content with the piecemeal niceties of street patterns for new plats and the pretty colored lines that separate single-family districts from multifamily districts on zoning maps. Very few are permitted to think about master designs for the detailed uses that should be made of all the fields and pastures on metropolitan outskirts that are positively destined to eventual urbanization. The civic architect is buried under the minutiae of spot planning without the benefit of guiding concepts of how the whole community should grow. No responsible person would invest in a projected office building for which there were no blueprints, yet every property holder in practically every city is an investor in a community which has no detailed blueprint for what lies ahead. A building contractor would lose his mind if he had no master plan and at every stage of construction a different architect showed up to insist upon structural innovations that had occurred to him the night before. Yet this is the way additions are made to cities.

While usually there is no basic concept of community organization to guide the growth of a metropolis in a rational manner, there is a plethora of ideas about the design of disjointed parts. There are superb plans for each new subdivision, and each new shopping center, and each new school. But these are only pieces to the total puzzle. The fact that they are ultimately destined to fit badly, with no reasonable suggestion of over-all design, seems to be no one's concern. The fact that the whole should be an entity superior to the sum of its parts is universally ignored by cities. Planners could do this job easily and well. That is their profession, but they are not given the green light. While hack work is turned over to these professionals, the basic decisions which really determine a city's future are made by speculators and politicians. The growing metropolis is in the curious position of allowing its future to be determined by amateurs and promoters, while specialists stand on the sidelines to give the game some semblance of respect. Yet this is the home of the American people. It is the environment in which they live out their lives. It is the backdrop which colors each day's existence. It is the setting for the private dwelling, and the stage upon which every social function is performed. This is the environment which arouses our emotions and influences our thoughts. There is no function without form and if the form is cockeyed the function is bound to be screwy. We could do better but we refuse to give the professionals a chance.

In areas where large cities lie close together there is no co-ordinated effort whatever between these neighbors to plan together so that they do not bump into one another. In fact when two cities such as Philadelphia and Trenton are only a few miles apart, there seems to be a fatal impulse to close the gap. Such "urbitraction" may be temporarily forestalled by active farming in the space between, but there is a limit to the farmer's ability to hold out until communities come to their senses and realize that space is an exhaustible resource that should be allocated with the most cautious respect rather than with a promoter's eagerness "to get things going" so as "to close a deal." The disappearance of farms on the urban fringe is not the "farmer's problem," but it is a matter of health or disease to the city. It is like the passage of years to an aging organism. Something irretrievable is gone, and the span of what remains depends almost entirely upon whether the past was spent in health or dissipation. Let the young city with big ideas look at Boston and its suburbs to study the frightful consequences of metropolitan growth without order or discipline. Let the young city on-the-make study Boston's tax rate and take heed lest it too travel the same road to bankruptcy.

USE ACCORDING TO CAPABILITY

The ways cities and suburbs consume farm space in their ever-spreading growth should be guided by the physical capabilities of the land and by the human needs of the community. Without a grasp of these principles and an adherence to them in planning, the eventual cityscape is certain to be sheer potluck or deliberate abuse. People need space in which to reside, work, shop, move around, play, pray, study, exercise, relax, love, entertain, and carry on government. The more people there are, the more space is needed for all these activities. A metropolis will be off-balance just as a diet may be off-balance if any necessary ingredient is omitted as the organism grows. Any landscape which is brought into metropolitan development through suburbanization must plan for all human needs by an allocation of space for their purposes. Just a casual acquaintance with the way suburbia is growing in most places will reveal neglect of fundamental human activities and civic needs. Only at the risk of drying up the diversity and vitality of American life may we neglect to provide space for every human exercise.

Attention to the bare subsistence details of housing and shopping are not enough. No community could get along without water, yet how many suburban communities have set aside space for reservoirs that will assure an adequate water supply when present populations have quadrupled? Where would they expect to find the space for reservoirs when the time comes when there will be four times as many houses, shopping centers, factories, schools, streets, and service stations scattered around? In December, 1957, soil conservationist Edwin F. Owens made a reconnaissance study of land use on 41,000 acres of the Wissahickon-Sandy Run Valley, which is on the outskirts of Philadelphia in Montgomery County. Among the suburban towns in the area are Roslyn, Willow Grove, Ambler, and Flourtown. The purpose of Mr. Owen's study was to locate, if possible, open areas where several water impoundments could be made without condemnation of houses or the relocation of power lines and roads. As suburbanization has progressed in the valley the rate of storm water run-off has increased. Roofs and pavements of new suburban areas, by shedding water more rapidly than farm land, have hastened flood discharge that has damaged urbanized areas farther down the valley. Land use at the time of the survey was found to be: agricultural, 25-30 per cent; forested, 10 per cent; urbanized, 35-40 per cent; idle, 25 per cent.

The idle land consisted chiefly of abandoned farms and pieces of farms which had been sold to investors and were waiting urbanization. Many years may pass before all this idle land is utilized, but because it is scattered among built-up zones it has already lost much of its value as far as regional planning is concerned. Of seventeen possible sites for the construction of impoundment areas, only three were "open." That is, these were the only places with enough acres grouped together to make a catchment basin where there were no houses to condemn or roads and power lines to relocate. Urban-suburban construction on thirty-five to forty per cent of the land is so sprinkled through the old farm country that the opportunity to acquire undeveloped space for flood control and water-storage reservoirs has almost disappeared. There is no point in training professionals in the principles of urban planning if their brains are used only to write expert post-mortems.

In 1958 the suburban town of North Providence, Rhode Island, had about fifty per cent of its land developed and fifty per cent awaiting someone to build on it. However, the two types of land were so intermingled that the town, in looking for a school site, could not find five acres of open land in one piece in a suitable location. The same community wants light industry to improve the tax base and provide employment. Yet with all its parcels of open land it does not have sufficient in any appropriate location for commercial construction. The best sites for industry, which are fairly level areas near railroad tracks and above the natural flood plain, are sprinkled with an assortment of residences, stores, and small factories. Only the latter are where they logically belong.

This kind of conglomerate development is happening in hundreds of communities at the present time. Clutter and scatteration distinguish their landscapes whereas there should be orderly separation of incompatible types of development. When space is abused and wasted in this way, a community is likely to be functionally obsolete before it is half finished. It will resemble a bargain basement stocked for a remnant sale. The customers it attracts will certainly not be the most affluent or discriminating. The city that wants to attract the best will have to practice snob appeal in its use of space or, like an inept swain, it will be rejected by the most desirable damsels.

Not only must there be a place for everything that communities should provide, but the place for each activity should enhance the value and function of all other places for all other activities. This calls for intelligent arrangement and a subtle consciousness of what goes into the physical construction of a community so that human lives will not be underprivileged. It enhances the value of a residential area to be within reasonable commuting distance to work, but certainly the place where people live should not look like a factory district nor should it be so close to one as to smell like it or sound like it. But there are new housing subdivisions around Gary and Hammond, Indiana, where people will never know what it means to live in a residential neighborhood. Schools do not belong in commercial districts, but practically every large city and some new suburbs have built them there. On the other hand a school may enhance the function of a park and a park may protect the function of a school. Certainly a church would be a more delightful place for contemplation and worship if it were set apart on a green landscaped square rather than at a highway intersection or next to a supermarket. This is a horse-sense concept as old as the colonial New England village, the physical charm of which is eternal in the annals of church location, but now seldom copied.

Planners know how to compute the additional space needed to accommodate properly every increase in urban population. They are aware, too, that everyone does not have the same income or taste. They can make allowances for all the normal variations in human desires and for inequalities in ability to pay. They are realists, and, if they were permitted, they could design communities that would be functional, attractive, and accommodate people of every cultural and economic level. With this basic grasp of what people do and need in communities, the problem of planning resolves itself into exactly where to allocate the necessary space for each facility. It is at this point that the natural landscape should become the guide rather than what the speculator wants and the politician approves.

The concept that land should be used according to its inherent capabilities has been well developed in agriculture but it is practically unheard of in urban planning. The nub of the idea is that any large area of earth surface shows natural variations and these natural variations should guide the way land is used. For instance, a dairy farmer with two hundred acres of land and fifty cows knows he must have so much pasture, raise so much corn, and harvest a certain amount of hay. He needs space for home, barns, sheds, roads, and a wood lot. As permanent structures are built on the farm over the years, they are located for the greatest utility and convenience with respect to the total area, its shape, and the undulations of its surface. Land areas reserved for woods include those where flooding occurs, where soils drain slowly after rains, or where the surface slopes so steeply that a permanent vegetative cover is necessary to prevent damage by erosion. The best soil with good drainage and the least slope is reserved for intensive cultivation. Poorer lands with intermediate slopes are reserved for pastures and fields of perennial hay.

Roads are built on the farm where drainage is good and the risk of erosion is at a minimum. This reduces the cost of construction and maintenance. The natural contours of the land, the variations in soils, and the steepness of slope are considered carefully when the shapes of fields and the locations of fences are determined. Drainage ways are left in permanent sod or trees so as to prevent gullying. If a pond to water livestock is desired in a pasture, its location is fixed by the undulations of the land, soil type, and the extent of the watershed above. If these natural determinants were not respected the pond might not hold water or a flash flood might wash it out. Unlike a public community a farmer cannot afford to fight nature. He has no taxpayers to underwrite mistakes. He must tailor his desires to Nature's dictates or he will be in constant trouble. If he uses his land with respect for its inherent capabilities, then management will be easier while every purpose to which he allocates space will be better served. Such planning for land use is the very foundation of productive and efficient agriculture and its principles are respected by the most progressive farmers. It has been largely due to such wise use of land that the rate of soil erosion has declined in recent years and the basis of a vigorous agricultural economy is maintained despite the gradual loss of space to the advancing city.

While the agricultural economy of professional commercial farmers gains rapidly in health and productivity as the years go by, the economy of urbanized areas pokes along more slowly. Official reports by the United States Departments of Agriculture and Labor indicate that in the decade 1948-58 productivity per man in agriculture increased 84 per cent while labor productivity in manufacturing increased only 26 per cent. While farmers are able to raise more with less land and less manpower, cities gain in numbers but lag in efficiency. Today the average American farmer raises food and fiber to satisfy the needs of twenty other citizens with more to spare for underdeveloped areas overseas. In Colonial times there were ten farmers for every urbanite. The modern commercial farmer's managerial abilities and efficiency have commanded worldwide respect and envy. In a very real sense the extraordinary productivity of the professional commercial farmer in the United States has created a labor surplus and an accumulation of material fat that allows the city to be profligate without disastrous consequences. But as cities grow larger and farms fewer, it will become impossible for the farm to stock the city or to compensate for urban waste.

When Fairfax County, Virginia, was caught up in the

maelstrom of suburbanization that swirls around Washington, D.C., it had no plan for normal expansion, let alone for the explosion which occurred. Between 1940 and 1957 the county's population increased from 40,000 to 185,000. Houses were built on flood plains and in drainage ways which should have been avoided. Suitable rights-of-way for commuter routes to Washington were not acquired by the public. Good development sites were by-passed in favor of poor ones which were cheaper to buy but which turned out to be more costly to use. Parks were not acquired where people concentrated, so that now most residential communities are on one side of the county and most suitable areas for regional parks are on the other. There are 2300 houses in Fairfax County with septic tanks that have oozed onto the surface of their yards because the subsoil is impermeable. After the once rural landscape was hacked to pieces in this irrational manner, Fairfax County finally came to its senses. The damage will not be undone except in the most critical places, but the lesson learned can help in the future and it could serve as a warning to other counties that are similarly unprepared for growth.

Fairfax has become the first county in the nation to put a soil scientist on its payroll as a permanent employee. This man had previously served with the Virginia Agricultural Experiment Station and had had experience advising farmers on the use of land according to its natural capabilities. A detailed soil survey was made of Fairfax County, and it is now impossible for a builder to secure a construction permit in areas that are naturally unsuited. Ignorant of these new regulations a real estate developer recently paid a farmer $600 an acre for his 100-acre farm. Two fine highways serve the area; the view is agreeable. The developer erected a temporary office on the tract and hung out a sign that he had lots for sale. Then he visited the county courthouse to secure approval for his plat. When the soil survey was checked it was noted that septic tanks would not function on this property. As it is located almost twelve miles from the nearest sewer connection development is out of the question. The temporary office building and sign have been removed and the land remains a poor pasture worth, perhaps, $100 an acre.

Without inquiring into local drainage conditions the town of Annandale acquired a twenty-two-acre school site at a cost of $1000 an acre. When the school was built it was discovered that the ground was waterlogged and foundations required special support to prevent collapse of the walls. The additional cost was $233,870, or more than ten times the original price of the land. Experiences such as these have made private citizens and public officials wary. The latest plans for future development in Fairfax County show in detail the area and location of natural drainage ways. As new plats are presented by developers it is recommended that drainage ways be reserved for recreation. To compensate the developer for this loss of land the county allows him to divide the bulk of his property into lots of minimum size. By considering the capabilities of land before plats are approved and before building permits are issued, Fairfax County has found a way to reduce the future incidence of some types of urban decay.

THE CONTROL OF METROPOLITAN SPACE

The dream boat of state is wrecked upon the shoals of reality. The abstract idea, that the development of space in metropolitan areas should be guided, sounds nice, but a community can do very little without controls. There are strict limits to a community's authority over landowners and what they should do with their real estate. This is as it should be for, otherwise, the very ownership of property would be a delusion. It would be clearly unethical and illegal for a public authority to permit one farmer to sell his land for great profit to real-estate developers and to deny this right to his neighbors on the assumption that their acres should be conserved as open space until the community approved conversion to other uses. This would be an arbitrary and a discriminatory exercise of police power out of keeping with constitutional guarantees.

Certainly it is unrealistic to expect that the average farmer or land investor would forego voluntarily the speculative advantages of possession. Population increase is the best guarantee that land values will increase substantially in metropolitan areas, and the average owner naturally wants to cash in on a good thing if the spread of suburbia comes his way. This is certain to happen in approximately two hundred metropolitan areas in the United States which comprise about seven per cent of the nation's surface and where sixty per cent of the population lives. Within these areas about half the land is still in farms but their life expectancy is limited for the rate of population growth is running seven times faster in the suburbs than in the central cities. If these communities wish to protect their futures, they must buy that protection from the landowner or buy the land itself just as they would buy any other commodity or service. If a city or county is too stingy to pay space insurance, it will have to suffer the consequences. It is not the duty of farmers or land speculators to save the health of the community. Theirs are legitimate businesses and they have as much right as anyone else to try for as much profit as they can possibly make. The community that seeks salvation must save itself.

While no large landowner in a metropolitan county has lived through the past decade without being intoxicated by the real-estate boom, the voting public remains pretty much in the dark about the kick in that potent brew. Most citizens have no acquaintance with real estate beyond their F.H.A. and G.I. insured mortgages. Under the circumstances they do not realize how fantastically open land increases in market price as it passes from farm to suburban development. Given time, which is another way of saying, "Let population pressure develop," an acre that is worth no more than $400 as cropland may sell for $4000 as house lots or $40,000 if it is in a choice commercial location. This can and does happen very frequently in a matter of ten or twenty years.

A man from Montgomery County, Maryland, who has had some pleasant experience with this sort of thing once told how fortune had blessed him. "I'm not a farmer," said he, "and I don't want to be. I'm only having fun with land. Never any farmers in the family as far back as I know my ancestors. I just always wanted some land of my own to walk on or ride on. Twenty years ago I started with forty acres on the edge of Washington. It was open country all around me then, and dirt cheap. Some friends of mine did the same and on Sundays we used to fox hunt on our places. We never did anything else with them—just played. Then after the war the building boom started. Each of us that bought pieces like that are millionaires today."

If communities want to get in on the ground floor of their own future they, too, will have to "play with land" and they will have to get at least a twenty-year head start. If communities want to plan their growth and dictate the way space should be used when it passes from farm to city, then they will have to do more than pass ordinances. They will have to gain control of the land. To get control they will have to buy it just as any individual would. Cities do not normally engage heavily in the real-estate business but they will have to if the pattern of their future growth is to be rational. Planning without control is idle dreaming. There are several ways by which a community could purchase control. It could buy land on the open market when it is in farms and hold it until it is ripe for development. It could then sell its holdings with restrictions in the deeds so that developers would have to build whatever the community would have planned for that particular space. This approach would be impossible for most cities or counties. They are already in debt for current needs and could scarcely find funds to invest in properties they could not use or sell for twenty years.

William H. Whyte, Jr., one of the authors of *The Exploding Metropolis*, has proposed that communities purchase "development easements" from farmers on the urban fringe. By the sale of such easements farmers would surrender the right to use their land for anything but agriculture. Space would then lose its speculative value because developers would scarcely care to collect cornfields and pastures if that were all the land could be used for. Possibly only farmers, who want to continue farming on their present properties, would be interested in forfeiting development privileges. Many estate owners who are harried by mounting taxation might sell such easements if their preference were to live on their properties indefinitely rather than to sell them for a profit. Local real-estate taxes would certainly be lower on farms and estates stripped of their speculative prospects because their market values would be comparatively low.

The "development easement" idea is a good one and a farmer who would sell such rights need not necessarily be a financial dim wit. Either he could charge a high price for parting with the speculative value of his land or he could afford practically to give away development rights if he were to reserve an option to repurchase them for a nominal fee at any future time the community should decide that his farm space were needed for urban development. By these devices a community could be protected against premature and disorganized expansion. It would gain control of its own future growth pattern because it could specify the uses to which the land might be put when it eventually released the rights which it had held in trust. The farmer would not be chased away until his land was urgently needed and meanwhile he would enjoy low taxes. Also the farm community could not be infiltrated and split up by other types of land uses if all farmers in the vicinity were to make similar sales of development rights simultaneously. Obviously the time for a community to buy development rights is not when the land is almost ripe for urbanization but when that day is twenty, fifty, or a hundred years away. The more remote the prospect, the easier and cheaper it should be to acquire them.

There are other ways to skin the cat. A community could establish a revolvi.g fund with which it would purchase farms on the urban fringe. Once they were in legal possession, then restrictions could be written into deeds that any change of use would have to conform to the development plans of the community. With these restrictions recorded the land could then be resold immediately into private hands for farming or speculation. Such a program would be senseless unless the community had a comprehensive plan for its future expansion. Another device would be for private citizens to establish a corporation either for profit or as a nonprofit foundation which would acquire farms and sell them with restrictions in their deeds that would conform to uses designated in a community's master plan. By processing properties in such ways as these relatively little capital would need to be tied up at any particular moment. Also, the chances are that while farms are in the temporary possession of the processing agency they could be rented so as to return a reasonable interest on the invested capital.

The basic reason for any approach to rational space design is that expanding metropolitan areas are so large that controls must be of a similar magnitude. Such space design on a large scale and fortified with legal teeth could go far beyond the capacities of zoning ordinances and actually blueprint specific patterns of future land use that would stick. No speculator could cry "foul" because he would buy land with its future clearly specified on the label.

The capital-gains tax on real estate is the logical source of the funds with which communities either might buy space for future public needs or acquire land temporarily in order to write development restrictions into deeds. These capital-gains taxes, which can amount to as much as twenty-five per cent of profits made on real-estate transactions, are now collected by the Federal Government as though they were ordinary revenue. Capital gains on real estate are actually the product of local community growth and should properly be collected by the community which created them rather than by the Federal Government. Either that or the Federal Government should return these revenues to the communities which produced them with the proviso that they be used only for planning and for the acquisition of land. They should be spent to buy space for future roads, parks, reservoir areas, school sites, airports, disposal areas, and other public facilities. These funds should also be available to buy development rights from landowners.

Revolving funds built up out of capital-gains taxes on real estate could be used to buy and sell land in order to amend deeds so that they would conform to master plans for future growth. The capital-gains tax on real estate should be regarded not as revenue but as a vital instrument with which to obtain control over the way a community grows. It is no mystery why the Federal Government has preempted the capital gains tax, which should have been a local privilege. Most local communities do not take planning seriously enough to realize that the way they grow either makes or breaks the real-estate market and that if they grow in a rational way then they, and not the Federal Government, should get the credit. Planning the ultimate use of space is one of the most important, if presently neglected, functions of local governments. Usually they have not progressed beyond the kindergarten stage of zoning. It is therefore no wonder that they have not reached the sophisticated level where they feel competent to control their own growth or realize what is the origin of capital gains in land.

CHAPTER 8

Space and Circulation

HIGHWAY ROBBERY

"A highway is a true index of our culture." With that bite the late critic and commentator, Bernard DeVoto, chewed off a mouthful. Certainly anyone can tell a lot about a community's cultural level and whether or not he would care to live there by a drive along its streets and highways. It is a national trait, particularly obvious in the new suburbia, to expose the details of our personal lives to passers-by. Few Europeans would think of revealing at the roadside so much of their private environments. Nor would they permit a stark strip of concrete to become the guide line of community evolution. Only because we, as a people, are peculiarly enamoured of highway facilities (since we are so dependent upon them), have we permitted highway engineers to distort traditional patterns of community arrangement and to dictate new grotesque shapes into which we must now fit our lives. This wonderful power to design the format of American living must swell the egos of ambitious highway authorities, but it is a power that they are incompetent to wield. They have acquired it by default, and it must be recaptured by communities so that it may be exercised with better sense lest their cultural levels drop to new lows.

Next to the authority to tax, the authority to spend tax monies is the most awesome privilege of government. These twin authorities in effect proclaim that the state is wiser than the citizen and that for his own good the government should take his earnings and spend them for him. The biggest single expenditure by state governments is for the construction and maintenance of highways. Budgets of highway departments are so fat that often they become the tail that wags the political dog of state. Highway funds seem easy to come by not only because every adult behind the wheel is held for ransom but also because most of the money is spent on contracts, and these attract some very hungry and important fish which would never snap at so insignificant a bait as a public salary. Then, too, highways can make or break a businessman or a speculator; thus, their design and location are matters of more than academic interest.

Even such impressive fiscal power is not a fair measure of the strangle hold that highway departments have upon the outstretched public neck. It is the power of road builders to mold the everyday environment that makes them a truly fearful force to reckon with. Because of a growing national penchant to arrange our private and our public lives along the roadside, the judgment of highway engineers has more to do with the present and future shape of America than that of any other group in government or private life. Even Congress and the Presidency have less to say about what America should be or become in so far as its physical arrangement and appearance is concerned. What the individual, city planner, or professional architect would like is all but ignored. This authority to lay out the arteries and veins of circulation is the authority to establish the guide lines of future real-estate development and the whole course of evolution of the landscape.

That such a fateful responsibility should have fallen into the laps of highway engineers and those curious new offshoots of government, the bridge and tunnel authorities, is one of the most unfortunate political delinquencies of our time. As matters now stand these men of special but narrow technical competence are allowed to locate the bench marks of the future for the whole metropolitan organism. All subsequent construction must follow in the ruts pioneered by the highwaymen. Their technical tasks are limited; but the influence of their design, their choice of location, and their consumption of space is almost boundless. Though they are held responsible for the quality of their engineering, they are immune to censure for the powerful impact which their decisions make upon the environment. The fact that a good but misplaced or misused road can destroy a city neighborhood or condemn a lovely rural landscape to future ugliness is usually dismissed as no concern of theirs. Theirs is the task to build but apparently not to reason why beyond the obvious need to make roads. It is no wonder that the work of most highway departments, while technically admirable, is sophomoric in its social concepts and often creates more environmental problems than it solves. Instead of demanding that roads be built so as to contribute to a rational organization of space in metropolitan areas, the community has let its highway engineers take the initiative while it passively accepts the consequences. The community allows highway planners to route traffic anywhere to "eliminate the bottlenecks." Yet after each costly elimination it is discovered that the trouble has only been shifted to another location.

By acquiescing to one traffic emergency after another, as though only a little face-lifting were necessary, metropolitan areas have allowed themselves to be overpassed, underpassed, widened, straightened, and segmented by "gasoline gullies" and "Chinese walls" *ad infinitum,* yet the headaches of congestion grow faster than the fresh supply of asphalt aspirin. The blame has been pinned on the automobile, but it can go only where there are roads—and it cannot talk back. If machines create congestion it is because street and highway departments route them where they should not have been routed in the first place, or they allow things to be done to their streets and roads that permanently ruin them as thoroughfares. Misplaced and misused roads account for more traffic jams than automobiles do. A new four-lane divided highway along which commerical and residential construction is permitted soon is reduced to little more than the main aisle of a strung-out shopping mart. When this happens, the highway ceases to be a road and becomes an obstacle course to test the endurance of brakes, transmissions, and human tempers.

The Massachusetts Highway Department is a specialist in this form of "carnival-midway" highway construction by which roads are built for the benefit of the sideshows rather than the motorist. Practically every major free road in the congested eastern part of the Commonwealth is patterned after the bone structure of a Boston codfish—a central spine bristling with so many commercial and residential ribs to turn into and out from that a free flow of traffic along the main drag is impossible. The purpose of highways is to prevent congestion, not to create it; but that is not the way Bay State engineers see their mission. They apparently operate on the sound bureaucratic principle that the more confusion they create, the more money they will get to "straighten" and "widen" their way out of it—and the blame is put on the automobile.

Highway departments usually fail to make hard and fast distinctions between a highway and a service street. In this day and age any road that attempts to be both is a miscalculation from the start. It is a mongrel that can only breed trouble in the civic kennel. It took an outside firm of professional consultants to reveal to the Virginia Highway Department that it could build a new eight-lane, limited-access highway cheaper than it could widen old Arlington Boulevard from four lanes to eight lanes as it runs from the Potomac River through Arlington and eastern Fairfax Counties. To condemn buildings and widen about ten miles of the old boulevard (which had degenerated into a service street-highway hybrid) would have cost approximately $62.8 million dollars, whereas to buy an entirely new right-of-way and to construct a brand-new road would have cost between $27.3 and $59.4 million dollars depending on the route chosen.

Distance was not the main factor in any of these calculations, for all the proposed routes were of approximately equal length. Land costs and demolition charges were the principal reasons for the spread in estimates. Even with these figures in its hands, however, the Highway Department remained hesitant about switching to the construction of a new restricted-access road despite the fact that it could thus get eight new lanes for less than the price of four. For some strange reason highway builders are handicapped by a compulsion to be service-street builders. Apparently they would rather breed scrubs than thoroughbreds, yet it is often the mutt that eats the most and in the end has little value.

Possibly highway departments fail to insist upon wide rights-of-way when they start a new project because they are service-street fanatics. A wide right-of-way would help to keep civilian construction at such a distance from the pavement that it might be discouraged entirely. In fact wide rights-of-way would permit the planting of lateral buffer strips that would positively prevent access from the side. This, of course, is the principle of the toll road, which aims to keep traffic rolling on the pavement and to prevent the escape or entry of vehicles from abutting private lands. Pavements protected from cross traffic and from the marginal friction of cars turning in and off to shops and homes are infinitely more efficient than those where the driver must keep bouncing his foot from brake to throttle. If state highway departments would stick to highways and leave the street-making business to cities and suburbs, the terrible waste that results from trying to make hybrids that are neither could be drastically reduced. For one thing most cities and suburbs are too poor to afford all the mistakes that states are so happy to construct inside their limits.

The main reason for trying to clarify the difference between street and highway is to make more efficient use not only of highway funds but of the dwindling amount of space that remains in metropolitan areas. The time is coming when it will not be possible to find new rights-of-way through the ever-widening suburban fringe up to the city line. Even now it is hard to find one that does not require the demolition of many buildings. This situation can only become more difficult and expensive as time goes on. Therefore it is important at this moment to take the widest possible rights-of-way and to protect them from every form of lateral cluttering. The rewards would be twofold. Pavements could be widened in the future without demolition and traffic could proceed along such roads at top speeds. With the hazards of cross traffic and side traffic removed, cars could only keep going because there would be no neon-lighted, car-hop emporiums where drivers could stop.

Of course, there is always a danger that reform itself may become a sin. The new Connecticut Turnpike has all the protective features that a good road should have. Its right-of-way is wide. Access is controlled. There is no cross traffic and every lateral enters or leaves the main stream by a parallel side strip. Since it is possible to zip along at a predictable speed, there is really no obvious cause for frayed tempers unless it be the frequent toll plazas which consume more pocket change than a pin-ball machine. In fact the "pike" is such a joy to drive that many commuters have converted their cars to mobile dining halls for the morning run. Relieved of the tensions that tie limbs and minds in knots on the ordinary highway, these happy innovators enjoy the luxury of extra morning sleep while they shave and breakfast on the pavement at sixty miles an hour.

With a little advance preparation, orange juice, coffee, vitamin pills, hard-boiled eggs, and oatmeal in the form of cookies are not too difficult to consume one-handed. The radio substitutes for the newspaper and there are no dogs to let out or cats to let in during the course of the meal. Plug-in electric razors are standard equipment. But this do-it-yourself valet-buffet service has the state police in a tizzy. Says Lieutenant Walter Foley, "Driving on the turnpike requires the full attention of a driver and he should not be distracted by eating while operating a motor vehicle." After years of tussling with the wheel and brakes on lethal U.S. 1, the new turnpike looks so easy to most old-timers that probably they feel they could even take a curve and a morning shower at the same time. Business will really perk for Lieutenant Foley when drivers with hide-a-bed cars decide to try for the office without even waking up.

A MATTER OF SPACE

There comes a point at which space for new roads in a growing community must be rationed. Otherwise, at the very moment when more room for circulation becomes necessary, less will be available. Unless states wish to face the prospect of spending more and more for less and less they cannot ignore the fact that it takes a bigger appropriation to run a bulldozer down Main Street, clipping off store fronts, than it does to cross a pasture. Even aside from this budgetary consideration, communities have need of space for other things besides streets and roads unless it is desired to convert them into black-top deserts. If highway engineers are permitted to carve up rural space between metropolitan centers as though it were inexhaustible and to blast their ways through cities simply because they have the technical showmanship and the funds to do so, then we must not be surprised if the result is a sick landscape and a sick taxpayer.

It is impossible for highway supply ever to get ahead of

demand if our engineers continue to recommend and build the kinds of uncontrolled access roads which they know are a waste of money and space—because they are obsolete before they are finished. As populations multiply in cities, the outlying farms will continue to ship them food, but the rural countryside will never be able to send gift packages of space to relieve the congestion that is certain to smother metropolitan districts to an extent and intensity far beyond present imagining. It is perfectly possible to plan for growth but not by sticking to old habits. Governor Abraham A. Ribicoff of space-scarce Connecticut recently warned every town in his state that it faces "fantastic traffic snarls" if it does not take municipal planning seriously and soon. "Towns that do not plan for their growth within the next ten years will have no future whatever," the Governor has eloquently warned.[1] Of course, the state government itself should set an example in every road it builds by making certain that access is highly restricted so that in perpetuity it will carry maximum traffic with the least friction. To plan a road for a useful life of anything less than forever is to plan for trouble. This is the basic principle of the railroad right-of-way and the reason that the railroad is still the most efficient way to get into and out of the hearts of cities despite the fact that some tracks were laid a century ago. As it is, Connecticut has a better than average record for a metropolitan state. Its Merritt Parkway, built during the depression years of the 1930's, remains one of the best designed roads for private cars in the United States. It is truly a road that is good forever. Of course there is a limit to the volume of traffic it can carry, but the highway itself will never become obsolete for its size and purpose, which is to route private cars, without cross traffic or marginal friction, through the suburban countryside that parallels the state's southern industrial cities.

The Merritt Parkway is a model of good taste in practically every detail. Its designers refrained from excessive blasting and bulldozing. Knowing they were not constructing a level-grade route, they left the gentle hills and valleys along the right-of-way relatively undisturbed. The landscaping is superb because it is all of indigenous trees and shrubs with no billboards. To traverse the Merritt is to take a long journey through an exquisite park, for there is no countryside in America more beautiful than New England when it is not butchered. But this parkway is no cultural accident. It is the result of a long and bitter planning-stage feud between the Garden Club of Greenwich Town and the state highway authorities. The club fought for controlled access, the undulating traverse, the landscaping, billboard proscription, and even the detail design of every overpass, but it did not win its battle without paying a price. To get what they wanted the people of Greenwich and all of Fairfield County had to sell bonds in the good name of their own county in order to raise money to give to the state so that it could build according to their specifications. The state said it could not afford such frills, yet the Merritt Parkway is the only road of its vintage in Connecticut which is as good now as when it was opened. The nominal tolls charged on this road are used to pay off the county bond issue.

Traffic congestion is the first serious symptom of a coming population congestion. If the inanimate machine cannot be handled efficiently, then there can be little hope of accommodating properly the droves of self-willed humanity that are in the offing. That is the really frightening aspect of the highway problem. It is the first severe test of man's capacity to organize space for the population crush that lies ahead. It would be folly to think that the management of hordes of people is something that government could solve easily. The highway problem has revealed how weak and inept government is when it comes to planning and construction. It is patently unfair of government to deride the private land-owner for slum conditions in housing or industry, as is done in many cities, when government itself sets the pace by the creation of slum streets and slum highways. The way a street is laid out in a city, with or without central boulevards, lateral lawns, or tree plantings, sets the tone of whole neighborhoods. A city government which tolerates potholed, ill-kept streets and allows them to be littered with utility poles, which could just as well be placed underground or in the rear of lots, is in no position to ask its citizens to spruce up their properties.

The bad taste and the extravagant waste of public funds on the usual kind of street and highway is the strongest possible argument against giving government greater authority in the field of planning and construction, yet no private agency has the power or wealth to assume it. Thus far, with a mountain to move, government has developed neither the vision nor the leadership for the job. Now the time has come either to practice vehicular birth control or to declare certain developed areas off limits for additional highway surgery because space is exhausted. It has been estimated that if an additional 75,000 daily commuters were to try to get from New Jersey into New York City by automobile it would require ten more vehicular tunnels under the Hudson River and twenty more lanes of expressways into the city. Once across the river in Manhattan there would have to be 250 new acres of parking space. What such an additional influx of cars would do to streets that are already jammed is anybody's guess; but doubtless the Port of New York Authority (a toll-collecting agency that builds bridges and tunnels) would be only too happy to give it a whirl and let the people worry about the consequences.

New York City's construction co-ordinator, Robert Moses, recently recommended to the Board of Estimate that $83,-000,000 be spent to build two and one-half miles of elevated highway in lower Manhattan so that traffic might flow from the Holland Tunnel and the West Side Highway to the Manhattan and Williamsburg bridges across East River. This, in the words of Mr. Moses, would be "a key to the resurgence of the entire downtown area."[2] The price tag on this job of municipal vivisection is an all-time high of $33,000,000 a mile. Of course, the idea is expected to catch fire because the Federal Government presumably would authorize itself to pay ninety per cent of the bill for such a Chinese wall by labeling it a National and Defense Highway. Just what a National and Defense Highway should be doing perched up on stilts in the midst of the most densely cluttered real estate in the nation has not been explained. On no possible grounds could it be approved as an evacuation device for this road is designed to route more traffic into the center of lower Manhattan than comes there now. The snarls that in an emergency would develop on the up and down ramps would paralyze all circulation in the neighborhood. Nothing could be a better set-up for bedlam than an exposed elevated highway in such a location. If Federal highway funds are to be released for ill-conceived and extravagant projects of this kind, then Congress would do well to keep its hands in its pockets a little while longer until the problem of populations, space, and circulation are better understood by engineers.

Before human congestion increases to the point where every parcel of space in metropolitan areas is more intensively used, piecemeal planning will have to cease. Highway and street construction will be ordered to conform to a detailed plan of land use for the whole community. The age of *laissez-faire* for street and highway departments will be at an end. They will continue to lay out the guide lines for community growth, but they will be told where to build and what designs to use by whatever agency is responsible for the allocation of space for all community needs. In the community-wide plans of the future so much space in specific locations will be allocated to circulation. Highway and street departments will have to stay within the space budgets granted to them. Regardless of their impressive financial strength they cannot be permitted to use tax monies to buy up space without restraint. Space, not money, will be tomorrow's most essential ingredient for community health. The metropolis that uses it wisely will flourish. The one that ignores the limitations of space will hit the skids.

With such restrictions placed upon the land that can be committed to circulation, there will come a time when even the best street and the best highway will become too crowded. Population increase makes that prospect inevitable. It is only a matter of time and reproduction. Then restrictions will have to be placed on the use of roads and streets. During rush hours the private car will have to stay off the public ways. Commuters will be obliged to travel by public conveyance. Shoppers will be permitted to travel in their own cars during the slack periods of midday and in the evening. Just as some cities now regulate the hours that a lawn may be sprinkled for lack of pressure or water, there will be regulations as to the times that roads may be used. Some major traffic routes will have to share their rights-of-way with rapid transit trains so that the same space can be made to carry greater volumes. Present planning should be done with these eventualities in mind. They are certain to come with population increase; if they are planned for in advance they will be more functional in design and infinitely easier for the taxpayer to support.

The present format of cities was established centuries ago when both urbanized areas and urban populations were small. Until motor transit was invented in modern times city people simply walked from one part of town to another. Persons of wealth rode horseback or in carriages but they could have gotten around like anybody else, on their two legs, if it had been necessary. Today, everything about cities is different in scale. They are taller, wider, and they have more people. The fused complexes of cities and suburbs, which are called metropolitan areas, are obviously too vast for foot travel and a horse that today ventures into town or onto the highway is the object of universal awe. Nevertheless, in so far as their relation to total urbanized space is concerned, streets and highways are laid out in just about the same way now as they were in ancient times. Structurally they are different and their pavement is superior, but the amount of room they take up in relation to the total urbanized environment is in just about the same proportions as in ancient Rome. In fact some Roman streets and squares are still a jump ahead of the average in size. Capacity is obviously less than need.

In the hearts of old cities this is understandable because they were created before the automobile and rapid transit. But that this urban pattern should be repeated in suburbia, where people are committed to daily long-distance travel, is beyond all reason. In the city where population density is increasing while the pattern of narrow streets prevails, there are two possible solutions to the traffic problem. Either buildings can be torn down to make way for broad thoroughfares and elevated highways at a cost of up to $33,000,000 a mile, à la Moses, or public rapid-transit facilities can be developed which will give such good service that they will be preferred to the private automobile for "in town" circulation. The latter would be advantageous to the city because it would not call for demolition of taxable private property and, for each person served, the overhead would be much less.

In suburbia, where open land is still available, very wide rights-of-way for future controlled-access highways should be purchased so that the private automobile could still be used for some decades if people preferred. However, even in suburbia, greater human densities must be expected ultimately. Then it will be necessary to convert parts of these rights-of-way to public rapid transit. One of the obvious sacrifices in living standards that everyone will have to make in the future, as human densities increase, will be a restricted use of the private automobile. To tear down cities and suburbs just to keep building roads for the private automobile has already reached the point where it is uneconomical in some places—the New York-New Jersey-Connecticut metropolitan area is one of them.

Increasing population pressure is more than matched by increasing piston pressure. While the human population of the United States is expected to increase 18 per cent in the next ten years, predictions are that motor vehicles will increase by 40 per cent. At the moment automobiles are being born at a faster clip than taxpayers—which means fiscal trouble. Today there is one motor vehicle for every three persons. Within fifteen years there will be one car and truck for every two human beings. If now we cannot keep up with present needs for roads except by bond issues that are claims on future taxes, then it is hopeless to expect that the future job of financing roads will be easier when the ratio of cars to people has increased. Even these tough statistics do not predict the whole story of tomorrow's costs and frustrations. It is well known that it costs more to build roads in metropolitan areas than in rural districts, yet both people and cars are concentrating in cities and suburbs while they are thinning out on the farms.

These are some of the rubber-tired facts of modern life: A single lane of surface street, subject to cross traffic in front and marginal friction along the sides, will allow about 1600 persons in private automobiles to pass a given point in one hour. Trains running on a single track, whether above or below ground, can carry from 40,000 to 60,000 persons per hour depending on whether they run as locals or expresses.

Translated into space requirements these figures are staggering. A single railroad track, used for trains that stop briefly every half to three quarters of a mile, is worth 25 lanes of ordinary street. A single railroad track, used for trains that stop briefly every one to three miles, is worth 23 lanes of turnpike or elevated express highway. To replace one double-tracked railroad entering a city would require 46 lanes of Chinese walls. It would be amusing to contemplate,

if the situation were not so tragic, why it is that cities are
literally performing hari-kari by ripping open their bowels
with elevated highways at fabulous cost while railroads,
which already have rights-of-way into the hearts of cities,
are going out of the passenger business. This has not happened by chance. It is the consequence of deliberate high-
level decisions to stifle a tax-paying private industry into
submission while substituting for it a colossal tax-supported
public-spending program which can never transport people
as efficiently and will always lag behind in providing the
service that gullible motorists have been led to expect.

In 1925 there was a flow of 161,000 persons from New
Jersey across the Hudson into New York City every week-
day morning between 7:00 and 10:00 A.M. In that year 96
per cent of the traffic came by train and ferry, for there
were no vehicular tunnels or bridges linking the shores in
those days. By the Year of Progress 1955, the average morning traffic between New Jersey and Manhattan had declined
by 10,000 persons although by that time there were two
vehicular tunnels and a bridge across the Hudson. No one
knows why this decline has occurred, but it is thought that
the wear and tear of commuting has become so severe that
many people have simply given up and switched to suburban
jobs that are easier to get to. In 1925 most of the travelers
lived in towns near railroad stations. By 1955 suburbia had
sprawled all over northern New Jersey, so that people needed
a private automobile just to get to a depot. During all these
years, while public authorities might have tried to connect
New Jersey commuter trains with the New York City subway
via a railroad tunnel, they have concentrated instead on
the spectacular vehicular facilities: Holland and Lincoln
tunnels and the George Washington Bridge. Now they are
in the midst of spending $183,000,000 to double deck the
George Washington Bridge and extend its approaches in
Manhattan and New Jersey. At present these tunnels and

bridge have a total of 18 traffic lanes, yet their capacity to transport people is not equal to two railroad tracks.

If, now, commuter traffic from New Jersey into Manhattan is 10,000 a day less than it was thirty-five years ago, there must be something wrong with the way money has been spent to build facilities. Between 1925 and 1955 railroad and ferry commuting declined from 96 per cent of the total to 50 per cent, while travel by private cars increased from 4 to 18 per cent. Buses, which offered no service at all in 1925, carried 32 per cent of the load in 1955. Obviously government-sponsored vehicular tunnels and bridges have knocked the tax-paying rail system in the head. Yet, despite all the spending on highway facilities, the drop of 10,000 in the average number of daily commuters in a third of a century indicates that traffic snarls have actually discouraged circulation. If America's greatest metropolis is losing commuters from just across its own water front, it had better review its policy toward railroads and subways before it is further cut off from the outside world by its own strangling web of elevated highways and vehicular bridges and tunnels. Though the happy toll-collecting authorities may be enjoying excellent fiscal health, the city itself is suffering from a severe case of traffic indigestion that calls for a different prescription.

In 1957 the Metropolitan Transit Commission of New York and New Jersey unveiled a $345,000,000 plan for linking the New York subway system with the northern New Jersey highway and railway commuter network. The scheme calls for two railway tunnels under the Hudson River: one opposite Battery Park at the tip of Manhattan; the other opposite 59th Street and connecting with Columbus Circle. These tunnels would be linked in Manhattan by about five miles of the present Broadway-BMT subway tracks and in New Jersey by about nine miles of new double-track surface rails. The whole loop, including tunnels, would be approximately eighteen miles long; and trains would run in both directions so that passengers could enter or leave the city by either tunnel. In the words of Arthur W. Page, project director for M.T.C., the new line would intercept in New Jersey "every Hudson River-bound rail line and every highway either now in existence or built in the future south of George Washington Bridge."[3] It would be the kind of facility that should induce people who can travel by rail to make the whole trip with one easy transfer. For automobile commuters it would eliminate a river crossing by car and a parking problem.

It is thought that a rail-highway-subway connector of this sort would be so efficient and convenient that it would help to revive railroad commuting which has dropped to one half its 1925 level chiefly because of suburban dispersion and the old ferry bottleneck at the banks of the Hudson. It was for lack of a tunnel into Manhattan that the Baltimore and Ohio, oldest railroad in the United States, finally discontinued all its Washington-New York trains in 1958. The Lackawanna, which is one of the major commuter railroads in northern New Jersey, was recently authorized to drop forty-two regularly scheduled runs because of deficits. While $345,000,000 is a pile of money, it is almost peanuts when compared with the costs of present and projected schemes for encouraging commuters to drive into New York in their own cars. In 1957 the third two-lane tube of the Lincoln tunnel was completed at a cost of $95,000,000. It would take up to thirty Lincoln tunnel tubes of two lanes each to accommodate as many commuters traveling in private automobiles as the two-tunnel rail circuit proposed by the M.T.C. Buses and cars are disgorged onto congested city streets while subway trains roll on unnoticed beneath the pavement. This is the kind of economical use of space which could speed circulation without destroying the superstructure of the city. It employs the ancient principles of surface and subway railroad engineering which are much more capable of solving transportation problems in congested metropolitan areas than a superimposed network of elevated highways. It is unfortunate that the public ever let itself be maneuvered into the position of using taxes to destroy a tax-paying utility that was doing a better job than the more costly and less functional facilities that have replaced it.

A MODEL OF THINGS TO COME

Los Angeles and its suburbs are the metropolis of the future existing in the present. This, the third largest metropolitan area in the United States, grew up, not in a baby carriage, but behind the windshield and the steering wheel. In 1890, in the heyday of the railroad and the trolley, Los Angeles County was little more than an orange grove with but a seed of a city. The town itself had 50,000 people in those times. Seventy years later the City of Angels and its suburbs could count a heavenly throng of 6,000,000 souls and its automobile population numbered 3,000,000. Los Angeles is the first major metropolitan area in the world to attain the fabulous ratio of one car to every two inhabitants. Thus it is truly the prototype of things to come—a living model of what American metropolitan life could be like fifteen or twenty years hence unless the rest of the country should choose to change its style of transportation before it gets as deeply committed.

By 1980, when other cities have caught up to the present Los Angeles car-man ratio, this civic motordrome will be still farther in the lead. The metropolitan area expects to have a human population of 15,000,000 by that time and one car to every 1.7 persons. To serve its citizens and their chariots, the Los Angeles metropolitan area now has in operation, or under construction, about 650 miles of freeways, which are limited-access highways that curve, swoop, and loop up, down, and around through the vanishing countryside. By 1980 the district expects to raise this figure to 1600 miles of freeways plus about 550 miles of expressways, which are a super-colossal,

double-feature version of the freeway. At that point the
Metropolitan Transportation Engineering Board believes
even Los Angeles will lag behind its own needs, having run
out of space for more adventures in highway building. Then,
in desperation, rapid transit will be called to the rescue.
Recently Swedish industrialist, Axel Wenner-Gren, offered
to build and give to the metropolitan area a 600-mile monorail rapid-transit system worth $800,000,000. In exchange for
the gift the community would be expected to supply Mr.
Wenner-Gren with a franchise to operate the network
together with permission to construct the monorail system
along the rights-of-way of the present freeways. Whether or
not this particular offer is accepted, the future solution to
circulation in the Los Angeles area will probably call for
some such rapid-transit system parallel to and on the property of the controlled-access highways. If this is a fate that
even Los Angeles anticipates, then other cities, not so
wealthy or so vigorous, might well ask themselves if they
should not turn now to rapid transit before having bought
themselves into bondage for vehicular skyways that will
never solve their mounting troubles anyway. Cleveland, one
of the best managed cities in the East, is prepared to test this
thesis.

Cleveland has two rapid-transit lines. One is an old but
rejuvenated interurban; the other is a new $35,000,000 in-
vestment—a fantastic bargain in these days of elevated
highways. The secret of its sweet reasonableness is that
there was room for a rapid-transit line parallel to an existing
railroad where there would not have been space for a
highway—thus no big bill for demolition; no condemnation
of taxable property. In the future Cleveland hopes to do
even better. It is completing arrangements whereby railroads will let the city run rapid-transit trains on their
present rails. The city will get service; the railroads will get
revenue. While this seems like a novel idea today it is just
the same old idea that put railroads in business in the first

place, but which somehow got misplaced for a quarter of a century while highway departments edited the headlines.

Other cities are looking at Los Angeles and Cleveland while reassessing their own strategies. Detroit, citadel of the automotive age, is subversively considering monorail. At present Detroit has about 1200 rail commuters while nearly 300,000 automobiles can be counted on its streets on week-day afternoons between 3 and 6 P.M. These are terrific odds to overcome. Detroit has considered subways but they cost up to $15,000,000 a mile while monorail, including the price of separate rights-of-way, would cost between two and five million dollars per mile.

Philadelphia's Mayor Richardson Dilworth, who acts like the hardest-thinking big-city mayor in the business, recently proposed that the public treasury should help to modernize the railroads and pay them to improve commuting service in a big way. This is quite a switch from the old policy of taxing them into obsolescence. To start with the City Council in 1958 gave a subsidy of $160,000 to the Pennsylvania and the Reading companies so that they would run extra trains into suburban Chestnut Hill. The Pennsylvania Railroad increased its daily trains from 24 to 36. To encourage week-end shopping the Reading doubled its Saturday runs from 15 to 30 while the Pennsy did almost as well by running 27 instead of 14. Extra feeder buses were put on suburban routes to bring patrons to the rail stations. Big parking lots were built at the depots for the convenience of those who chose to use their own cars to catch trains.

After a year's trial the city is convinced that greater effort should be made to increase commuter traffic on all lines operated by the two railroad companies. At present these lines carry an average of 100,000 commuters daily, and the annual deficit borne by the railroads is $7,000,000. Now there is to be a city-financed rejuvenation of its railway systems, including the purchase of new equipment. It is expected that increased patronage will reduce but not eliminate the railroads' deficit, which the City of Philadelphia, through a non-profit corporation, will underwrite to the extent of more than $2,000,000 in 1960. The non-profit public corporation, known as Passenger Service Improvement Corporation, is the first in the nation to arrange with railroads for deficit-free improved service within city limits. In 1958 Philadelphia paid $27,000,000 out of general revenue for highways. If a smaller payment to railroads would prevent highway subsidies from climbing, it would be a good deal. As Mayor Dilworth has said, "I feel that the people would return to public transit if we gave them a good clean ride at a reasonable rate. We just cannot give them the highways it would take to carry everyone to and from center city every day. We cannot afford it and we don't have the space."

The non-profit public-corporation approach to transportation subsidies can be a dangerous weapon when it gets into irresponsible hands. Philadelphia, under Mayor Dilworth, will probably make it work as efficiently and economically as possible, but Massachusetts has had some sad experience with this device which indicates that the idea is not foolproof. If care is not exercised, such a transportation authority may run for the benefit of political friends rather than the public.

Martha's Vineyard and Nantucket are two photogenic piles of glacial gravel that, during the past ten thousand years, have been separated from the Massachusetts mainland by a slow but steady rise of sea level. These islands, now some miles offshore, are like picturesque antiques in the attic of an old New England mansion. They still have the look and accent of 19th Century whaling days. Each summer they are invaded by urbane urbanites who welcome a chance to walk barefoot on Main Street and attend clam bakes for charity. Martha's Vineyard has a native population of 6000 "islanders" who make a living off 40,000 "summer people," who come in June and depart by Labor Day to put their children back in school. The job of ferrying this

migratory horde and their automobiles across the waters to
and from the islands is a lush business for three months of
the year. It is done profitably by the New Bedford, Woods
Hole, Martha's Vineyard and Nantucket Steamship Authority—a non-profit transportation corporation established by
act of the Bay State legislature and subject to its orders.

However, the three-month profit of the steamship authority is regularly converted into a twelve-month deficit
amounting to hundreds of thousands of dollars each year.
Political pressure groups are able to keep the boats operating on superfluous schedules nine months out of twelve—a
practice that would bankrupt any private corporation. It
would be as if the New York Central were obliged by an
irresponsible management to maintain its full schedule of
commuter trains on Sundays so that more friends and relatives could be hired to operate them. The deficit incurred
by the steamship authority is paid by a state-authorized
assessment upon the real estate of the communities serviced.
In some years the taxes upon homes on Martha's Vineyard
are increased one third to reimburse the steamship authority.
After the 1958 levies were announced a few owners with
elaborate old-style mansions on the ocean front threatened
to tear them down and build cabins to escape from confiscatory penalties in the future. A taxpayers' association foresees a general neglect and deliberate razing of developed
real estate as long as these unwarranted deficits are charged
to the towns. Despite strenuous effort by local representatives to get the islands off the hook, the Commonwealth's
General Court thus far has refused to curb the wasteful
practices of the steamship authority.

Irate citizen, Charles G. Norton of Vineyard Haven,
summed up popular resentment when he wrote in the Vineyard Gazette, "If a vessel requiring a crew of 60 men making
one trip from New Bedford daily carries an average of 5
passengers, 2.21 automobiles, and 2.6 tons of freight, how
many trips would be required to make the operation profit-

able?" The people of Martha's Vineyard recently voted in secret ballot 2167 to 136 to urge the Commonwealth to cancel the superfluous trips to New Bedford but their wishes were ignored. A community might be better off to make flat annual subsidy payments to private transportation corporations and be assured of responsible management rather than try to put the public into a business it cannot handle properly.

WHY THE RAILROADS WANT TO QUIT

The railroads want to abandon passenger operations because they put an otherwise profitable business in the red. Howard Hosmer, an Interstate Commerce Commission examiner, has predicted the end of all railroad passenger service by 1970. If rail travel continues to decline as it has in the past decade, Mr. Hosmer believes that parlor and sleeping car service will end by 1965 and coach service will be out by 1970. Commuter trains, which carry one half of all railroad passengers, will be the last to go. They rack up the heaviest losses for the railroads but the public howls louder as they are gradually withdrawn. In 1957 passenger trains on all American railroads ran up a deficit of nearly three quarters of a billion dollars, yet passenger tickets account for only seven per cent of all railroad revenue. Freight, which is profitable, brings in ninety-three per cent of railroad income, but the deficits on the irritating passenger business are so wildly out of proportion to its status that they soak up half or more of the profits made on freight.

In the first eight months of 1957 passenger losses suffered by the Pennsylvania Railroad, the nation's largest, wiped out fifty-two per cent of the profits made on freight. During the same period the New York Central saw sixty-one per cent of its freight profits go down the drain to subsidize passenger service. The railroads not only lose money on the measly passenger business; but it takes the whole heart out of what would otherwise be a thriving industry that could go to the banks for credit to modernize, like any other respectable member of the business community, and pay its stockholders dividends commensurate with their investments.

Many things contribute to the heavy losses that railroads have experienced. Although they are a public service, their facilities are heavily taxed; and all passengers but commuters pay ten per cent more for tickets than would otherwise be necessary because of a Federal "luxury" impost on rail travel. While the Federal government thus penalizes the railroads, it underwrites from fifty to ninety per cent of the costs of major highways. The rising price of tickets, partially due to taxes, is a factor in the decline of patronage, which has obliged railroads to run trains that are only partially filled while potential customers take to the pavement in their own cars. Despite the rising cost of railroad tickets, many commuters apparently do not recognize a bargain when they see it. The New Haven Railroad recently made a study of comparative costs of commutation by private car and by rail from Mamaroneck, New York into Grand Central Terminal. The costs of automobile transportation were computed on the basis of a Chevrolet used over a five-year period. Allowances were made for 5000 miles of non-commuter travel per year which reduced the depreciation charge-off to commutation. According to the New Haven's calculations, the annual fare by automobile was $1500 while tickets on the railroad would have come to $262.80. Obviously most commuters are not accountants. If they were to compute costs on the basis of gross income before Federal income taxes, they would realize that the $1500 may have actually cost them closer to $1800 or $2000 in salary.

Ninety per cent of all present intercity passenger traffic in the United States is via the private automobile. About 3.5 per cent is carried by rail; a little less by bus; a little more by plane. Total annual commuter traffic on American railroads dropped from 340,000,000 in 1945 to 247,000,000 in

1957. At the present time about 164,000 people commute to New York every day by car or bus and about 209,000 come by train, but practically every railroad except the Long Island wants to get out of the business. The Long Island is the only major railroad in the United States which makes a profit on passengers. George Alpert, president of the New Haven, has said that if his company does not get higher fares, tax relief, and public subsidy, it will have to abandon its commuter lines serving New York and the suburbs along its right-of-way. The Lehigh Valley Railroad has publicly stated that it wants to get out of the commuter business entirely. The New York Central has offered to cede its tracks inside New York City to the public so that it can rent them back for less than present taxes. In 1956 the Central and New Haven railroads paid New York City $11,500,000 in taxes on less than six miles of right-of-way and the Grand Central terminal. Meanwhile the city was breaking its neck to build more free skyways for automobiles and buses.

Deficits incurred by commuter trains are heavier than losses from passenger service in general because expensive equipment is used for only a few hours morning and evening; then it remains idle in the yards the rest of the time. About ninety per cent of all the Pennsylvania Railroad's suburban trains are used only during rush hours twice a day. The New York Central commuter facilities are used fully only thirteen per cent of the time. Labor featherbedding also adds unnecessarily to the operating costs of railroads. The brotherhoods still insist upon putting aboard trains the size crews that were needed in 1919 when steam locomotives were the source of power and a whole batch of current safety devices were unknown. Daniel P. Loomis, president of the Association of American Railroads, has pointed out that engineers on the 225-mile run between Washington and New York earn two and one-quarter days' pay in four hours because of a distance-quota system. Railroad wages, which averaged 75 cents an hour two decades ago, were $2.60 an hour in 1958.

All these things have caused the companies to cut service whenever possible, and this in turn has antagonized patrons and alienated public sympathy. If the railroads are allowed to slip out of the passenger business, it will be only for an interlude until the highway situation in metropolitan areas gets to be too much even for the docile American taxpayer to support. When it does, the railroads will be invited back with all the concessions they have asked for; but, by then, the cost to the public of resuscitating a defunct operation will be far greater than if a little oxygen had been given to the gasping giant when it still had strength of its own.

Meanwhile, as public commissions, labor unions, executive confabs, and politicians try to thrash out the deep problems of an ailing industry, the Mercury International Company, which provides coin-operated luggage lockers in depots, is going ahead optimistically with its own inspired program to restore a better atmosphere. Mercury International has a new "quilted" surface, stainless-steel locker that is fitted with an automatic deodorizer that releases a "fresh out-doorsy aroma" into the cabinets each time they are opened. To express its faith in the future of railroading, Mercury is replacing old dingy gray-enameled storage boxes in depot waiting rooms with this dream installation. In the immortal words of W. Richard May, president of Mercury International, "We want something the ladies will like. They use half of all coin-operated lockers. We haven't found the right odor yet, but we'll try anything short of Chanel No. 5."[4] Why the intrepid Mr. May draws the line there is not explained, but then there are other vital points about railroading that are not too clear either.

The world's biggest job of commuter railroading is done by the New York subway systems, which carry three times as many passengers annually as all 131 of the nation's first-class railroads—for fifteen cents a ride. Yet the subways are

losing their clientele; their patronage today being only half
what it was in 1942, when a trip anywhere in town cost a
nickel. Of course, in those times, the city subsidized the
subways but now the subsidy is on streets and highways
while the subway is on its own. The chances are that
fares will climb to twenty cents or a quarter in a few years,
and even more people will switch to private automobiles. At
present nearly five million passengers each weekday push or
get pushed through the token turnstiles and the automatic
doors of New York's underground trains.

The subways do their fabulous job so cheaply for many
reasons. One is that it takes only one motorman and an
engineer to operate a train, as compared with a normal crew
of five on regular railroads. The subways pay no taxes, and
five million passengers every weekday are still quite a substantial trade to bank on. Upkeep overhead is held dangerously low; some of the coaches have not been replaced since
the system was inaugurated in 1904, and their windows
appear not to have been washed in the interval. The crowding and the filth of the dim, cavelike stations are notorious,
for they present as seamy an aspect of urban decay as the
old-time Bowery. The wages of subway trainmen are de-
cidedly substandard for the railroad industry and will doubtless have to be adjusted upward in the near future. In 1957
subway motormen averaged a lower annual wage than either
city police patrolmen or sanitation corpsmen. This is the
low level to which the world's best patronized railroad has
been reduced.

THE FEDERAL HIGHWAY PROGRAM

On July 1, 1956, President Dwight Eisenhower signed into
law a Federal Highway Act under which a 41,000-mile
system of roads is scheduled for development by 1971 at a
cost then estimated at $27 billion. All these figures are now
obsolete. Fewer miles will be developed in more time at

greater cost, and *system* is probably the wrong word to apply to the project. A very large portion of this program, accounting for about a third of the distance and more than half the funds, is intended to widen and straighten present major rights-of-way and to replace old bridges with longer, higher, and broader models. Thus a vast share of the new hope is a face-lifting job to patch up the past.

It is a rather startling feature of this gigantic Federal investment that there is no specific master blueprint to guide its development. It was not conceived with concrete ideas as to how and where traffic should be routed either in detail or on a nationwide basis. Instead state highway departments are individually invited to submit their most urgent needs and projects for review. There will be co-ordination at the Washington level, but what the nation's highways need is some very tough refereeing and some strict ground rules that will preclude a repetition of past chaos. It will help very little to co-ordinate obsolete ideas so that they will agree with one another as they meet at state lines. A tough policy is not in the cards as they are now cut, but a really critical policy is what America's major highways have long needed, even more than they have needed money. As now conceived the national program will be limited by state vision and state politics, which on the whole have created in the past more problems than they have solved.

John T. Howard, Professor of City Planning at Massachusetts Institute of Technology, has detected the most critical deficiency of this, the largest single effort to organize the use of space in our national history. Too much money, according to Professor Howard, will be "spent for the wrong things in the wrong places." The 1956 law, says the professor, is "silent on planning and deals almost entirely with engineering and financing." As he sees it, and many others will agree, this program forces highway engineers to "make decisions that have impacts far outside their fields . . . It does not belittle them to say that, just as war is too important to leave to the generals, so highways are too important to leave to the highway engineers." Professor Howard recently told a national planning conference that over the course of the next two decades the highway work done under the 1956 act would have "more effect upon the form and pattern of growth, and therefore upon the character and structure, of our metropolitan areas, than all of the metropolitan planning done by any city planners in this country between 1945 and now."[5] These words of warning doubtless will go unheeded, but no prediction could be more certain of fulfillment. Yet a national project of this weight and scope is itself without a philosophy or a plan.

City after city is perverting the basic intention of the law by trying to get Federal highway money as financial aid in urban renewal. Appeals are being voiced to route roads through slums as a justification for condemnation and compensation. To the extent that road monies are thus diverted from building roads to reclaiming urban real estate, the whole program will suffer. Not only will there be fantastic raids on the funds themselves but, worst of all, roads will be built where they should not be built in the first place. By this time every city knows that circumferential and by-pass routes that divert through traffic so that it never enters the heart are the only types of roads that effectively cut down vehicular congestion as much as thirty per cent in metropolitan business centers. Nevertheless, despite such evidence, some of the first and most expensive projects approved under the national program are bringing interurban traffic into the hearts of cities, which many drivers would avoid if they had an alternative. One mile of such street widening may cost as much as five to thirty miles of first-class, controlled-access, four-lane, divided highway in the country. If motorists were faced with the facts and had a choice, they would probably vote for more and better roads rather than for glorified arterial streets.

One of the best features of the national highway program, as it is developing, is its strong emphasis upon use of the controlled-access principle in construction. Controlled access is the only satisfactory means by which to avoid obsolescence due to cross traffic and marginal friction. This aspect of the program will do more to illustrate the basic principle of space conservation in highway construction than any amount of educational appeal to state legislatures or the motoring public. Daily, nationwide experience with this kind of functional highway eventually will develop popular support, so that all serious future road construction, under whatever auspices, will incorporate this feature. Strange to say, there is little that is fundamentally new in highway design that was not understood in a theoretical way before the automobile age was out of knee pants.

As far back as 1911, T. Coleman du Pont of Delaware conceived of a road such as the state has not built to this day, yet he devoted the best years of his life to this project and invested much of his personal fortune to get a highway started that would run from the Pennsylvania line in the north to the Maryland line in the south—and would never become obsolete. Had this road been built as Mr. du Pont conceived it, Delaware would have become the most progressive state in the union in highway construction. But his ideas were so far ahead of his time, and ours, that they were actively opposed and sabotaged by public and politicians alike. As much as present Chief State Highway Engineer Richard A. Haber would like to use certain principles of design first proposed by Mr. du Pont a half century ago, he has not received the support he deserves either in the State House or from the little man with a driver's license.

T. Coleman du Pont, born in 1863, had become a national figure in finance and business by 1911 when he embarked upon his venture to build a road with private-investment funds. He planned to give this road to the State of Delaware in return for certain rights to control and charge for access from abutting properties. After the appearance of the automobile, and foreseeing great expansion in this form of transportation, Mr. du Pont made surveys of road systems in Europe and the United States. As a result of what he saw and what he could imagine the future would require, this engineer of extraordinary vision conceived of roads with 200-foot rights-of-way when horses were still the chief means of conveyance in the Delaware countryside.

This 200-foot strip, according to du Pont's blueprints, was to be divided in its cross section in such a way that both edges would be shrub- and tree-lined borders fifteen feet in width. These borders were to be the buffer zones that would protect the road from lateral entry except at points where entryways were to be leased to abuttors. The plantings were intended to enhance appearance. Being a man of taste and culture, du Pont did not consider the possibility of billboards despite the fact that his venture was designed for profit. In the center of the right-of-way there was to be a paved road for automobile traffic. That road was to be flanked on each side by rail lines for electric interurban trolleys, and by separate roads for trucks and separate roads for horse-drawn vehicles. Parallel to the vegetated border strips there were to be sidewalks for pedestrians. In between each type of roadway buffer strips were to be reserved for safety, and for shoulders and culverts. Much of the center strip for automobiles was actually built by the private investors, but, before it was finished, both Federal and state aid began to be voted for public highways and the project was eventually turned over to the State of Delaware for completion. Needless to say, most of its visionary features were never translated into fact.

TURNABOUT

Many years ago, on summer evenings, people who lived in a red-brick apartment house on Thompson Street, south of Washington Square in New York City, looked out of their

windows onto the cobblestones below. There they saw a
steady procession of horse-drawn wagons and carriages cluttering the streets. The cursing of the drivers with reins and
whips in hand and the jostling of the traffic made the people
who looked down from their windows a little sad to think
that a horse must live such a hard existence. Today all that
is changed. There are only a few horse-drawn vehicles left,
and only a few horses to pull them. Consequently life is a
little better for those beasts. People are more considerate;
they admire the mild-mannered mares and geldings as relics
of the past. On Thompson Street the apartments in the red-
brick building have been vacated by their human occupants.
Stairways have been replaced with ramps while bedrooms
and parlors have been converted into stables. This is where
some of the last weary dray horses of New York come at
night. Following the ramps they walk up into the dingy
building to get their oats, hay, and a night's rest. On warm
summer evenings, when it is stuffy inside, some of the old
nags stick their heads out of the windows and look down on
the streets below. There, like the human tenants of old, they
see a steady procession of traffic cluttering the streets. They
hear what they may suspect is cursing above the din of
motors and they are a little sad to think that people live such
a hard existence.

CHAPTER 9

Parks and Playgrounds

Public parks and playgrounds are among the casualties of modern community design and modern community culture. The Victorian notion that a proud and progressive city should have within it many preserves of open space, for play or contemplation, is becoming obsolete. The new stripped-down efficiency-model community consisting of a shopping center surrounded by housing developments is generally devoid of parks, libraries, and playgrounds. Even schools and school yards are consolidated and put off into remote spots accessible only by buses which leave right after dismissal. The new citizen learns at an early age to become a commuter, and he learns also to do without the games and exercises that once were a part of childhood when parks and playgrounds, or simply a vacant lot, were centers of after-school fun. In today's efficiency community there are no vacant lots and usually no public space except the curvilinear streets, where the parked car takes precedence over youthful exercise.

Parks in Victorian times, and even up until the 1930's, were municipal status symbols. They were the touch of elegance that softened a stark commercialism which had made the best cities prosperous but threatened the well-being of their inhabitants. The sprawling suburbia of the mid-twentieth century had not yet opened the safety valve of spacious private house lots to the mass of urban workers. Consequently cities felt some pressures to conserve bits of the natural landscape within their bounds. Thus every citizen who wanted physical exercise or emotional relaxation would not feel alien in an environment that was too full of people and the artifacts of everyday business. In the new suburbia the need for public open space, particularly for children, was not recognized in the beginning. There seemed to be unlimited open land on the edge of each development. By the time new subdivisions had surrounded the old (and were themselves surrounded by even newer mass housing), the pattern had been set and it was discovered that people could get along without. This discovery that most people will settle for less and less of the amenities that once were considered essential to good community life is the touchstone of suburbia's amazing growth. Capital is quickly drawn to enterprises in which nothing is wasted on overhead and every improvement is marked for sale and profit.

Until the rise of suburbia and the decline of cities, men of prominence in private and public affairs felt a social obligation to demonstrate good taste by helping to make cities healthful and attractive, as well as sources of livelihood. Wealth and political distinction implied that the man who enjoyed them also possessed cultural insights. Such a person was expected to contribute both money and effort to community improvements because his predecessors had themselves established that tradition. This sense of civic duty was a hangover from times when the public responsibilities of royalty were assumed by the business fraternity. In the absence of a king, the leading merchants of a 19th century American city often accepted the social impositions of wealth. These solid citizens did not reproduce the Gardens of Versailles but they did create worthy projects, among which parks were prominent. The successful businessman and his city lived together and were associated in the public mind. It was a symbiotic relationship—each doing better than either could have done alone. The patron gained prestige; the patronized acquired public amenities. Nearly every American city has a park that was donated by a senior citizen or his family; many bear the names of these benefactors although who they were and whatever else they did are now forgotten.

Today, organized professional welfare activity has largely replaced private conscience and private taste. Parks and playgrounds fare badly at the hands of present city budget makers and in the programs of Community Chests, which concentrate upon the supervision of misfortune rather than upon the elimination or avoidance of its causes. Again, this switch in focus reflects a switch in society's own conscience. The rise of professional, cash-payment welfare as the chief business of the largest cities, and of distress administration as the principal concern of organized charity, has pretty well doomed any serious attention to the physical structure and design of the city or to the economic and cultural causes of human misery and community decay. The emphasis now is on adjustment to hardship rather than upon its prevention. That the deterioration of the environment may have anything to do with the deterioration of people seems to have escaped the minds of professional rehabilitators who evaluate themselves by the weights of their case loads rather than by what they do to correct the circumstances which help to breed degeneration.

The job of creating an environment in which man would feel fit is far more difficult than to administer tranquilizers that temporarily quiet a misfit man. Apparently one of the major causes of juvenile delinquency in large cities is a lack of opportunity for physical expression and exercise except through violence or sex. Considering the city's environment it is surprising that teenagers are as respectful as they are of today's adults, who, in their youth, had better opportunities for outdoor play and exercise than they now provide for their own children. It is a very old and respected observation that parks and playground programs help to preclude delinquency. As far back as the early part of this century, St. Paul, Minnesota, discovered that where there were playgrounds with active recreation programs, there juvenile delinquency decreased substantially, but in neighborhoods where there were no supervised playgrounds delinquents were numerous. A district attorney of Philadelphia many years ago analyzed the record of juvenile delinquency in a neighborhood where playground recreation programs had been available for five years. He discovered that there had been a fifty per cent drop in delinquency during that period as compared with a similar five-year period before the supervised playgrounds were established.

No reasonable person would suggest that more parks and playgrounds would solve the problem of what to do with children until they are old enough to be put to work or put in jail. However, to provide youth with the facilities for healthful amusement and exercise in their leisure time is a social obligation as important as to give them schools. Good citizenship in the younger generation can only be the product of responsible guardianship by the older generation. Civilization and culture are not born in the individual but are nurtured and instilled by family and community. The community or the family that simply propagates its young and leaves them to their own devices without further attention or concern except in the matter of formal schooling is itself delinquent.

City building has not stood still in recent years, yet the loveliest city parks and the most ample public playfields are found almost invariably in the old-fashioned neighborhoods. They are holdovers from the times when people tried to make their cities attractive and when it was believed that the city could be the noblest environment in which a cultured human being might live. Nothing remotely comparable to these sometimes fabulous relics are being set aside or developed by the public in newer urban sections or in the conventional suburb. The reasons are partially financial, but more particularly social. As the physical nature and human composition of the modern community has changed, enthusiasm for public parks has been superseded by other interests. Also the whole cultural pattern of living has undergone a metamorphosis.

Public parks do not fit into the modern recreational picture of privileged persons as universally as they once did. In fact as urban populations have tended to become predominantly poor-white and colored, other more privileged people have lost interest in the organism as a whole. Either they have abandoned the city entirely for the suburbs or they have crawled off into little corners where they try to preserve or restore some neighborhood quality. In Washington the Georgetown, Chevy Chase, and Embassy Row sections remain as oases. In Baltimore the Homewood district is still delightful. In Philadelphia Society Hill is coming back and in Manhattan some of the midtown East Side is desirable. On the whole, however, the old-fashioned city has been deserted by persons of means and cultural advantages so that few are left who would be willing to insist upon civic excellence or to pay for it. It is one of the most ironic twists of our times that the city has been abandoned by the very elements of the population which could afford excellence, and the shell has been left by default to the underprivileged who are unable to keep it in repair.

The tastes of potential users of parks and playgrounds have changed as much as the tastes of potential sponsors. Police patrol and playground supervision are not as effective as formerly. Usually there are no attendants or regular groundskeepers. Thus many parks are not so safe or so pleasant as they once were. Most of New York's Central Park and Philadelphia's Fairmount are "off-limits" at night and parts of them are wisely avoided at all times. When parks degenerate to the point that they harbor vandals rather than deter vandalism, then they have lost their value to the community. This is not owing to any deficiency in the physical park but to a deplorable cultural degeneration of city administration. It is perhaps impossible to tell precisely whether the dwindling interest in city parks and playgrounds is because the facilities have deteriorated and thus have lost their former appeal and social status, or whether the desire for open space and an outdoor place to play is fading from the consciousness of the modern urbanite. Possibly a once blithe spirit is at last subdued and now is reconciled to the cage.

Today parks do not have the prominent advocates who formerly secured results at City Hall. Recently it took all the power of Carmine De Sapio and Tammany just to prevent the widening of a street through New York's Washington Square. Formerly such a combination of political influence could have created a Central Park. Now it is easier for citizens of means and culture to forget the public and to take care of their personal needs through subscriptions to private parks and clubs. There is an understandable reluctance on the part of the wealthy to foist their preferences upon the community or to ask municipal bodies to share their tastes. Citizens of stature who formerly donated land and money for the embellishment of public parks are losing interest for obvious reasons. Since many of this class no longer live in cities they have shifted their allegiance to the suburbs. Also, taxes being what they are now, a man of respectable income more than pays his social debts in hard cash and there is less compulsion to donate amenities. Since the public has already put its hand in his pocket without an invitation, his conscience is hardly overburdened. It is not his fault that bureaucrats and legislators choose to spend public monies in ways that seldom inspire pride in the environment.

Politicians should know that a city which neglects its own face and figure cannot expect to inspire passion among its inhabitants. The dowdy can never be proud. The unlovely will not be loved. That is a kindergarten lesson in civic loyalty. The city, the state, or the nation which neglects the quality of its environment does so at great peril. People respond with deep emotion and affection to what they see and admire. The citizen must see beauty if he is to love his country. He must witness elegance to believe that his is the favored land. God's eye is not blind. The blessed are not the wasters and spoilers. Faith has its roots in the wonders of life rather than in exhortations and abstractions.

The bulk of urban citizenry, being thus abandoned without leadership in matters of culture and aesthetics, does almost nothing and gets almost nothing. Professional politicians, to whom has fallen the chief responsibility for city development and environmental charm, are not particularly gifted or active in matters of taste. Thus parks seldom assume significance in their strategies. Libraries, museums, historical monuments, botanical gardens, zoos, and planetaria are other cultural facilities that fare badly in the hands of the artless politician who is so wrapped up in managing government that he neglects the welfare of the governed. In the New York metropolitan area, which once had an admirable record for park development, the rate of land acquisition for this purpose has dropped sharply in recent years. Between 1901 and 1940 park-land accessions within the metropolitan area by states and counties averaged nearly sixteen acres for every increase of one thousand in population. Between 1941 and 1955 the average dropped to seven acres per thousand increase in population, but even this was good compared with the nation as a whole. During the latter period suburban expansion was pronounced and large areas of previously open country came into more intensive use. On the basis of newly developed areas, parks fared badly. In the 1901-40 period, when urban-type compact growth had been dominant, twenty-seven acres of park were established in the New York metropolitan area for every one hundred acres of new real-estate promotion. During the 1941-55 period, when suburban sprawl had come into its own, the allocations for parks dropped to one tenth of the average established in the earlier part of the century. Only 2.7 acres were set aside for public recreation for every one hundred acres that were developed. A prosperous people had learned to cheat themselves when there was the least excuse to do so. That was the penalty of being without a leadership conscious of the role that the environment plays in a human being's physical and psychic condition. This neglect practically assures the newer neighborhoods of a faster deterioration rate than was experienced by older parts of the metropolis.

Rome is not called the "Eternal City" because it hired a public relations counselor to coin the phrase. What makes Rome eternal is the eternal respect of Romans for their city and its respect for them. Its physical façade is as perishable as that of any city, yet it is admired and preserved, whether it is as old and weather-beaten as Trajan's Column or as recent as the newest parks along the Appian Way. Twenty centuries and more of history greet the eye on a morning's walk. It is there in ruins and restorations. It is in St. Peter's Cathedral and in the fluted columns of temples to more ancient gods. It is in fountains, triumphal arches, cobblestones, and palazzos. It is in the gardens, boulevards, parks, and sports arenas of all periods since the beginning. As a people most Romans are very poor, but no city is richer in its public trophies or happier in the pride of its citizens in their citizenship.

Now Rome is experiencing a fantastic expansion in population. In the past ninety years it has grown from 25,000 to 2,000,000. This human multiplication has also increased the physical breadth of the city. Suburban development has erased open vistas on the old urban fringe. But, instead of mourning change and passively accepting it, aroused Romans have forced the Italian Ministry of Public Works to draft a master plan that provides for a reservation of open space for public parks, playgrounds, and sports fields in every district of the city. Under this plan up to thirty square feet are set aside for gardens and playgrounds for every inhabitant in new quarters of the city. This allotment is three to four times the average allocation of recreation space in New York's newest public housing projects. Along the Appian Way there has begun a vast park development which in area will be as extensive as all the existing park lands that have made Rome one of the greenest cities of the past. To provide for the pedestrian in the land of his namesake, a network of footpaths is contemplated which will be eight miles in length. Rome's eternity is thus reinforced by regard for its all too temporal citizens. Possibly a goodly share of the next million Romans will be sojourning Americans who may wish to sample a sophisticated urban environment even if they must go across the seas to a spot over two thousand years old to find it. The rest of Europe also lives in the 20th Century, and it knows something about automobiles as our imports show, yet Europe is not disposed to downgrade parks and playfields in community development simply because it has acquired other interests.

FUN FOR THE MILLIONS

New York City has ten municipal golf courses for 8,000,000 people. The Dyker Beach course in Brooklyn is the most popular. There golfers, who wish to tee off at 5:30 A.M. on a Sunday morning, start to line up for the privilege in the stillness of the night at 2:30 A.M. By five o'clock a radio policeman arrives to maintain order among the come-latelys who may mill around for as much as nine hours before it is their turn to knock the ball over the eighteen-hole course. A five-hour wait for a turn to play is par for Dyker Beach. Players who live nearby have an advantage for they can register, pay their fee, and pick up their admission number. Then they can go off to church, shop, or do chores around the house while time rolls on. The experienced can guess to within half an hour when they should return with their clubs. However, night owls from more distant lofts cannot register until the municipal cashier arrives about dawn. These eager drivers establish their claims in line by leaving club bags to hold their places while they visit a snack bar or try to finish a night's sleep in the back seat of the family car. At times like this claim jumpers sometimes shift bags to insert their own and that means business for the cop. As one of New York's finest was heard to comment at Dyker Beach, "Have you ever seen a crazy golfer when he wakes up from a snooze in his car and finds his golf bag has been moved under a tree or something? . . . They're—peculiar." One refugee from Dyker Beach says he can drive to Bridgeport, Connecticut, play eighteen holes and get back to Brooklyn in less time than it would take to play in his own neighborhood.

Some city people who go to suburban parks may be headed for disappointment. Westchester County has five public golf courses for half a million persons—a ratio that is eight times more favorable than New York City's. In self-defense Westchester has chosen to exclude nonresidents from courses at Saxon Woods and Scarsdale; otherwise natives would be squeezed out of their own territory by an overflow of New Yorkers. In 1958 Westchester's Board of Supervisors also closed to outsiders its conventional public parks at New Rochelle and Yonkers after a "license-tag survey" revealed that nine out of ten visitors came from outside the county. This brought an angry retort from Bronx Borough President, James Lyons, who sought to have the City Council prohibit the parking of Westchester automobiles on Bronx streets. It is the habit of the county commuters to drive into the Bronx, leave their cars at unmetered spots, and continue their journey to work via subway. In this way they travel faster and pay no parking fees. Apparently getting into each other's hair (or trespassing upon one an-

other's space) is beginning to irritate urbanite and suburbanite in reciprocal measure.

In the absence of legal restrictions only distance and a
quota system deter the masses from bursting out of the
park-hungry city into public open spaces beyond. Bear
Mountain Park on the Hudson River is eighty miles from
New York City. There are 150 tenting sites at Bear Mountain which are in constant use throughout the summer season. A family which manages to get onto the assignment list
may occupy one of these tent sites for two weeks: eight
dollars a week for a wooden platform; six dollars for the bare
ground. Only the limited number of sites restricts the number
of families which otherwise would respond to the call of
the wild.

Mr. and Mrs. William Cameron of New York City are
experienced at this sort of thing, and they are willing to go
through some rather hectic transportation acrobatics to
satisfy a summertime urge to get away from eight million
people for a brief communion with the chiggers and mosquitoes. Mr. Cameron continues to work each day at his office
in the city even while they vacation at Bear Mountain Park.
He and Mrs. Cameron are up with the birds by 5:00 A.M.
After rustling breakfast they drive south to the New Jersey
state line at Suffern, where they part. Mr. Cameron goes on
by bus and in less than an hour he has arrived in the city.
Meanwhile Mrs. Cameron drives back to camp, does the
dishes and shopping and manages a swim before she goes
back to Suffern to pick up her spouse. Hopefully there will
always be some rugged souls who will not be deprived of
Nature—no matter what the obstacles may be.

Professional recreationists recommend that communities
acquire a minimum of twenty acres of park land for every
increase of one thousand in population. At the present rate
of growth in metropolitan areas that means at least 40,000
acres should be added annually to city and suburban park
systems. There is now a national accumulated total of about

three quarters of a million acres in community parks—about a third of the minimum required. Only about 1800 out of more than 17,000 municipalities have this kind of facility; obviously some communities are well off while others are destitute. This is a fantastic indictment against a rich nation which apparently is unable to keep up with its own minimum needs for space for outdoor physical exercise. In this matter of local parks and recreation grounds, the United States is a poor underdeveloped country, yet park land in strategic locations could be purchased for as little as $1000 per acre—some might cost as much as $5000 or $10,000 an acre. To buy 40,000 acres of local community park land annually and thus keep up with population growth would require a national expenditure of approximately $150,000,000 —just ten miles of elevated highway constructed in any major city could cost that much or more. It is not juveniles who are delinquent, but the adults who decide how public monies should be spent.

The physical and mental health of the nation is related to its outdoor facilities for decent exercise and temporary relief from the common causes of tensions in a metropolitan world where most of the day is spent inside home, school, car, office, factory, or shop. The really somber aspect of this neglect to acquire local community park space as the population grows is the fact that it cannot be bought later. A community which fails to act while it is growing will never catch up later because the open space that might have been a park will have been built upon. Parks must be established during the course of a community's growth or forever after it will be an underprivileged neighborhood. To a child who must play near home if he is to play at all, it can hardly be much consolation to know that someday the family may drive to Yellowstone while on a two-week vacation. A glimpse of Old Faithful will not erase the scars of an entire childhood passed in a blighted community where there is no proper place to play. Perhaps nothing is more important for the future health of the nation than abundant, convenient, everyday play and exercising grounds for all citizens, who, otherwise, will be unnecessarily soft in body and warped in spirit.

Winthrop Rockefeller, board chairman of Colonial Williamsburg, predicts that by the year 2000, when America's population will have doubled, it will need perhaps four times the number of city parks and playgrounds that it has now. It will require sixteen times as many regional parks and lakes close enough to urban areas for a day's outing, and roughly forty times the amount of land now in national parks and scenic areas. Mr. Rockefeller foresees the day when the use of parks and visits to historic places may have to be rationed unless more open space is acquired while it still exists and unless more historic shrines are protected and preserved now. "We are faced with an opportunity that has no parallel in history—the opportunity to invest wisely in an unprecedented amount of leisure time. There is no doubt in my mind," says Mr. Rockefeller, "that the use we make of this gift will have a profound influence on our national character."[1] The importance to the welfare of the state of sound bodily health and mental relaxation is something that politicians from the local to the national level had better heed with action and not relegate to committees for futile surveys and unused plans.

If it were not for several million acres of national parks, forests, and game refuges which cater to over 200,000,000 visitors every year, the opportunities for recreation on public land would be slim indeed. About 2000 state parks also serve approximately 180,000,000 guests annually. However, these national and state parks are somewhat removed from major urban centers. Their purpose is not to be everyday exercising grounds but rather week-end and vacation retreats in the kind of primitive and picturesque environments that are antidotes to brick, concrete, and human congestion. The daily demand for exercising grounds, particularly by children, must be satisfied by local parks within easy walking distance of the home, but it is precisely these facilities that are now neglected. It would seem that the home community is doomed to thwart the happier, robust side of life. City fathers are too distressed by the agonies of welfare services, harassed by traffic pressures, and embarrassed by inadequate public schools to dwell on the more pleasant aspects of existence which parks and playgrounds represent. These facilities seem to be regarded as frills rather than as the absolute necessities which they really are.

PRIVATE SOLUTIONS

Under such discouraging circumstances people who can afford to buy their own parks, playgrounds, and recreation clubs are banding together for self-protection. They are letting the public stew in its own negligence while they take care of themselves. Private golf clubs already in existence are adding tennis courts, swimming pools, and playgrounds for the younger set. Sportsmen are buying their own hunting preserves. Private beach clubs, ski clubs, riding clubs, athletic clubs, wildlife refuges, and picnic grounds are mushrooming in suburbia. For those who are willing and able to pay the initiation fees and annual charges, there is no limit to the excellent facilities available in some of the better neighborhoods. In fact the finest developments are constructed around private recreation areas—the houses come later. This kind of arrangement is far easier to achieve in a new suburban community than it would be in a city because of the abundance of land that is available in the beginning. Then, too, the economic segregation that characterizes suburbia brings together people of comparable means and tastes. When he moves from the city to a new community on the fringe, a person may choose not only the kind of home he can afford but also a social and recreational life commensurate with it. This do-it-yourself-for-yourself approach brings fast results for those who have means. The rest of the population is left to do without mainly because it lacks initiative to plug for public facilities.

A new housing development on the outskirts of Washington, D.C., recently got off to a fast start with a sumptuous built-in recreation layout. In its advertising, a fictitious housewife informs a friend by phone that she and her husband have "always considered where we plan to buy a home as more important than a new car or a trip to Florida . . . so we're going to buy here where I know our leisure-time activities, friends and the children's playmates will be what we want. Listen to what they are planning for recreation facilities: an eighteen-hole golf course, an Olympic-sized swimming pool, a clubhouse, tennis courts and a big playground with swings and everything. Oh, yes, they've preserved the rolling terrain and created acres of wooded park land around a chain of three lovely lakes which wind through the golf course." All this without the grace of a city council or the county commissioners.

The new emphasis upon private recreational facilities is hastening the withdrawal of private lands from public entry. Every kind of space near growing communities which has any recreational potential is now capable of returning an income to the landowner. As he looks over his rising tax assessments, he is understandably disposed to nail up no-trespassing signs and to rent recreation rights to those who will help him pay the taxes. Thus the amount of private land around cities that was once open to the public has begun to shrink rapidly. Even in the open spaces of Rocky Mountain Colorado, the number of trout streams available to the public has declined in the past decade from ninety per cent of the total to fifty per cent. During the same years the number of fishermen looking for a free trout has quadrupled. The time is perhaps not far off when the small landowner who permits public entry upon his property will be a freak, yet most persons of middle age today will remember that in their youth they could hunt, fish, and camp just about anywhere because, in those days, it was custom to allow strangers to come and go as long as they behaved themselves. Of course, there were fewer strangers and thus comparatively more space in those times. Taxes were low and no one dreamed that he might be paid for granting recreation privileges. The closure of private lands to public entry is throwing a greater burden than ever on national and state parks. Only the most stupendous increase in those facilities could begin to compensate for the exclusion that private landowners must now practice if they are to have any privacy themselves.

Federal conservationist Neal Munch of Monmouth County, New Jersey, says that many farmers in that area on the metropolitan fringe have converted their land into private game preserves. On what were once fine potato fields these modern agrarians have made plantings of trees and shrubs that provide the best cover and feed for wild life. Pheasants, quail, and rabbits propagate rapidly under these conditions; also the natural fauna are generously supplemented in some cases with cage-reared specimens. A hunter's chances of success are considerably improved when his quarry is released before his gun sights at a proper signal. Also the farmer pockets a tidier profit from the sale of an unplucked pheasant full of buckshot than if it were a well-dressed chicken without a blemish. In addition to upland game tracts under private management, large areas of marsh have been converted into ponds that are stocked with bass and trout.

Fish ponds, if properly screened with appropriate vegetation, are excellent lures for migratory waterfowl. There are now some 525 ponds of this sort in Monmouth County alone. Practically every farm with marshland along the Atlantic flyway between New York City and Norfolk, Virginia, has been closed to the public by owners who rent gunning rights at attractive fees to individuals and clubs. Hunting on closed private lands is highly preferable to the mass competition encountered on the limited, and often too exposed public lands. On private reservations the number of hunters is restricted by the size of the fee. Blinds are well located and comfortable. For $50 or $60 a day a sportsman is practically assured of two wild geese or three ducks unless he has 0:0 vision and a case of palsy.

Even the private Shangri-La is not always a foolproof solution to the quest for recreation. Great Captain's Island is a postage stamp of rocky space just off the Connecticut coast in Long Island Sound. Some years ago it was bought by the Aerotec Corporation of Greenwich, Connecticut, as a leisure-time refuge for its two hundred employees and their families. There they may swim, picnic, and sun-bathe on lazy summer afternoons. Though Great Captain is not more than four miles from Greenwich by land and by sea, it is also within thirty-five miles of Times Square. Not even an island is unto itself when it is that close to a metropolis. Instead of simply being surrounded by water, Great Captain, on a fine holiday, is just as likely to be surrounded by a swarm of sea-going litterbugs. On a single summer Sunday some time ago seven hundred uninvited guests moored two hundred small craft along its beaches and made themselves at home without so much as politely offering "Please." Being well informed in law, they knew that ocean beach between the high-tide mark and the surf is public domain if it can be reached—which is no trick at all in a motor boat when the sea is calm. In desperation the Aerotec employees' club has been obliged to hire a policeman just to see that these modern buccaneers take their beer cans and pop bottles with them when they return to the mainland after their Sabbath forays.

Doubtless one organization which is not likely to be bothered with gate crashers is the Police Recreation Center, Inc., at Elka Park in New York's Catskill Mountains. This is a 600-acre resort run by the Empire City's finest for their brotherhood of nearly 5000 members. By operating their own the policemen say they can enjoy a first-class vacation with their families at a discount of forty per cent below the going commercial rates. Nestled in the forest the patrolmen have a 120-room hotel as well as some cottages and guest houses. A swimming pool, tennis courts, a baseball field, horseshoe pits, and courts for volleyball and badminton are on the grounds while three golf courses are available nearby. When a guest checks in he also checks his rank, so the law and its keepers may rest assured not even an advantage will be stolen.

The most impressive private contribution to recreation for the American public is provided by major timber companies which own seventy-four per cent of the country's private industrial timberlands. These manufacturers of lumber, paper pulp, and other forest products permit hunting in season on ninety per cent of their 46,000,000 acres. Seventy per cent of these vast holdings are open to all visitors at all times and fishing is permitted on nearly 56,000 miles of lake and stream banks. Berry picking, picnicking, swimming, camping, hiking, riding, skiing—even rock collecting and fern picking are allowed in some places. Sixty-five of the major lumber companies have established 132 public parks and the number of these facilities is expected to increase. This generosity is part of a public relations program that is designed to educate the public in forest care and appreciation. Almost all owners of large timber tracts now practice sustained-yield forestry, so that everywhere a new crop is growing no matter what its age may be. Under these circumstances a guest who is respectful of the woods and cautious about fires is preferred to an irresponsible trespasser. The only drawback so far as most people are concerned is that these fine facilities, like the national parks and forests, are located too far away from growing metropolitan areas.

THE WOODLAWN TRUSTEES

Over the years a great number of philanthropic endeavors have sought to improve the environment of American communities. The gradual accumulation of these amenities through time lends individual charm and character to each particular locality. It is rare, however, when ideas born of philanthropy benefit a community and earn money so that they become more effective as time goes on. Back in the last century William Bancroft of New Castle County, Delaware, owned a textile mill in the historic Brandywine Valley, which begins in Pennsylvania Piedmont and finally runs through the City of Wilmington out to Delaware Bay. While Mr. Bancroft was a prudent businessman he was also an humanitarian, both characteristics being consistent with his Quaker faith and education. During the later years of his life this considerate gentleman became concerned about what should be done with his wealth and what would become of his loyal employees upon his death. After some serious but practical thought, Mr. Bancroft began to buy farms along Brandywine Creek in New Castle County whenever they came on the market at a reasonable price. Eventually he left these lands, together with other wealth and a plan, to a group which he called the Woodlawn Trustees, who were instructed forever to "create suitable country homes that could be bought at a reasonable price by ordinary working men." In his day suburbia was yet unborn and Mr. Bancroft was appalled at the dwellings of workmen in such cities as Wilmington and Philadelphia.

As the years passed the Woodlawn Trustees kept faith with their founder's purpose. Their program accelerated as it eventually dovetailed with the popular housing movement in suburbia. Few counties in the past decade have sprouted subdivisions and developments more rapidly than New Castle County, which rather unexpectedly has found itself in a swirl of growth. The almost simultaneous construction of Memorial Bridge across Delaware Bay and of Bay Bridge across the Chesapeake suddenly put this once pastoral region into the main stream of East Coast economic expansion, and it has scarcely caught its breath since. But the Woodlawn Trustees were ready. The old farms they owned greatly increased in value as they became choice suburban properties in terms of both location and beauty. In making subdivisions of farms near Wilmington, the Woodlawn Trustees have been particularly careful to co-ordinate each new housing development with broader master plans. Inasmuch as their purpose is not real-estate profits but good homes in good settings, they have employed the best taste. Lands immediately bordering the Brandywine have been reserved for parks. Green belts of woods and meadow are left between individual subdivisions. Within the developments there are reserves of ample space for roads, playgrounds, and parks.

The persons who profit from this generosity are the people who live there. As the most expensive land close to Wilmington is developed, earnings are used to buy cheaper farms farther out. These are rented as farms until the day shall come when they, too, will be made into homesites. According to the present master plan about 800 of the approximately 3000 acres now held by the Woodlawn Trustees in their land bank eventually will be reserved for parks. The remainder will be used for homes and roads. Old miller-philanthropist Bancroft might well be both pleased and amazed were he able to see how his idea and his modest investments have brought better living to individuals as well as a plan for the use of land in a part of Brandywine Valley that guarantees a well-organized and pleasant environment in perpetuity.

PARKING IN THE PARK

The adult who loses the eyes of a child has lost the way to his own soul. The city that loses its parks loses its children and those adults who have not forgotten how to play and enjoy Nature. Not only are cities of the 20th century failing to meet 19th century standards in park development but they are backsliding into wholesale park vandalism. Raids on parks by street and highway departments, boards of education, mayors, and city councils are common thievery no longer considered scandalous by a people who have grown callous through long abuse. The Connecticut Society of Public Park Administrators was recently goaded into uncomplimentary epithets because of the contempt in which public parks are held by an increasing number of municipal officials. "One would think that open spaces, representing park land on a planner's map, were magnets drawing the planner's pencil," the Society observed. "Of course we need schools, hospitals, roadways, and so on but must a community give up park land . . . ?" The assembled administrators did not overlook their own weak hearts. Park executives, they said, have done a "poor job in fighting off encroachments of park properties."[2]

In city after city municipal parks have been embezzled by the very office holders appointed to defend the public interest. Eager to get on with pet projects regardless of consequences, a street department will not hesitate to annihilate a park if it can get away with it. In Portland, Oregon, new highways are proposed which would slice up twenty-one of the city's public parks. In Andalusia, Alabama, an entire city square was converted to asphalt for a parking lot. In Holden, Massachusetts, the city fathers did the same to the best piece of public open space in the business district. That this could happen in New England, where the village common is supposed to be the symbol of community culture, shows how culture has lost face where it used to count. In New York City public officials had planned to pave a piece of Central Park to enlarge parking facilities at a public restaurant until they were foiled by irate mothers wheeling baby carriages.

Thoreau's *Walden* is a landmark in our literary heritage because it is good natural history as well as a strong dose of fresh, independent philosophical thought of the kind that gave America stature in a century of extraordinary world-wide intellectual ferment. The environment of Walden Pond was important to the thinking processes not only of Thoreau but also of Ralph Waldo Emerson, who once owned the eighty acres of woods that almost surround that dark pool of water. It was there that Emerson walked, thought, and worked on his own immortal essays for many years before he offered the use of Walden to Henry Thoreau. At one time after his friend's death, Emerson was urged to sell his property because, by then, the Fitchburg Railroad Company, which owned but a single acre on the shore, had moved in and built a commercial honky-tonk with bath-houses, dance hall, and bowling alleys to which it ran excursion trains. The original peaceful character of the whole pond area was for a while suppressed by the interloping Fitchburg Railroad and its boisterous patrons. Emerson held off with characteristic forbearance. Later the railroad's hot spot burned down and, since it was not replaced, Walden Pond and the woods around it reverted to the primeval simplicity which the two writers had appreciated deeply.

When Emerson's daughter, Edith, died in 1922, she left all the family's valuable Walden holdings to the Commonwealth of Massachusetts as a memorial to her father and Thoreau, with the proviso that the lands be kept forever in their natural state "for the public who wish to enjoy the pond, the woods, and nature." According to her wish picnicking and bathing were to be permitted as long as no trees or other vegetation were destroyed for access roads or buildings. These conditions were accepted by the Commonwealth on behalf of its people and the citizens of Concord Town, as well as by all others who might wish to visit that quiet remnant of old New England. At Walden it has been possible to walk within a few minutes from the busy life of our time into a bit of the last century, where the natural landscape is just as magical as every American school child for generations has imagined it to be.

Early in the spring of 1958, without any public notice, the Middlesex County Commissioners, egged on by the local Red Cross, suddenly descended upon Walden; and in two days of frantic effort, before most citizens of Concord could discover what was happening to their shrine, chain saws had felled nearly two hundred noble pines and oaks as well as a wide clearing of other vegetation. Bulldozers had pushed forest humus and top soil out into the water to construct an artificial beach. Contrary to the wishes of Edith Emerson, and with contempt for all those who cherish Walden's simple natural beauty, the Commissioners and the Red Cross planned to erect a cinder-block bathhouse one hundred feet long and to build a black-top access road to the main highway. Where children and their parents had previously been free to swim when and as they wished, their activity was now to be organized and supervised by salaried do-gooders on public property where they had no legal right to go into private business. The contemplated construction might have come to pass, had it not been for the vigilance of the Thoreau Society which at its own expense has since carried on a hard legal defense against desecration of a public heritage through collusion by the very officials entrusted with its protection. Contracts of any sort, whether they are deeds of property or constitutions, are only as good as the willingness of citizens to defend them in the courts. For those who want the bathhouse type of organized swimming there is other pond shore in Concord Town which may be purchased. Like Mount Vernon or Bunker Hill, there is only one Walden to be preserved, and if it is not then the heritage of every American will be that much the poorer.

In Toledo park lands have already been taken for Y.M.C.A. buildings, a Coast Guard installation, a police pistol range, a private yacht club, a sewage disposal plant, and a factory parking lot. If each generation hacks away at parks on the scale that is currently fashionable in most cities, the only uninvaded green spaces in congested districts are likely to be cemeteries. It will take the dead to protect the living from their own folly. Mrs. Evelyn Wiseman is manager of beautiful Woodlawn Cemetery in Toledo. For years she and her two daughters occupied a fine house on the landscaped grounds at Woodlawn, where there is a reflecting pool and a meandering creek. "I've always loved Nature and I wanted my daughters to love it too," explained Mrs. Wiseman when asked about her choice of locale. "There are more than three hundred types of trees on the grounds and the wildlife includes rabbits, squirrels, raccoons, swans, ducks, and geese." After a look at most of the rest of the city one would be inclined to agree with Mrs. Wiseman that "you can't find surroundings more beautiful anywhere in Toledo."[3]

Almost every city has a cemetery which is the only green accent in what is otherwise a congested area. Trinity Church Yard near the towers of Wall Street is the most famous. It is not just a stable moment of antiquity in an age of fluctuating values briefly recorded on ticker tape. Trinity and its gravestones of slate and marble are symbols of eternity itself in a world that has almost forgotten eternity. There at noontime through the iron gates and along the quiet paths stroll clerks, secretaries, and the giants of finance, whose day is made a little better by having visited the hallowed ground. Perhaps no one but a city planner would think of converting Trinity Church Yard, or others like it, into parking lots.

What is good for General Motors is good for America—

sometimes but not always, as the stunned people of North Tarrytown, New York, learned when the local Chevrolet plant tried to buy eighty-odd acres of Kingsland Point Park for factory sites and a parking lot. It was not enough that tax-hungry town fathers had previously permitted G.M.'s heavy industry to bed down next door to Kingsland (at one time cited as a model of fine recreation development), but in addition Mayor Gabriel P. Hayes also favored this sale of public property. Had the proposal been approved as first announced, the public would have salvaged nine acres out of an original grant of ninety-three acres from the Frothingham family, which stipulated in its deed that the land should be restricted "for all time" to use as a public park. By legal maneuvering the conditions of the Frothingham deed and the spirit in which it was accepted were both violated. Strong local opposition restrained to 29.5 acres the final G.M. raid which was unanimously approved by the County Board of Supervisors.

General Motors and Nature have tangled before. In 1958 the director of its proving grounds came up with the observation that thirty-one per cent of all car deaths involve vehicles running into objects off the highway, mainly trees. To the proving-grounds director the solution was not better driving or safer cars: "The obvious thing is, of course, to remove the hazards." The official also pontificated, "Many of our rural roads and main highways are lined with trees that constitute a terrific hazard for the driving public. Trees are being planted in the right-of-way of our new national highway system. In fact, at the Highway Research Board Roadside Development Committee meeting in Washington in January some representatives of Southern States were proposing to plant tree farms along the highway right-of-way. Such plans must be stopped, for they only create additional hazards and loss of life in the future."[4] G.M. did not offer to discontinue roadside advertising so as to discourage hazardous billboards along rights-of-way. And somehow it overlooked those people who enjoy natural scenery and are not in favor of surrendering their pleasure to drivers and cars that cannot stay on the pavement.

Perhaps it is unfair to expect too much from the unenlightened when molders of the mind themselves are led into temptation. The University of Pennsylvania, richly supplied as it is with various departments of city planning, architecture, public administration, and classics, is not itself above parking in the park. At almost the same time the University recommended that the Philadelphia suburbs should acquire more park land, its own vice president, John L. Moore, asked the city for permission to convert a two-acre playing field into an accommodation for 450 automobiles. This small plot of public land had been given to the city in 1894 "to be held forever as a museum and botanical garden and park." Since that original condition had been violated some years ago, the University perhaps felt no qualms about a further slip from grace. As everyone in the home of brotherly love knows there is an abundance of slum property around the campus which could not look worse if made into parking lots but that would cost money. Public open space, although it is a scarce commodity, is sometimes easier and cheaper to acquire than slums.

Regarding the subject of land-use planning, it is not at all uncommon for Alma Maters to flunk their own courses. The University of Wisconsin, which at one time possessed one of the most beautiful campuses in America, has managed to construct parking lots along its lake front and to chop up its exquisite woodlands near Muir Knoll to make building sites. Yet these violations of good taste were committed during a period of great economic prosperity when Federal aid might have been secured to remove slum properties on the city side of the campus, where new development would have upgraded rather than downgraded the environment.

The sky above America's parks is full of hawks and buzzards peering for prey to pounce upon. Recently a group of fund raisers announced that they would like to promote a church on the rim of the Grand Canyon to impress the Almighty with the wonders of man's architecture. The Armed Services delight in stretching summer bivouacs on public vacation grounds into permanent military installations. Mining companies want concessions in the national forests. Oil companies seek to drill among the egrets on coastal wildlife refuges. Lumber companies plug for admittance to public parks. In this day of advanced multiple-purpose designs, it is downright reactionary to think a park is a park.

Regional forester Charles A. Connaughton of San Francisco has reported to the Society of American Foresters that tensions are building up in national forests between timber cutters and recreation enthusiasts; between wilderness hikers and those who want to rough it by car; between people who want streams for recreation and the advocates of hydro-electric power and irrigation. Everyone has a pet scheme for the wisest use of the public domain. "The land manager," says Mr. Connaughton, "must try to reconcile these conflicting demands to retain public goodwill." Robert Jones, an airplane pilot who tows five-by-fifty-foot advertising streamers through the public sky sees no reason why he should not carry his messages over bathing beaches while patrons lie on the sand looking at clouds or training for the Miss America contest. However, the Long Island State Park Commission contended in First District Court that it controls the air "as high as you can go" and at least temporarily restrained Mr. Jones from engaging in such missions of enlightenment. It would appear that in the future when a keeper of public space begins to think he has reached the point where he is able to reconcile conflicting interests, then he himself should be about ready for a keeper.

Ordinary John Q. Citizen can hardly be blamed for not doing right by parks when his own congressmen, whose business should be to create them, have become snatchers instead. Recently four identical bills were sponsored by key members of both parties on the Senate and House Interior Committees which would authorize the National Park Service to lease a choice piece of park land for ninety-nine years to the Congressional Club as a site for a new $350,000 headquarters building. The club's members are chiefly wives, daughters, and mothers of congressmen. According to Mrs. W. F. Norrell, the club president, members had scouted around for three years before they turned to the Park Service. The result was the selection of a park on Massachusetts Avenue in the Embassy Row district which a local real-estate appraiser estimated to be conservatively worth a half-million dollars.

Representative Wayne N. Aspinall, Chairman of the House Interior Committee, acknowledged that some Washingtonians ". . . couldn't understand why the wives and daughters of congressmen had to be given some of Uncle Sam's property for a site like this."[5] However, Chairman Aspinall probably melted the objectors' stony hearts when he explained that the club compensates the women while they are in Washington for being deprived of their customary social life back home. The new headquarters, as he said, would help the women by offering them a place where they could work for charity as well as find relaxation and recreation.

PHYSICALLY SOUND

Physicians and other students of human biology seem to agree that modern man and his child do not get the kinds of animal exercise they require. A developed country is all too likely to be inhabited by underdeveloped people. Nerves apparently are overwrought while muscles are allowed to languish. Dr. Richard T. Smith, Director of the Department of Rheumatology of the Ben Franklin Clinic in Philadelphia reports, "The population of the United States is becoming more sedentary, more dependent upon wheels for motion and consequently more physically unfit." Of 500 patients who were examined in his clinic fifteen years ago, 13 per cent had fibrositis or muscular pains due chiefly to inactivity. Recently 500 comparable patients were examined and 31 per cent were found to have the same malady. Dr. Smith sees a connection between his clinical records and the announcement that, in a series of physical tests, American children failed at a rate of 57.9 per cent whereas European children failed only 8.7 per cent. He thinks this may be an outgrowth of the motto, "Don't walk if you can ride, don't stand if you can sit, don't sit if you can lie down and if you get the urge to exercise, lie down until it passes off."[6]

Parks and supervised playgrounds are not the cure-all for physical inertia; but as long as communities are without ample and convenient facilities of this kind the physical education of American youth will remain stifled. A few periods a week of calisthenics in a school gymnasium are no substitute for hours of vigorous healthy play by which the mind, spirit, and body are all enthusiastically exercised every day. The supervision is essential to prevent rowdyism and intimidation by juvenile gangs. A park is of no social value and can be a menace if it is appropriated as a "turf" by hoodlums. The supervision of children becomes the obligation of the community when parents abdicate. Where there is no such public conscience, the conscientious parent must continue to retreat to "safe" communities, whether they be in the suburbs or in the few surviving privileged neighborhoods of cities.

It will be rather remarkable if children who are brought up under fears of attack by other children should grow up to be socially sympathetic or co-operative. Cleavages between the bestialized and the civilized in childhood are quite likely to be perpetuated in adulthood and such moral degeneration cannot help undermining the whole community. A society which neglects to guide and inspire the fullest development of the child will itself be neglected by the thwarted adult who eventually emerges. Physical fitness calls for facilities equal to the need and the goal. Children are much more likely to develop drugstore posture than health if there is no place to go and nothing to do after school but to limber up the pin-ball machines and to engage in straw drill at the soda fountain. Adults are as badly stymied and probably one reason they do not provide opportunities for their children is that they do not know from personal experience what they are missing or how essential physical exercise is to normal health.

Colonel Theodore P. Bank, President of the Athletic Institute in Chicago, says that we are getting "softer and softer" because our advanced technology eliminates much of the physical activity that kept our forefathers in shape. To Colonel Bank one of the most important challenges before today's political and social leaders is the need to provide adequate space for recreational needs. As it is, he feels that turning the electric blanket from high to medium is the peak of exertion for some people. Out of all New York's millions of males only about 15,000 hold memberships in the little rub-down parlors known as health clubs that are equipped for the hand-ball, steam-bath, and sun-lamp regimen. Yet four fifths of these patrons, who are among the vanguard of urban athletes, find self-propelled exercise too exhausting and generally settle for a sweat bath and a massage on the theory that they might as well rest while their pores and capillaries take the workout.

Dr. Lester S. Blumenthal, Chief of the Headache Clinic at the George Washington University Medical School, says things have come to the point that leisure itself gives some people pains in the head. "Letdown headaches," he explains, may strike office workers on week ends and clergymen on Mondays. This discomfort is the result of relaxation after a week of tension during which blood vessels in the head are constricted. According to Dr. Blumenthal, the dilation of blood vessels, which occurs with a letdown on the day of rest, may irritate nerves so that a person may actually feel worse than if he were under tension. But a constant regimen of tension does not seem to be the solution either. Dr. Richard E. Gordon and his wife, Katherine K. Gordon, recently reported to the American Medical Association an analysis they had made of admissions to the Englewood Hospital at Englewood, New Jersey. There they found that tensions and emotional difficulties are associated with various diseases such as ulcers, heart attacks and other psychosomatic disorders. Englewood, according to the report, is a fast-growing suburb where people are busy getting ahead. Many may be struggling to achieve higher incomes and to advance in social status. These private ambitions are frustrated by everything from crab grass in the lawn to high taxes. Such frustrations tie people in psychic knots. According to the Gordon report, "The rapidly changing community itself, with its higher taxes and overloaded schools, roads, recreational facilities and other resources, may contribute to a patient's overburdened psychophysiological functioning."[7] Apparently when people lack normal outlets for their energies and emotions they can get into all kinds of trouble.

Mr. Martin R. Gainsbrugh, Chief Economist of the National Industrial Conference Board, thinks a longer work week would not only reduce the problem of how to spend leisure time but would be best for national productivity. He believes Americans should place a higher priority upon output than upon leisure. At least one out of twenty workers agrees with him for, according to the Bureau of the Census, five per cent of the employed are already "moonlighting"— holding down two jobs instead of one. If only the other ninety-five per cent of the adult working force could be persuaded to turn to extra jobs, and if child labor could stage a comeback, then the problem of parks and playgrounds would be automatically solved. Inasmuch as one third of

America's married women are employed outside the home, it might not be an exaggeration to say that each one of them and her mate already has a job and a half apiece. Doing housework is a time-honored means of getting more exercise than most human beings find necessary. By dividing this chore between them the working couples achieve a kind of balanced life. Such persons probably do not need parks for physical fitness and do not have time for "letdown headaches"; but their children certainly have a greater need of supervised playgrounds than those whose parents have time and a place to play with them. Although the working mother has become commonplace in the past two decades, there is as yet not even the germ of a nationwide program for after-school fun and exercise for her children. That the hardest working parents should have the most neglected children is scarcely an admirable civic oversight.

Big suburban house lots are, of course, the answer to the recreation needs of the playpen set but most of these areas have very poor records for developing the kinds of parks and playgrounds needed by older children and adults. Between 1950 and 1958 New Castle County, Delaware, acquired 70,000 new residents—an increase of about 32 per cent. But the most remarkable aspect of New Castle's recent growth is the fact that it is almost entirely suburban. The City of Wilmington's 1950 population of 110,000 climbed to only 115,000 by 1958—an increase of less than 5 per cent. However, the county, outside its major city, put on a truly remarkable spurt by leaping 60 per cent. Wilmington is laid out according to the traditional pattern of the 19th century American city with rather generous allocations of land to parks in the better residential neighborhoods. In addition to nearly 1000 acres of parks and playgrounds, there is a municipal golf course of 148 acres. Together these are almost ten per cent of the total area of the city. There is one acre of public recreation ground for every one hundred inhabitants—low, of course, but better than the ratio in many cities.

New Castle County outside the city is in a shocking condition for lack of public recreation space. Despite the fact that the suburbs are inhabited by the better paid members of the community and are predominantly white, they have only 101 acres of county parks for their 174,000 citizens or one acre for each 1700 persons. This example is unfortunately more typical than it is exceptional of the new suburbia where the well-paid middle-class taxpayer has not done as well for himself and his children in the way of public recreation space as did the old-time low-paid worker in a mill city where a few wealthy philanthropists provided the public with recreation areas. It is a rather sad commentary on our times and cultural values that with the rise of a large and rather affluent middle class the standards of community recreation have declined rather than improved except among the few who have their private playgrounds.

CHAPTER 10

Covering the Water Front

SALT

Fifty years ago it was possible to buy land facing the open sea for as little as fifty cents a front foot. Even in 1935 twelve inches of sandy beach with a backdrop of high dunes could be purchased for one or two dollars. By 1954 a few scattered water fronts on off-shore islands remained price-tagged at twenty dollars a foot. Today, anyone who finds so much as a rocky promontory for sale at fifty dollars per foot has discovered a bargain. These are prices for completely undeveloped land without roads, electricity, telephone, or any other modern facility. They are values that have been put on land that is in the same condition today as it has been since the present shore line was created by tectonic shifts of the continental basement and the rise of sea level.

No raw land, unchanged by human investment, has increased in value so fantastically as the seashore. It is the outstanding example of what population pressure can do to the market price of space. It is also an index of the desperate desire that a too civilized humanity feels for a place "away from it all"—a desire that intensifies as cities and suburbs become more crowded and contacts with the natural world become fewer and less accessible to the greater portion of the population. In the past fifty years, while ocean frontage has increased in value 10,000 per cent, the American population has doubled from 90,000,000 to 180,000,000. Fifty years hence, if there is such a thing left as undeveloped seashore, perhaps $500 a front foot might look like a steal. The ocean beach is one commodity which will not stretch. Rivers can be dammed to create vast and beautiful lakes such as Lake Mead behind Hoover Dam. Swimming pools can be installed wherever there is water to fill them. But the creation of an ocean and the land's rim around it is still beyond the genius of man. The sea coast that exists now is all that is likely to exist for the balance of human time.

As measured by the Coast and Geodetic Survey, the East Coast of the United States from Calais, Maine, to Brownsville, Texas, is nearly 3700 miles long. A mere 240 miles of this total (about 6½ per cent) belongs to the public and not all of that is available for general use. Were it not for military acquisitions in strategic places, there would be even less ocean shore within the public domain. More than half of the 240 miles of public sea front is confined to three reservations: Acadia National Park in Maine, Cape Hatteras National Seashore Recreational Area in North Carolina, and Everglades National Park in Florida. The balance is scattered among thirty-six smaller areas in fourteen states. Four states with ocean frontage have no Federal or state parks on the sea. A few municipal and county beaches are all that they have salvaged of their original heritage. On the Pacific, not including Alaska and Hawaii, there are 1743 miles of general shore line of which 295 miles are in state and Federal reserves.

Congestion along the ocean's edge is unlike congestion anywhere else because time is fast running out when something really effective can be done about it. In so far as this particular water front is concerned, the public appears doomed to fight a rearguard action from here on out. It may salvage a few more scraps as consolation prizes, but the

really big opportunities to satisfy its needs lie dead on the
forensic battlefields of the past. Once there was brave talk
of saving the seashore for all time for all generations, but the
major burden of these speeches fell upon the clerks who
recorded and filed them. Neither legislators nor citizens
were moved to action; and it is doubtful, if the same opportunities existed today, that voters or their representatives
would do differently. There is a conviction on the local
political level that it is wrong for the Federal and state
governments to remove seaside from the local tax roll even if
it is to be set aside for public use. "What has posterity done
for us that we should clip our tax base for posterity?" is the
cynic's sharp query. Such a thrifty philosophy has broad
popular support and in seaside communities it has gone far
to frustrate the acquisition and development of Federal and
state water fronts. After all, the Federal Government could
pay a hundred dollars a foot for all the still desirable but
undeveloped seashore on the Atlantic and Gulf coasts and
the bill would not come to one half of one per cent of a
single year's budget. By recent count there were still over
600 miles of ocean beaches that would make excellent national recreation reserves, and most of those vast stretches
could be bought for less than a hundred dollars a foot.

It is not a lack of purchase money nor the lack of opportunity to buy which has deprived a growing nation of ample
ocean frontage. It is a conflict in tax policies between local
and Federal governments and a woeful lack of understanding on the part of public officials at all levels of government
as to their responsibilities for the well-being of the total
citizenry. The average person is utterly without an articulate
concept of the American landscape as to its dimensions and
variety, or what is now happening to it under the onslaught
of population increase and real-estate speculation. It is hard
enough to grasp what is going on in a single city or suburb
without trying to visualize how the nation is put together in
space. Yet any kind of rational approach to the wise use of

water front demands such concepts. Perhaps it is too much to expect that the average citizen could ever be well informed in this matter. His education and his daily duties preclude a comprehension of anything so intricate as the design of his nation's landscape. But for the conscientious legislator such understanding is a professional obligation if he is to act wisely for the public good. If insight is not developed at the level where decisions are made, then the coming population deluge will run rampant for lack of proper channels to guide its gathering currents.

Property taxes are the fountainhead of local revenues whereas the Federal Government by-passes that overworked source for richer pay dirt. Beach-front taxes are almost pure gravy for counties and towns because summer cottagers are usually nonresidents—they pay taxes but call for relatively little public service. Their children as a rule do not attend local schools. They come in June and by Labor Day they are homeward bound to city apartment and suburban split-level. Also, the beach-front landowner is hardly a pauper. He is more likely, through his taxes, to be a dispenser of local welfare rather than a recipient. Ocean shore towns have a good thing in low tax assessments for local residents on inland house lots and high tax assessments for summertime cottagers on the water front. Assessors, being local residents, are often kind to the natives and generally not averse to milking the summer people. As a tax assessor on Martha's Vineyard Island once remarked, "After a sale we don't know exactly how high we should go. The safest thing to do is to raise until there is a squawk." When the Island's town of Gay Head was challenged in the Appellate Court for such a policy, it was ordered to rebate to the level of assessments on similar properties held by islanders. Yet even while under a court order the town persisted in its policy. A subsequent investigation by state adjusters revealed that many Gay Head natives paid but token taxes and five per cent of the land in the town enjoyed a free ride because it was not even entered upon the tax roll. Counties and towns in such a lush position to be subsidized by summer vacationists are not eager for the Federal Government to buy their beach front and remove it from the tax roll. Generally they will bring all possible political pressure to prevent it.

In 1935, only two and a half decades ago, the National Park Service made a survey of the Atlantic and Gulf coasts, looking for unspoiled seashore that might serve as public recreation areas. At that time there was still an abundance of unspoiled beaches that could have been bought at depression prices. When the search was completed the National Park Service recommended that twelve major strips, containing 437 miles of the ocean's edge, be acquired as national reserves. In the quarter century that has since elapsed only one of these sites, the Cape Hatteras National Seashore, has been bought. Meanwhile all the others have gone into private and commercial development—destroying for all time their wild, unaltered beauty. They are on the tax rolls, paying more taxes than ever, but they are closed to the general public. If local citizens thought they could keep beach land on the tax roll and yet enjoy the privilege of free entry, they were mistaken.

Local commercial interests often buck the transfer of land from private to public domain for fear that customers will be lost. Before its inception the successful Cape Hatteras project ran the gauntlet of usual challenges by associations of taxpayers and businessmen, and was almost submerged by their opposition. Cape Hatteras as of now is the only ocean shore-line reserve established by Congress. It came into being in 1953 after eighteen years of patient effort by the National Park Service and its supporters on Capitol Hill. When Senators Richard Neuberger, James Murray, Clinton Anderson, and Paul Douglas proposed in 1959 that the Federal Government purchase other seashore reserves while they were still available, a howl went up among taxpayers, cottagers, and businessmen in the designated areas. One of the major prospects, Oregon Dunes, is in the late Senator Neuberger's home state. Controversy over that proposal reached such intensity that the Eugene *Register,* an enterprising newspaper near Oregon Dunes, sent a reporter and a photographer at its own expense to the opposite side of the continent to learn at first hand what had happened at Cape Hatteras.

The *Register's* reporter, A. Robert Smith, discovered that the arguments against the North Carolina project in its early days of struggle for acceptance were identical to those now being raised all the way from Oregon Dunes on the Pacific to Cape Cod on the Atlantic. However, Mr. Smith wrote that many of the original adversaries of the Hatteras reserve had since become its most enthusiastic proponents. Businessmen have benefited from an influx of summer visitors that rose in five years from 100,000 to 348,000. Real-estate values on private properties near the national reserve have soared fifty to one hundred times. This spectacular increase in land values brought property-tax receipts to new levels that more than compensated for what had been removed from the rolls. A leading banker revealed that previous to the Federal reservation the local economy had been on the decline. "If it hadn't been for the Hatteras park, I don't know what we would have done," was his grateful endorsement.

There is nothing that so enhances the tourist value of an attractive natural landscape as to be designated a national park. Between 1916 and 1958 attendance at national parks rose from 400,000 to 58,000,000 annually. Senator Neuberger said, "If this rate of increase should continue, not even the twenty national shore-line parks sought in our omnibus bill will be sufficient to assure Americans of the future the travel opportunities which ought to be theirs."[1] As resort keepers are already aware, the American public in substantial numbers is beginning to move off the United States mainland onto beaches in Caribbean countries, Mexico, and Canada.

What they cannot find at home they now seek abroad and their dollars go with them.

From Sandy Hook to Cape May, the Atlantic Coast of New Jersey is a succession of once magnificent barrier beaches that for the most part are plastered with a hard shell of seaside cottages and commercial swim emporiums. This 130-mile stretch of white sand and salt water is the happy destination of millions of summer visitors who pour in torrents from surrounding metropolitan areas in quest of fun and frolic with other lucky escapees. While most of the seemingly endless shores of these sand bars at the ocean's rim now are closed to public access, every major city has reserved some public beach where hot weather throngs can congregate by the tens of thousands. Atlantic City alone attracts each season more than 20,000,000 devotees of sand, surf, and pulchritude. Fifty-one other Jersey shore communities play the profitable host with undiminished zeal to lesser numbers. Being vacation land to the 52,000,000 people who are within an overnight drive is one of the Garden State's biggest businesses, for in summer New Jersey easily pre-empts Florida's role as the East Coast's favorite bathhouse.

Just north of Raritan River the Garden State Parkway climbs into the sky over the high arch of a viaduct. Beneath that sleek bow of steel and concrete runs the New Jersey Turnpike. If one were to come upon this busy intersection from the north on a Sunday night in midsummer, he would see extending many miles to the south several lanes of paired headlights lined up so closely one behind the other that they form a continuous belt of glittering amber slowly crossing the black background of the night. Traffic from the Garden State Parkway veers off at this point to take the Turnpike into New York City. If one were to comment about this incredible procession at a toll gate he would be told, "It's been moving like this since late afternoon and it'll go on past midnight without a break."

If anyone wishes to participate in a typical urban attack

upon the limited seashore, let him join such a bumper-to-bumper conga line into and out of Tom's River, New Jersey, on a summer week end. Tom's River is a bridge town which commands access to Island Beach—a magnificent twenty-three mile sandbar in the Atlantic Ocean just off the mainland. Being sixty-one miles from Philadelphia and sixty-seven miles from New York City, Tom's River is in a perfect spot to be assaulted from both directions. Present beach facilities there are overtaxed, but preparations are under way which eventually will accommodate 10,000 more automobiles and their passengers at a newly created state park. If, someday, these 10,000 automobiles were to begin moving one after another and were to keep a distance between them of only half a car length, they would form a continuous line of traffic all the way from Tom's River to the Holland Tunnel. Conceivably the day is not too remote when several hundred thousand cars will move out of New York and Philadelphia on Friday headed for New Jersey's ocean front. On the following Sunday afternoon at 5 P.M., if only one hundred thousand of these automobiles were to start moving back into New York and they were spaced thirty feet apart, it would take at least until 1 A.M. for ten lanes of uninterrupted parkway to handle the crush. Just this beach traffic alone would tax to capacity all available lanes across the George Washington Bridge, as well as the Lincoln and Holland tunnels.

If a million people in 250,000 cars were to get the crazy notion simultaneously to go to the New Jersey beaches some certain summer afternoon, they would not only throw the present highway system into a state of paralytic shock, but, assuming they ever got to the beach, there would be one and a half persons for every foot of ocean front all along the 130 miles of the sand-strewn coast line. A million bathers are not many among the present urban hordes. New York and Philadelphia together number more than ten millions and there are over five millions in New Jersey itself. The

Garden State is second in the Union in human density, with twice as many persons per square mile as there are in India. The prospects of finding more room in a closet than at the seashore seem to be improving. The rising tides of humanity begin to assume proportions that make even the vastness of the ocean seem less than formerly.

Human ingenuity can be counted on to create as well as to obliterate. While natural shore line goes out of circulation, beach-club swimming pools increase. At a cost of $1,300,000 Westchester County recently built a public tank that is 900 feet around the rim and accommodates 2000 bathers. This is an average capital investment of about $1400 per foot of "shore line" or $650 per swimmer. If now the sound of surf has a somewhat antique wave length, it is because the ears of modern thousands are attuned to the broadcast beat of rock 'n' roll while lolling in an Olympic pool. With today's crowded beaches hep families shy away from shore picnics of sandwiches and sand. The smart-set mother on Long Island herds her kids into the station wagon as soon as the beds are made and the switch is flicked on the electric dishwasher. By ten o'clock she and her brood are in the parking lot at Capri Club, Malibu, or one of a score of other membership swim-and-fun establishments where the seasonal cost is no greater than that of a summer vacation away from home base. All these elaborate beach developments have some ocean shore but that stage setting is only an excuse to introduce such fancy manmade improvements as ceramic tile ponds lined with cabanas, supervised day nurseries for toddlers, teen-age dance pavilions, bars to revive flagging fathers who arrive after work, cafeterias, and even night clubs for those that can stand the wear, tear, and tariff. As the majordomos of these happiness emporiums profess, "We are not just beach clubs; we have created a new way of life."

The old-fashioned seashore was never like this. Atlantic Beach, the first town on Long Island to develop such a private club, now has fifteen. Lido Beach has six clubs on "The Strip." The idea is as contagious as a virus and a lot more diverting. Malibu Club, one of the largest and most recent, occupies 33 acres and 850 feet of ocean front. It has a membership of 4000 and parking space for 2000 cars. Malibu's main pool is 150 by 50 feet and, in addition, it has a diving tank and three smaller tanks. It is equipped with a day camp, a dining room with outdoor patio, snack bar, and cocktail lounge all done in modern decor. Featured entertainers have included Cab Calloway, Eartha Kitt, Frankie Avalon, and Fabian. With such delights as these to behold who could care less about the vanishing shore line or about building sand castles or looking for starfish?

For the little man who does not have everything there is Jones Beach, the salt-water haven of the multitude. Jones Beach is a New York state park of 2413 acres and six miles of ocean shore, where the average seasonal attendance runs beyond ten millions and the biggest single day found 212,600 heat-struck swimmers passing through its turnstiles at the rate of seventy-five cents a carload. For those who find Jones Beach a little overrun with humanity, the town of Oyster Bay has developed overflow Tobay Beach immediately to the east. Thus the isolationist who wishes to escape from the common throng can pass on to this quieter preserve for an additional one dollar per carload. By this simple process of the double fee 2000 carloads of swimmers at Tobay Beach are separated from 22,000 carloads at Jones Beach. Even the names connote their differences from each other and from the far-off dream world at Malibu. Seaside standards and culture patterns have now reached such stages of refinement that it is possible to judge a man's status, tastes, and income by the beach he attends as easily as by the more conventional clues—and there is nothing in the animal kingdom quite so maladjusted as the human fish in water that is either too shallow or too deep for his social stature.

At the top of the ladder are such sophisticated mansion-

and-cottage colonies as fashionable East Hampton, Long Island, where uniformed chauffeurs occasionally appear but where it is etiquette to be rustic and simple in Ivy League knits and tweeds. To hunt down an authentic seventeenth or eighteenth century salt-box cottage and move it to East Hampton's shore is an expression of good taste *cum laude.* Honorable mention goes to those who drive to the beach in an antique Stanley Steamer or a Delauney Belleville. The man who does both is a social king-maker and his garden fence is certain to be strung with honeysuckle and roses. Old East Hampton Club is the resort's most exclusive with a membership said to be limited to those whose families have summered at the colony for at least two generations and which pass the inspection of specialists in ancestral dendrology. Rental of a socially acceptable summer cottage "on the dunes for the season" may run into five figures but it is worth it to find out if one's future grandchildren are likely "to fit." In the best circles the rooming-house week ender and two-week vacationer are as welcome as panhandlers.

For New York's millions who have not yet made a million, there are the Rockaways-on-the-subway, to which there is a daily non-stop underground train that pulls out of the Forty-Second Street station of the Eighth Avenue Line at 9:30 A.M. and "all purchasers of a ticket are guaranteed a seat." Passage to Rockaway Beach costs $1.55 and is good for the round trip plus $1.50 worth of rides at an amusement park. This joyriding seashore express is especially equipped with a loudspeaker system for piped music and pretty girls have been known to spray the cars with flowery deodorants as passengers climb aboard. The train, which makes the sixty-four-minute trip in thirty-eight minutes, offers the most unsubwaylike ride in the New York area. Everyone embarks for a holiday in a holiday mood, and the fact that no one pushes for a seat or stands on his neighbor's feet helps to maintain the festive spirit. For the man who is long on family but short on family tree, this is the one way to make a splash without going overboard.

SWEET

"Water, water everywhere and not a drop to drink until chlorinated"—thus amended, an old sea dog's phrase describes today's polluted inland lakes and streams. While it is all very nice to have an ocean beach here and there to play at, the most important water is the everyday kind we drink. Now even this simple, unassuming commodity is getting more expensive and harder to come by in a clean natural condition. It is a wonder of our age that water used to wash the streets, bathe the industry, and flush the plumbing of one city on a river bank can be reclaimed and run through the faucets of the next town downstream without disastrous consequences. Even a river like New Hampshire's Merrimack, which at points becomes so filthy that fish cannot live in it, may be laundered so that men drink from it again many times over before it reaches the sea. Sedimentation tanks, coagulators, filters, aerators, and chlorinators, by their magic action, have become part of the very underpinning of modern civilization. Without them we might have run out of a useful water supply long ago.

According to quiz-kid calculations the daily use of water in the American home averages about 150 gallons per person of which only two quarts are actually drunk. It takes five gallons to wash hands, shave, and brush teeth. Each time the toilet is flushed, at least four gallons rush through the pipes. A shower consumes five gallons a minute and a tub bath normally demands twenty-five gallons. For families with swimming pools several thousand gallons are needed when it is time for a change. A minimum charge for an automatic clothes washer is six gallons while dishwashers, lawn sprinklers, garbage disposals, and air-conditioners help to run up the quarterly bill for H_2O.

Despite growing demands for water the United States seems quite amply endowed for a long time to come. Where there are shortages, the central problem is generally not one of original supply so much as it is inadequate distribution, expensive storage, or pollution. It is the cost of clean water which rises with population increase that makes it a major problem in many growing communities. Even in most arid regions more water could be had, but the expense of saving it and distributing it generally exceeds its value so that these areas remain deserts. The greatest of our western streams— the Columbia, Colorado, Sacramento, Missouri, and Rio Grande—all originate in high mountain areas where rains and snows feed them copiously. Every one of these rivers passes through some dry zone before it discharges into the sea and every one could contribute more of its annual flow to irrigation, industry, and homes; but it is the increased cost and diminishing returns from dams, pumps, and canals which have so far dissuaded man from doing the full job. There is a point in the economics of water supply when it is no longer feasible to build more dams on a river just to increase storage. As explained by Luna B. Leopold, chief hydraulic engineer of the United States Geological Survey, reservoir capacity in excess of a calculated optimum achieves no practical conservation because evaporation losses from expanded reservoir surfaces cut too deeply into total supplies. Another engineer of the U.S.G.S., Walter Langbein, states that "there is a limit to the practical gains which can be accomplished by building reservoirs on streams, and that limit already may have been reached, if not exceeded, in some of the western drainage basins."[2] This is fair warning that, on streams which have already been fairly well harnessed, any further development will show less results per dollar spent and water costs all along the stream may be increased.

In humid regions there is seldom an absolute shortage of water but rather a shortage of cheap clean water. In almost every instance of water deficiency east of the Mississippi River, the real culprit is not Nature but lack of facilities to make the best use of an enormously abundant but almost universally polluted supply. Since the earth is a sponge that soaks up rains as well as a drainboard which sheds them, the amount and quality of raw water in a humid area depend largely upon how the earth's surface is used. If the land is plastered with buildings, asphalt, and concrete then most of the rain immediately runs off into drainage channels. If the land is cloaked with forests and meadows the rain soaks into the ground to feed springs and wells. Since the hard shells of cities are water shedders, each metropolis must get its supply from man-made reservoirs or from lakes, rivers, or wells. In most places the local geology is such that water under ground would maintain a farm or a village but hardly a city. Where cities have grown, usually a polluted lake or a river is tapped, and citizens must be satisfied to drink and bathe in reclaimed water that once was unfit for human use but subsequently has been strained and chemically processed to make it safe. While disease is thus prevented, the unpleasant fact remains that millions must imbibe a hand-me-down product.

A smaller number of cities have been so fastidious and farsighted as to create reservoir areas in clean rural districts far away from the centers of population and pollution. Among the big cities New York and Boston have been particularly circumspect in providing clean virgin water to their inhabitants. Some of New York's reservoirs lie in the fresh green country of the Catskills scores of miles from any significant human pollutants. The shores of these municipal reservoirs, wherever they are located, are protected from indiscriminate use or contamination and their buffer zones are almost universally wooded to prevent silt from roiling the waters or filling the collection basins. Boston's spectacu-

larly beautiful Quabbin Reservoir lies eighty miles west of
the city in lonely pine and hemlock hill country that is beyond both the sight and sound of urban populations. Quabbin holds five years' supply of crystal-clear water that is
guarded with great care from any possible offensive surface
drainage. As Boston's supply is withdrawn it passes underground through tunnels blasted out of crystalline rocks so
that it arrives at the city in the most delectable condition an
urban resident could desire.

Unfortunately, for every metropolis that has such a fresh
source of virgin drinking water there are several which scoop
their supplies from contaminated streams and lakes into
which others have discharged their wastes. Not a city on the
Eastern seaboard is really forced to this unattractive expediency, for the Appalachian mountains and their Piedmont
foothills are everywhere within reach by a modern aqueduct.
Nevertheless adequate measures are seldom taken to acquire
sites for reservoirs or protected watersheds while these farm
and forest hinterlands are still relatively cheap and unpopu-
lated. To be sure there would be evaporation losses that
would add to costs but the water saved would be cleaner.
This lack of vision and appreciation of the engineering
measures that should be taken to cope with the population
deluge that is upon us will be paid for now and in the
future in inferior water at greater cost. The willingness of
cities to get by with the provisional rather than to plan
wisely and confidently for the best is one of the sorriest
aspects of modern metropolitan management.

As large cities and their suburbs continue to merge into
vast conurbations, the problem of floods will also become
more aggravated. On the one hand there will be a rising
demand for water and on the other catastrophic visitations
of too much. Whereas rains of the pre-industrial past soaked
into country ground, they now drain quickly from the eaves
of urban buildings and from the streets to create torrents in
depressions where other houses and industries have sprouted

in defiance of the law of gravity which guarantees there will be floods in low places at times of unusual run-off. The proper counterbalance to the increased run-off from cities would be a system of retention reservoirs in the rural sections of any particular watershed. As the urban drainage surface expands the remaining rural watershed should be harnessed to compensate. Two objectives could be achieved by the same engineering. The water stored by retention dams in rural areas to reduce flood discharge of tributary waterways could be saved to supply the cities with virgin drinking water. With proper care the forested and meadowed buffer lands around the reservoirs could be used as parks while the waters themselves could be used for recreational boating. But, as in so many other matters of rational land planning for metropolitan growth, there is a general apathy on the part of the uninformed and already overburdened taxpayer as well as a reluctance on the part of the politician to lead the way for fear of some controversy that might cost him a vote.

As time and progress bring better things, new challenges continue to poke scientists in the ribs. Once it was a simple problem to cleanse water but today's detergents seem to linger on. Old-fashioned soap suds would disappear in the fermenters and aerators of municipal treatment works, but not so the miracle froths of today's wonder cleansers. Chemist Jesse M. Cohen of the Robert A. Taft Research Center in Cincinnati recently reported to a meeting of the American Public Health Association that one of the simplest tests to determine if there is detergent in household water is to watch for foaming at the tap. So powerful are modern washing aids that less than one drop in a million drops of water will cause froth at the faucet. As Mr. Cohen reminded his listeners, if there are cleansers in the water there may be other pollutants as well. While it is one of the marks of civilization to be clean in body and raiment, any continued ingestion of modern detergents might not be appreciated by one's inner linings which are as sensitive now as they were in neolithic times, when seafoam was the closest thing to a bubble bath.

There was a time when our cities were young that the contaminants in streams and lakes were ordinary organic wastes that bacteria could consume if given time and oxygen. Today such simple natural products are the least of the water chemist's worries. Sylvan C. Martin, regional director of the United States Public Health Service, has indicated that there is a growing hazard in the "tremendous rise" of little-understood pollutants that defy ordinary sewage-disposal treatments. These contaminants, Mr. Martin explains, "can hardly be identified, let alone measured with present techniques and methodology."[3] It would seem that where everyone is taking in each other's wash water a mammoth biological experiment is being conducted without the hordes of participants being very much aware of how their stomachs, kidneys, and general physiological apparatuses are being tested for tolerance. Someday autopsies may reveal that what prolongs the usefulness of the garment may abbreviate that of the wearer.

It seems altogether remarkable that while there is proof positive that controlled additions of small amounts of fluorine to city water can promote dental health, there is often strong agitation against it while the same do-gooders are cotton-mouthed in the face of genuine contamination of the public drinking fountain.

But the picture is not all gloom. Two Wisconsin agricultural specialists have announced that sewage effluent has its merits as well as drawbacks. Professors C. J. Chapman and J. W. Clark found that by irrigating pastures with stream water carrying sewage effluent from the City of Madison's disposal works they increased the dry matter forage yield of a pasture by 400 pounds an acre. Chemical tests revealed that the effluent contained plant-nutrient elements at the rate of 24.8 parts per million of nitrogen, 25.7 parts of phosphorus, and 13.1 of potash. The scientists suggested that where the value of sewage effluent is proved it would be a simple matter to pipe it or run it through a ditch for disbursement on crop lands. Many years ago it was another Wisconsin scientist, F. H. King, who wrote *Farmers of Forty Centuries*, a classic work on soil management and fertility. That book is a report on Oriental agriculture as observed at first hand. Among his comments Dr. King remarked that no civilization can long afford to squander the life-giving elements of nitrogen, phosphorus, and potassium that Americans so thoughtlessly waste and which the Chinese and Japanese so carefully preserve. Professor King recognized the health hazards of applying raw sewage to crops used for direct human consumption and recommended that more progressive ways be found to salvage and utilize the enormous quantities of useful minerals that are annually lost in waste waters.

A wider use of sewage effluents on forage and industrial crops, feed grains, and tree farms will doubtless come in the future. If communities were able to plan their total land use wisely, they would zone some areas near their sewage-disposal works for perpetual farming or forestry and they would locate these works near rivers. Thus very little water would be lost and almost all useful minerals would be salvaged. The crops would get the minerals as the effluent would pass through the soil. The streams would eventually get the water through underground seepage. Such natural cleansing systems would be far cheaper for the taxpayer and more healthful to the future user of reclaimed water. But without total land-use planning for city and hinterland such practical ideas stand little chance of coming into general use.

In nearly every densely populated area the underground water table is dropping because of excessive withdrawal, yet little effort is made to recharge the subterranean reservoirs with sewage effluents, as probably would be done if scientists rather than politicians were to make the decisions about what is done with America's water supply. Some years ago the world's largest producer of frozen foods, Seabrook Farms of southern New Jersey, had a double water problem on its hands. It pumped from the ground over a million gallons daily to wash fruits and vegetables before packaging and freezing—an average of forty gallons is used by Seabrook Farms to wash each pound of strawberries! This liberal dousing threatened to lower the ground water table while disposal of the waste water at the surface became a puzzler in itself. When flushed out onto open land the wash water formed a marsh with offensive odors.

Eventually Seabrook's research division discovered that the wash water could be put right back into the earth where it came from and in the recycling process made as fresh and clean as ever. Through giant overhead sprays wash water from the packing plant was made to fall like rain into a nearby forest. The litter of forest duff acted as a blotter, soaking in the water and passing it on to the soil beneath. Apparently a forest will drink water faster than any cultivated field or pasture. Wherever the ground water table from which a municipal supply is taken may be recharged from above, there a city might be able to conserve part of its supply if it would maintain municipal forests and use them for effluent disposal according to the Seabrook formula. At least it is a possibility they ought not to dismiss without study of the geology of their areas. From the standpoint of national planning, water that goes into the ground anywhere is likely to be of eventual use to some community; thus no waste water should be discharged into a stream which might be salvaged unless that waste water is immediately essential to support navigation.

The United States was using 250 billion gallons of water daily in 1957. This amounted to more than fourteen hundred gallons for every man, woman, and child. By 1975 consumption will be up to 450 billion gallons. Despite such demand only a fraction of the rain that falls ever gets used even once. The rest goes off as evaporation or flows away untapped. The seventeen states of the dry zone from the Great Plains to the Pacific Coast allocate to irrigation about eight-five per cent of all the water they draw. Twelve per cent goes to industry and three per cent into the homes of about 45,000,000 people. Thirty-one states in the more humid eastern part of the nation use eighty-nine per cent of their drawn water in industry. Ten per cent goes into the homes of 135,000,000 people and only one per cent is used in irrigation. Industrial requirements are phenomenal but, of course, what goes into a factory must come out in some form or other: sometimes clean, sometimes contaminated but still reclaimable. A single large papermill demands more water than a city of 50,000. To make a ton of steel requires 65,000 gallons, and it takes 20 gallons to refine a gallon of oil. Three hundred gallons of water are needed to make a barrel of beer, which is what some people have suspected for a long time.

CLEANSING ACTION

Increasing populations require more of every resource used by civilized man. Even sand and gravel rise in value and ordinary rock has become a good commodity for speculation in metropolitan regions. City denizens have become so detached from nature and so completely surrounded by pavements that dime stores find it profitable to sell them soil by the pound in plastic bags. The time is not far off when masses of citizens will choose to buy water for drinking and cooking from bottlers who have wells and springs rather than imbibe the countless industrial and household chemicals now found in the public supply of many communities. Taste, health, and a simple desire to put a too vivid imagination at ease will prompt the discriminating to pay for what once was free and easy to get. This will not be a great financial imposition, but it will be just one more of the little burdens that make life more complicated and expensive in this age of congestion. While people themselves may be cheaper by the dozen, the per capita costs of public services reveal an almost uninterrupted tendency to rise along with human increase. We have long ago passed the point of optimum density for good living at low cost. From here on out public services are most likely to go up in cost and down in quality, chiefly because no community has yet learned how to organize itself efficiently for the kind of population pressure we have today.

As more people eventually turn to commercial bottling companies for drinking water of old-fashioned quality, cities will be free to concentrate on the provision of service waters for those household and industrial uses that can be satisfied with less fastidiousness. By the employment of better decontamination facilities ordinary service waters can be made biologically safe for external use in the vast quantities every city will need in the future. It is evidently uneconomical, and it is becoming less and less possible, for many cities to maintain desirable drinking water standards for everything that goes through the public mains. Since less than one gallon is imbibed out of an average daily per capita consumption of 1400 gallons, it is also manifestly unnecessary. It is a practice already common in Europe and almost universal in Latin America for people to buy what water they drink from commercial bottlers who have sources that are free of man-made contaminants and to depend upon public service for the rest.

Remarkable progress can be achieved within a very short time when serious efforts are made to treat sewage before discharging it into streams and lakes. Twelve years ago less than one per cent of the nearly 4,000,000 people who live along the Ohio River were protected from pollution by raw sewage. Today more than ninety-five per cent are safeguarded because sewage is properly treated by nearly every community in the valley. Maurice E. Gosnell, chairman of the Ohio River Valley Water Sanitation Commission, has noted with appropriate pride that "in this relatively brief period, the combined efforts of eight states, their citizens, and their industries have reversed the trend of half a century of river abuse."[4]

Better quality water in streams means a better life in different ways to different people. To members of Wilmington's Primitive Baptist Church it means a resumption of baptismal services in Brandywine Creek. A century ago it was a common practice among several congregations to perform the rite of baptism in the historic stream that flows from southeastern Pennsylvania into Delaware. Subsequently industrial wastes and raw sewage from upstream communities forced a suspension of the practice. In recent years through the valiant efforts of the Brandywine Valley Association both industry and the public have been persuaded to clean up. A report released by the Department of Interior shows that suspended sediment in the Brandywine declined thirty-eight per cent from the years 1947-50 to the years 1951-55. Those who have watched closely the improvement of the Brandywine say that progress continues toward renovating this beautiful stream, and that is good news to more than one hundred thousand residents of Wilmington who depend upon it for their daily water needs.

The rate of improvement is not everywhere so encouraging. Congressman Blatnik of Minnesota says the Potomac River, as it flows past the District of Columbia, is "the best-dressed cesspool in the country," and he has called for immediate steps to clean it up. This is more easily said than done. When Congress voted early in 1960 to spend $900,000,000 during the next decade to help local communities clean up their water supplies President Eisenhower promptly vetoed the bill. It is estimated that it would take $150,000,000 just to redeem the Potomac. Meanwhile suburban Fairfax County, for lack of a trunk sewer line, is toying with the idea of complicating matters with an "interim" treatment plant which would release effluent into the Potomac just above Washington's water supply intake.

This being the situation along the stream which flows by the Lincoln Memorial and the Nation's Capitol, it is scarcely to be wondered at that other less wealthy areas are also delinquent. For all the billions collected in taxes it is too often impossible to get the few millions allocated that are necessary to perform essential public services.

FROM SALT TO SWEET

The great hope of industrial cities near ocean coasts is that someday economical techniques may be perfected to remove salts from brackish and sea waters. Two such converters capable of producing five million gallons of sweet water daily are already in action in the desert sheikdom of Kuwait on the Persian Gulf, but the cost is such that only an oil-rich principality could afford it. Present conversion costs are said to be in the neighborhood of $1.75 per thousand gallons, whereas to gain acceptance in the average American community the price at the plant would have to be reduced to seventy-five cents or less per thousand gallons. Government officials in Washington believe that ways to desalt water at reasonable costs may be achieved before 1965, and President Eisenhower has proclaimed to the United Nations that the world's sweet water problem is on "the threshold of solution." Laboratories of the Bureau of Reclamation in Denver are now experimenting with a promising electrodialysis process that was developed in the Netherlands.

Basic to the electrodialysis process is the fact known to every high-school science student that salts in solution split into positive and negative ions and that, when an electric current is passed through the solution, the positive ions move to the negative electrode while negative ions travel to the positive electrode. To reduce the concentration of ions in part of a given solution partitions of plastic membrane are placed in the container. These membrane partitions are impervious to water but ionic particles, under the impelling force of an electric current, do pass through them. Thus water between membrane partitions and away from the electrodes becomes less salty while water outside the membrane partitions and near the electrodes becomes more concentrated. By passing a stream of sea water through a series of such electrodialytic cells its salt content may be progressively reduced. The trick is to develop membranes and a process that will not consume as much electricity as present experimental models use.

Until the millennium arrives and there is an abundance of everything for everybody instead of just an abundance of everybodies, one of the best ways to stretch a short supply of good water seems to be the old solution of eliminating the leaky faucet. One faucet with an opening of 1/32 of an inch will leak 76,000 gallons of water in a year. At the present price of municipal water in such a town as Newark, Delaware, this could mean a waste of $284. If hot water were involved the additional cost of fuel would be $38. Probably there are other ways of pouring money down the drain that are more fun.

CHAPTER 11

Space Between the Ears

The most important space in any civilized community is the space between the ears of its citizens. If that space is disorganized and cluttered with trivia, then the community and the design of its terrestrial space will certainly reflect it. There was a time when man made little impact upon the natural world around him. He was but one among the numberless species of living things struggling for a cave of security on a none too friendly planet. His job was to adjust as well as possible to avoid annihilation by either competing organisms or the rigors of an environment which he had not learned to shape. Today man is master of most living things and chief arranger of the inanimate landscape. Only a few stubborn viruses and bacteria still present a serious challenge. But even these cannot escape his scrutiny, for he has devised microscopes and other means of detection which in the end will enable him to hunt them down and destroy them whenever they pose a threat. With all other natural competitors subdued, or facing containment, man has only himself to reckon with. To make that final adjustment to his own swiftly multiplying kind without wrecking the civilized qualities of the environment will require the best possible use of that crucial space between the ears.

Some say that education of the young is the hope of mankind and that schools can do the job. If so, this is a rather large order from a people who, as a whole, look down their noses at the egghead. To expect teachers, who are the most underprivileged professionals in our society, to be the purveyors of its culture and the enlighteners of the young, is somewhat naïve. It is asking the discount house to give custom service. It is expecting those who have not tasted wine to appraise the vintage. To anticipate that the coming generation will do better than the present because of its schooling is wishful thinking and an excuse for mental laziness upon the part of contemporary adults. Wholesale reliance upon the conventional education of the young as a rocket to the intellectual moon may tax the pocketbook but it does not tax the mind. Illiteracy and its cure are one thing, but the development of wise and cultured human beings is far more subtle and difficult. The average school can cope with illiteracy but it is neither staffed nor designed to develop able and imaginative minds; yet these are truly the hope of mankind.

The two biggest issues on the current academic front from first grade through the Ph.D. degree are how much will an education cost and how many students will the schools accommodate. What may happen to the mind of the scholar at any level is much less important to the average citizen and most school administrators than what may happen to the budget. This is not strange; for, with the exception of its vocational aspects, conventional schooling does not really prepare a young person for life as an intelligent adult. It tests his perseverance and gives him entré to certain opportunities in the form of credentials and social contacts, but from there he is on his own. Every adult knows that ninety-five per cent or more of his time in school was spent stuffing facts into mental cubbyholes without much thought as to meaning. He also knows that forgetting most of these facts later imposed no handicap upon his career. Thus he quite realistically scorns the content of such an education for his children while insisting upon its certificates. It is of little consequence to most adults what children learn as long as they get their vocational training along with it and cultivate reasonable diligence. It is also quite essential to get grades which satisfy the family ego.

Inasmuch as this skepticism is founded upon the facts of life it cannot be dismissed. Quite obviously what the school really does and what it purports to do in the way of cultivating the intellect are not in agreement; otherwise, an academic education would not be so universally desired while the educated mind is so commonly suspect. There would not be so much honor for the quiz kid and such contempt for the intellectual. There would not be such approval of answers and such disdain for questions. There would not be such love of facts and fear of ideas. There would not be such comfort in repetition of the known and such reluctance to explore the unknown. The diploma would not be rated higher than a desire to learn by parent, faculty, and student. Nevertheless, as long as diplomas are in demand for very mercenary reasons, the school is assured of attendance regardless of its curriculum or the quality of its instruction. To satisfy a rapidly rising market for credentials, and the economic advantage which each sheepskin gives to its winner, schools must be built at an unprecedented rate in the future.

There are now about 45,000,000 students in the nation's schools. This is one quarter of all the population. Three fourths of these pupils are in the elementary grades. About 9,000,000 are in high school and over 3,000,000 are in institutions of advanced study of all kinds. Today over 95 per cent of all children between the ages of seven and thirteen are enrolled in school. During what might be considered the normal high school years registration declines from approximately 95 per cent of the fourteen-year-olds to about 40 per cent of the eighteen-year-olds. An amazing 35 per cent of all youths between eighteen and twenty-one years of age were enrolled in schools of higher learning in 1959. At the dawn of this century college registrants were only 4 per cent of their age group. There is no doubt that young people today recognize the importance that educational documents play in shaping their careers. Since 1951 there has been a 54 per cent increase in the total enrollment in college and other upper-level schools. This leap is due less to the birth rate than to a new appraisal of what education beyond the high school is worth in the growing competition for better paying jobs. The impact of the war babies upon college registration is yet to be felt.

For the most part the undergraduate college student is in school because it is a sieve through which those who pass are likely to find more lucrative employment and more desirable mates than if they took their chances via some other route. To a certain extent the high school serves a similar purpose but on a lower plane. The opportunity to gain an education beyond the grade school and the ambition to work for it are not everywhere the same. In South Carolina and Louisiana the average number of school years completed by all students is 7.6, while in California it is 11.6. For the United States as a whole one half of all students go into the sophomore year of high school or beyond, while the other half drop out somewhere along the line before they get that far.

The monetary value of passing each academic milestone is beyond question. Today the average working person at age fifty earns twice as much if he is a college graduate rather than a grade-school graduate. If he finished high school but did not graduate from college he earns only about sixty per cent as much as the college graduate, but approximately twenty-five per cent more than the grade-school graduate. These are the facts of life that persuade students to crack the books whether they like it or not and whether they improve their minds or not. The United States Office of Education predicts that by 1970 forty-five per cent of all jobs will be "white collar" and that professional workers will be the fastest growing occupational group. The only way to get out of overalls and into a gray flannel suit will be to stay aboard the textbook express down to the last multiple-choice exam, even if it takes a diet half benzedrine and half phenobarbital to do it. According to those who have looked into the earning power of the average college degree, it seems that for an investment of four years' time and six to eight thousand dollars a young man may earn $100,000 more during his employed lifetime than if he never sat on his alma mater's knee.

While the argument that education promotes earning power is persuasive, it has a tiny flaw—it does not work for the teacher. Like the unhappy tailor who could not sew or the physician who could not cure himself, the teacher has not learned the elements of subsistence as well as his students. Perhaps it really is not education after all that fattens the wallets of graduates, or possibly teachers do not care as much about wages as other people.

In 1959 college faculty members earned an average annual salary of $6711, according to the National Education Association. It was in that year that President Jean Paul Mather of the University of Massachusetts resigned in despair when he was unable to persuade the legislature of the Commonwealth to raise the salaries of his associate professors to the level of the average truck driver, who then made between $7200 and $7800 annually. If earning power alone were a man's objective he could as well end his academic career at his secondary school commencement as to struggle for a berth on a college faculty, since a fourth of all instructors earn less than $4600 annually and only ten per cent of all teachers earn over $10,000 a year. As a group the average college graduate earns about 33 per cent more than the average college professor while the average teacher in elementary and secondary schools does well to make as much as the average graduate from the eighth grade.

Superficially these figures might suggest to the taxpayer that the education he is buying for his children is the biggest bargain ever offered. To some extent that may be true, but only because he never learned very much about academic quality and his teachers did not enlighten him because the facts are not very complimentary to themselves. In a report recently completed by the New York State Department of Education, teaching was described as a "profession in which a premium is placed upon mediocrity." This conclusion was reached after a statistical analysis of the records of 1251 students who had enrolled as prospective teachers in sixteen colleges and universities in New York in the academic year of 1949-50. Of the original aspirants only 531, or 42 per cent, actually had become teachers by 1954. The study of their achievements revealed that in academic subjects the graduates who became teachers were only one cut above those who flunked out or were asked to leave. On the other hand the students who switched from vocational teachers' training to other majors tended to be superior in academic subjects and younger. The students who transferred to other fields also had developed those personal characteristics associated with effective teaching to a higher degree than the group which actually became teachers. Dean Lester Vander Werf of Northeastern College of Education has observed that "teachers are of a lower mental caliber than members of any other profession and are not intelligent enough for the functions they perform. Bright students are not encouraged by parents and teachers to become teachers."[1] The dean might have added that their brightness could be the very trait which leads them to stay clear of the academic life.

Amidst all the clamor for higher teachers' salaries, New York University Professor Roland H. Spaulding has ventured a minority opinion that many American teachers are "greatly overpaid." Dr. Spaulding, as director of aeronautical education at his university, is particularly interested in the quality of instruction in mathematics, and he was appalled to discover some time ago that only five of a group of thirty-two teachers of mathematics whom he addressed in New Jersey had studied beyond high school plane geometry.

"We can not inspire young people with the love of mathematics and science," he said, "through teachers who are not leaders and who are not themselves fully informed experts."[2]

Harvard's Professor Edwin C. Kemble has charged as recently as 1960 that only a small minority of today's science teachers know the subject well enough to teach it properly. The good professor probably knows that a great many of today's instructors in elementary and secondary schools are not necessarily expected to know well the subjects to which they are assigned. However, they must be proficient in issuing homework according to master schedules and they must be willing to grade tests as prescribed by the "answer book" which comes with the text. It is all very simple for a simple intellect unless a freak student should get interested by mistake and ask questions that are not in the answer book or, even more embarrassing, come up with a solution just as valid but which cannot be accepted because the authors skipped it. This being what often passes as teaching, it is no wonder that bright minds want to get as far away from it as possible and leave the field to the unimaginative scorekeeper mentality.

A schoolroom atmosphere that encourages questions and a teacher who is able to handle them without hiding behind an answer book are what an intelligent scholar would find most exciting. But that kind of teacher is likely to be weeded out as he goes through the hoops of many teacher-training courses, where he gets bogged down in classroom techniques, norms, percentile curves, and the art of assigning homework. As matters now stand in the District of Columbia, Dr. James R. Killian of the Massachusetts Institute of Technology, formerly President Eisenhower's advisor on science and technology, would not be permitted to teach eighth-grade arithmetic because he has not taken required courses in educational theory. Even Einstein, if he were alive, would be barred because he had no credits in "how to teach mathematics." In practically every community the teaching profession outside of the colleges and universities is now solidly in the grip of "educators" who must know how to teach even if they do not know very much about *what* they teach. No one has yet come up with a satisfactory explanation as to how children learn in such a vacuum, but that does not seem to be important as long as they develop leadership in their group relationships.

University of California chemist, Joel Hildebrand, has lashed out at this new breed of schoolroom record-and-attendance keepers who are glib about "life adjustment" but tongue-tied on subject matter. "One of our greatest dangers," says Professor Hildebrand, "lies in the anti-intellectualism fostered by school authorities who should be among its most valiant opponents. One expression of it is the pious cliché, 'We teach boys and girls, not subjects.' The superintendent of schools of a large city puts this into practice by assigning his teachers to subjects they have never studied, because, he says, he wants his teachers to be 'child-centered' not 'subject-centered.'" In asking for more basic studies in mathematics Professor Hildebrand adds, "I am not recommending that they replace other basic subjects. Let them replace things like 'how to have a successful date' and 'how can my home be made democratic' and 'how to predict business trends.' We need foreign languages now more than ever. We need history and geography. We need ability to read, write, speak, and think clearly."[3]

Quite obviously in the process of erecting their empires of functional buildings and certified staffs, modern school boards have forgotten that improvement of the intellect is the purpose of schools and that children do not attend classes to get cut-rate, amateur psychoanalysis by motivators who do not even know the subjects that the student is expected to take an interest in. There is nothing like the old-fashioned notion that a teacher should know his subject so thoroughly that he can stimulate the interest of a child to learn, reason, question, reflect, and imagine instead of pounding him with true-false achievement tests and rushing him off to the "guidance clinic" for a report on what it is about his home life that disturbs him when he does not measure up to norms set by some commercial testing service.

The young citizen who is put through years of busy-work assignments out of which he gains no real competence in any basic scholastic discipline or has never tasted the pleasure of mental speculation and argument has lost forever his best opportunity to acquire the kind of intellectual habits and aesthetic tastes that would stimulate and enrich all the succeeding years of his life. Also, by being raised in the presence of tutors who are not scholars but rather who fear and despise scholarship because they are unfamiliar with it and untrained in it, the student is never introduced to the vast world of ideas that only avid reading can reveal. President John A. Perkins of the University of Delaware in his hard-hitting *Plain Talk from a Campus* places an industrious and discriminating reading habit at the very top of attainments that a college should attempt to develop in its students. Without an eagerness to read, intellectual initiative will never shift into high gear and in later life the citizen is more likely to be influenced by opinion than by thought. Today's student seldom reads good books. His school busy-work prevents it. Dr. Francis H. Horn, President of the University of Rhode Island, has called for an end to the trend toward academic togetherness and a rebirth of the mind that is willing and able to think alone, independently of fashion.

Today's elementary and secondary schools keep the pupil so occupied with memorized trivia that he has little chance to read or to think, dream, argue, or speculate about a subject, should he have the inclination. Such a product is certain to become an ineffective adult in civic matters that demand analysis and judgment or which call for some sense of humanity that has been refined and articulated by acquaintance with the arts, history, and the literature of Western culture. Anything can happen to a raw present which is cut adrift from all moorings to the mature past. If the time is now at hand when the metropolitan community must undergo drastic revisions in its physical and social organization in order to accommodate the rising tides of humanity at its threshold, the citizen will have to be intellectually ready to perform new tasks for which there are no predigested instructions. It will be of inestimable value if he has some sense of eternal values because he is grounded in the ancient mental disciplines of the human race including mathematics, philosophy, and the arts. Familiarity with such classical subject matter as well as a grasp of the fundamentals of modern chemistry, physics, and biology will help men make their way with insight through the difficult intellectual marshes of our time. It is impossible to find a pat formula for the future wrapped up in a textbook of the past but a well-honed mind which has learned to tangle with ideas will be capable of discovery. If there is no depth or wisdom in the space between the ears, then the community space we live in will not be efficiently used or tastefully embellished. The quality of both our personal and community lives will suffer even though the school budget is doubled or quadrupled. Any basic improvement in the educational system will have to begin not with budgets but with the recruitment and training of teachers and a shift in emphasis from quizzing and testing to reading, analysis, and free discussion. Dean William Penrose of the University of Delaware's School of Education has stated that teaching techniques are of value only when a teacher is master of his subject. Graduates of his school must have thirty-six semester hours of instruction in their major plus eighteen in related fields.

The process by which many teachers are produced for primary and secondary schools practically guarantees the elimination of scholars. This is a consequence not of accident but of design. Too often in primary and secondary schools the act of teaching is now regarded as more important than mastery of content. Thus a man trains to become a teacher of chemistry rather than a chemist. He tries to qualify as a teacher of biology rather than as a biologist. He becomes an expert in everything that has to do with teaching except, frequently, the subject matter his students are assigned to study. The result in the classroom is a stifling of curiosity and of serious questioning by students while the teacher devotes himself to endless rote testing. Such a teacher is incapable of departing from the written text because he is not at home in his field of instruction. He cannot approach the details of his subject with vigor and insight because he himself is blind to its logic and scope. Students are loaded with fantastic homework assignments which keep them busy, bewildered, and intimidated. Too often it is assumed that the student comes to class not to learn but rather to inform the teacher of what he has memorized at home. Somehow or other the roles of parent and teacher have been reversed, and it is the parent who must instruct the child in subject matter and the teacher who lectures him on conduct and social attitudes.

If he is a product of the conventional secondary school, the college freshman who elects to train as a teacher will have subsisted up until that time on this kind of ersatz intellectual porridge. Although his brain may be in sound physical condition, it will be inclined to memorize quickly and forget just as fast. It will not be accustomed to puzzle, ponder, or speculate and the wheels will scarcely turn if it is asked to reason or debate. It will know how to take multiple-choice and true-and-false tests by the gross. It will match pat answers to stereotyped questions with astonishing speed. Adept as it has become at these games of mental bingo, if it is required to write a composition with the faintest trace of style or subtlety of thought it will flip.

When this brain gets to college there is still a slight chance that it may come into contact with the kinds of intellectual exploration that have brought man out of the stone age and created civilizations. The experience may be so overwhelming that all past intentions are discarded while new goals are set and fresh ambitions are generated. At this point some minds actually take off and there is no satisfying them until they are on their way to the bottom of things. If this happens the student will demand that his time be spent on learning and not on gimmicks. If he is a candidate for a teaching certificate, he may very well switch at this point to preparation for a different career. He may decide to be a specialist in spiders or atomic energy, in Sanskrit or Elizabethan drama. He may want to be truly proficient in mechanical engineering, human physiology, or the history of India. Whatever it is that captures his imagination the thrill of actually using his brain will make it spin like wine and he will never again settle for sanitary, "cellophane-wrapped," "prepared-package" learning. Since he thus disqualifies himself for teaching in primary and secondary institutions, he is safely removed from any possible disturbing influence upon the school system, and principals may rest in peace.

Dean John H. Fischer of Teachers College, Columbia University, says, "There are natural-born teachers, but unfortunately there are not enough of them."[4] As head of the most influential breeding ground for the profession in America, he believes the remedy is to make his students masters of educational techniques as well as of subject matter. The fly in this ointment is that the time spent taking courses in the techniques of arranging the bulletin board reduces the time available for solid academic subjects. Anyone familiar with teachers' training manuals knows they are as full of new styles as a fashion show and that they go out of date faster than an Easter hat.

When, almost by accident, a scholar slips through the barriers and becomes a teacher, disaster eventually may break loose. Such a calamity befell Fox Lane High School in Westchester County, New York, when James R. Worley, chairman of the English Department, decided he could be more effective if he made certain that his students were learning instead of going through the motions of preplanned canned lessons. He was fired for his pains. Preplanning is a dearly beloved technique whereby a teacher submits a written statement to his principal telling him exactly what detail of his course a class will cover on a certain date two weeks hence. This is supposed to illustrate the thoroughness with which the teacher organizes his class time so that every moment is accounted for. This paper work is important because it is put in a file and enables a principal to prove that he rides herd. It is also a device whereby a poorly informed teacher may plead, "We must get on with our work; there is no time for that" whenever a student raises a sticky question that is not covered in the text.

When Mr. Worley was called on the carpet for his refusal to file written plans for classroom studies, he explained that they stifle imaginative teaching and offered no apologies. Thereupon he was dismissed by his board of education which issued an eight-page summary of its opinion in which it was stated, "As a board of education we place high valuation on creative teaching, believing that creativity in the educational process is essential to the development of mature, inquiring minds. We subscribe to the principle that teachers should be accorded maximum freedom in the exercise of their professional capacity. . . . It has been acknowledged that Mr. Worley is an able classroom teacher, but in our opinion professional competence cannot be adduced as a rationalization for insubordinate behavior."[5] It was a document worthy of the fact that two members of the school board which swung the axe were professional public-relations executives.

When word of Mr. Worley's plight reached Dr. Jacques Barzun, provost of Columbia University, he expressed his surprise that "in a period when the rarity of good teaching is notorious and likely to increase, it is a rash administrator who would dismiss a competent and reliable teacher solely on the ground of not following to the letter a secondary obligation in this form of paper work."[6] Parents of two Fox Lane students, who apparently agreed with Dr. Barzun and who appreciated Mr. Worley's way of teaching, offered to employ him as a private tutor. Doubtless there were others who wished they could afford the same privilege.

TEST-HAPPY

In recent years educators have become test-happy. In the old days when teachers taught and encouraged questions or debate the test was used after a reasonable period of classroom exposition to determine if the student had been reasonably diligent. Now the test is becoming a device to check up on the student's homework. After spending the best hours of the day in the classroom getting nowhere, he is sent home with a load of books that is enough to make him prematurely hunchbacked. In the evening, when most adults would be willing to call it a day, the homework begins and it commonly covers new material which has not been explained in class.

The next day the hours in school are devoted to reviewing the homework and, in this task, the teacher is well armed with an instructors' edition of the textbook. This manual or "teachers' guide" suggests questions that might be asked to determine if the student has covered his assignments. It even gives answers. If the course is one in algebra, the manual will illustrate how the answer is obtained. The student may be sent to the blackboard to work out his solution while the teacher consults the "answer book" to see if it is correct. In this way an instructor in physical education can fill in as a math teacher since most good math teachers have now left the schools for better salaries on the outside. Every precaution is taken by the authors and editors of today's textbooks and teachers' guides to get the instructor through the course without embarrassment or difficulty, and they assume that he is not well informed about the subject. If parents ask questions the instructor can always fall back on the student's "group-consciousness quotient" and "sub-median study habits." If the student makes the grade without the help of an "answer book" he is considered bright or even a "genius." If the student should get tangled up and his parents are too tired or unable to help him, then he will become a statistic to prove that in all classes there are "poors" and "intermediates" as well as "superiors." Class grades must fall into a "curve" with some on top, some on the bottom, and most in the middle; otherwise it becomes quickly apparent in the records office that the teacher is either too easy or too hard.

Eric Groezinger, director of elementary education in the New Jersey State Department of Education, has expressed strong disapproval of the concept that the more time spent in the classroom and the more homework heaped on the student the better the school. Mr. Groezinger quite clearly distinguishes between work load and learning, and he has had the courage to challenge a current dictum that bigger assignments promote better scholarship. He does not subscribe to the popular school of thought that quantity makes quality. It is his conviction that "better schools can only come through better teaching that results in better learning"[7]—a simple thought but not popular.

Dr. Harold G. McCurdy, psychologist at the University of North Carolina, undertook a study of the childhood patterns of twenty recognized persons of special ability who included Goethe, Voltaire, Pitt, and Coleridge to determine what they may have had in common. He found that all of them had enjoyed a high degree of attention from parents and other adults, particularly in their education. They experienced privacy and isolation from other children. Also their sense of fantasy had been cultivated to a high degree. Dr. McCurdy observed that public education today is "a vast experiment on the effect of reducing all three of the factors to minimal values, and should, accordingly, tend to suppress the occurrence of genius."[8] Dr. McCurdy, of course, recognized the importance of inheritance and admits that not all youngsters, even under the most favorable circumstances, would respond in outstanding fashion. However, almost anyone of normal ability would be stimulated and encouraged by good adult tutoring and the privilege of privacy when desired. The twin desires of man to be at times gregarious and at times alone to dream, think, or read are evident in the school child, yet today's routine scarcely gives him a chance.

Another psychologist, Dr. Bruno Bettelheim, has flatly stated that school children should not be expected to work up to the full limit of their capacity. "Only in rare and special moments and in areas we thoroughly enjoy does anyone work up to his capacity. We, as psychologists, have a duty to tell teachers that to expect this from children is nonsense. . . . Fortunately most children have a healthy resistance to this. Education procedures should be geared, not to the needs of an assembly line, but to the needs of the human animal."[9] These wise words are almost universally ignored by the usual school system and is one reason why many children who are perfectly bright are overwhelmed and confused, and develop a passionate dislike for school. Some of the most able young minds are those which resent wasting their time in school. If teachers would really teach, then fewer hours of classroom concentration would be necessary to master daily lessons. The remainder of the student's day could be spent at libraries, museums, study halls, the playing field, or gymnasium. Physical exercise for the normal growing child is as imperative for mental and spiritual health as his lessons. Probably one of the best things that could happen to the elementary and secondary schools as the result of growing population pressures and rising budgets would be to force all formal classrooms onto a half-day shift under teachers who teach. The other half day could be spent under the guidance of librarians, homework tutors, arts and crafts instructors, and sports coaches.

When the criticism is made that primary and secondary schools neglect the "hard" subjects for the "soft," the intent is not to put the student under greater stress, as some educators seem to believe. The objective is to get schools to offer such courses as algebra, English grammar, foreign languages, biology, and chemistry in such a clear and lucid manner that students will catch on. A concentration on these subjects rather than on "personal charm" or "baby care" is desirable not because they are "stiff" but because, if properly taught, the student gradually will develop genuine mental muscle. Just as no athletic instructor would think of asking a man to run a half mile until he had trained for it gradually, no biologist would launch into genetics without preliminary studies of cell structure and function. Understanding of the complex is built upon understanding fundamentals. The half mile would be "hard" for the untrained athlete just as genetics would be "hard" for the student of biology who had not started with fundamentals. With proper coaching the average student could take the so-called "hard" subjects with greater ease and success than he now takes the "soft" electives that are chiefly bags of confusing, disorganized busywork.

It is no trick at all to make a course in "modern diet," "fashion design," or "garage mechanics" harder than a basic course in physics. It is as possible to get a student more tangled up in a test on "education theory" or "swatch identification" than on "the periodic table of the elements." It depends chiefly on how well the teacher understands and explains his own course and how diligently he tries to present it in an understandable way. The so-called "hard" courses need not be difficult for the normally diligent student. They even have the advantage that a clear logic underlies the arrangement of their factual material. Facts without meaning and relationship are out of place in such courses. To the mind that is learning by reason rather than by memorization such courses are not difficult and they are the only kind of study which give the analytical mind a thrill. By no multiplication of homework and fancy quizzes, gimmicks, or visual aids can a trade-school course in "budgeting the home" or "self-help in the tool shop" be considered the equivalent, although there is no doubt that such courses can be made very difficult indeed. A college course in "the teaching of geography" can be made tougher than a basic course in "physical geography" but the logic, if any, will be arbitrary and imposed. It will not be inherent in the subject matter itself. It may cultivate a sense of showmanship, but it will not add depth to the student's understanding of geography unless he knew very little about it in the first place. Usually, however, it is possible to get as much "credit" for one as for the other.

The modern educator has come to believe that his mission in life is to be a talent scout. He is a school-circuit Major Bowes on the lookout for academic tap dancers and trained seals. Armed with I.Q. tests, achievement tests, scholastic aptitude tests, and a raft of special tests (recently a half million students in 1400 high schools were subjected to a battery of 26 tests), he is poised to snag at the earliest possible moment "the particularly gifted child." With just as much zest he wants to put the finger on "the emotionally disturbed pupil." That this mania to quiz and failure to teach may be disturbing influences in the life of a school child, who would like to learn but not become a parrot, does not seem to enter the heads of the new breed of pigeonholers who are as keen about indelible labels as a commercial laundry. It does not disturb these advocates of vocational predestination that tests measure not what the student thinks but whether he thinks as the tester who is sometimes incorrect himself. In some school systems the point has already been reached where the result of an I.Q. test given in an early primary grade influences the entire future course of a child's school career. Every subsequent teacher is given the record to make her aware of the brightness or dimness of that first spark. The dossier, constantly fattened, sticks to the child as though it were his fingerprint, and it would be a rash instructor who would not be "oriented" by the evidence.

Recently a college professor was asked to review a high-school achievement test in his field of competence. The test had been prepared by one of the foremost educational testing services in the country and is now in circulation. The time allotted to the high-school youth for whom the test is designed is forty minutes. The professor finished after one hour and forty-five minutes. His own comments after taking it were, "I am not in sympathy with this method of checking either the factual knowledge or intellectual concepts of the student. The low-grade English used in phrasing the questions, and the emphasis upon speed with no encouragement of reflection or comment indicate a contempt for both the student's mind and the subject. The test fosters snap judgments and puts a premium on glibness. Some questions are unfair and the answers expected in a few instances are inaccurate. It sterilizes where fermentation is desired."

Colleges now are in such a dither about increasing enrollment that they, too, have turned to objective tests to weed out or pigeonhole their students. As the student-teacher ratio widens the professor is not expected to know undergraduates as well as formerly. Therefore the electronic digital computor makes their acquaintance in his stead. Perhaps it will not be long before letters of recommendation to a graduate's prospective employers will be cranked out by the machine, which already advises the professor as to what he should say. The professional testing services, which have a strangle hold on elementary and secondary schools, are moving in on the colleges with a vengeance. As they win college acceptance, they gain a prestige that makes them practically irrefutable at lower levels.

Not only are college board exams called upon to determine who should go to college and preferably where but even after admittance the student may look forward to periodic checkups via magnetic-pencil inquisitions shipped in by an outside scholastic-measurement outfit. Woe to the man or woman who falls below some supposedly impartial national norm set up by the quiz entrepreneurs who know in advance that there cannot be a norm unless half the students fall below it. When word comes back to the college revealing how its product stacks up with all others, professors will be expected to drill their classes so that they make a better showing on the next go-around. While this process may appeal to the score-keeping mentality of a records office, it looks as if the day were not far off when all undergraduate college curricula and class subject matter will be as standardized as any soap or cereal marketed from coast to coast. Teaching machines are in the offing; grading machines are already here. If only machines were designed to take tests, then colleges might dispense entirely with students and faculty and devote their full attention to writing catalogues, evaluating records, and soliciting contributions from alumni.

The Rockefeller Brothers Report on education which was released in 1958 states that "tests are most effective in measuring academic aptitude and achievement. There are certain other kinds of aptitude that they can measure, but with less assurance. And there are many kinds of talent that must go unmeasured because no adequate measuring instrument exists. In short, tests are effective on a limited front. Decisions based on test scores must be made with the awareness of the imponderables in human behavior. We cannot measure the rare qualities of character that are a necessary ingredient of great performance. . . ." This penetrating report scotches the notion that tests will segregate the "intellectually gifted" from the academic pluggers, pets, conformists, and literal-minded.

After a study of the records of three hundred leading scientists, artists, and writers, Dr. John Drevdahl, Oklahoma State University psychologist, emerged with a conclusion which challenges the idea that coming up with "right" answers is an indication of creative talent. He warns that should the nation champion the routine and fail to nourish skepticism and nonconformity in thinking on the part of young creative minds, then the richest potential source of scientific ability may dry up. Dr. Drevdahl contends that "it is only through continued scientific advancement, necessarily by creative persons, that this country can regain or maintain its position of leadership. . . . By forcing the potential genius to conform for the sake of conformity is a good way to bury his creative abilty."[10] This is the greatest danger of the current test craze. It equates ability with a capacity to give predetermined answers when the kind of talent which is really needed in these times of momentous change is one that can find pathways to the stars for which there is no map.

The rarest kind of knowledge is that which perceives the limits of what is known. The most valuable kind of intellectual effort is that which tries to fill the gaps in human understanding by setting out on cerebral voyages beyond established facts in search of new discoveries. This kind of mind can be intimidated and its usefulness forever impaired by the sort of brain-washing which insists that to be a parrot is to be intelligent. The student who becomes convinced through such academic conditioning that the objective of education is to know what is already known will not be inclined to go on from there when he is on his own after graduation. The teacher who can get a student excited about what is not known is worth a dozen who would fill him full of quiz-kid facts.

The professional testing services have sold the nation's schools such an impressive bill of goods that now the primary objective of most teachers is to drill students for scheduled tests. There is a competition between high schools and preparatory schools to see which can get the highest number of graduates into "name" colleges. Past college board exams are carefully studied and used as guides to the content of curricula. Students are drilled in dry-run exercises to make them familiar with the mechanics of the tests and the kind of information they are likely to deal with. The same questions rephrased are often repeated. Colleges and universities are aware of this, yet they generally believe the exams are useful. They, too, like to play it safe. Better to have a dependable grind than an unknown quantity that could turn out to be anything from top to bottom. Frank H. Bowles, president of the College Entrance Examination Board, recently informed a select group at Arden House in Harriman, New York, that only about one third of all high-school students applying for college now are being subjected to selective admissions tests, but that a new era is about to dawn. By 1961 he believes that two thirds of all candidates will take tests, while 1970 will find almost one hundred per cent being tested, if not for selection, then for sorting, placement, and "mass guidance." The days of the odd-ball, the square peg, the "late-bloomer," and the skeptic are numbered while streamlined mass production of the submissive organization man has begun in earnest.

The story of Cheng Guan Lim is the tale of a very bright youth who did poorly in examinations. One day in 1955, when he thought he was flunking out of the University of Michigan, he decided to hide away from the world. He was afraid to face friends and he thought immigration authorities would dispatch him to Taiwan in disgrace. For the next four years, without serious illness and without being discovered, Cheng Guan Lim managed to live as a church mouse in the empty lofts of Ann Arbor's First Methodist Church. It was an ordeal that required the highest degree of alertness and ingenuity—qualities desired in the best of scholars. Without any textbooks to guide him, Cheng Guan Lim analyzed his predicament. At night he scrounged for scraps of food in the rectory kitchen and managed to avoid beriberi. He made stubby stilts to cross a snow-covered roof in winter to avoid wetting his shoes. He jumped rope to keep his body in condition. Occasionally he took a sun bath on the church roof, but he had to watch out for planes that might have spotted him. He devised mental exercises to keep his mind from wandering. When, after the long seclusion, he was discovered, Cheng Guan Lim seemed to be sound in flesh and spirit. He was invited to return to the university, for it was apparent that even though he had not done well in tests he was quite capable of using his head.

MASTERS AND HELPERS

The nation's school bill is fabulous. The cost of running public and private schools at all levels in 1958-59 ran at the rate of $22 billion annually. Two thirds of this total was spent upon public elementary and secondary schools. That was $456 for every active pupil but the consensus is that even this amount is not enough; so fresh money must be found. Local governments now pay 56 per cent of the cost of public elementary and secondary schools; state governments pay 40 per cent while the Federal Government contributes 4 per cent. Michigan's Governor G. Mennen Williams says that state and local governments can no longer afford to supply the increasing quantities of money needed to handle today's avalanche of students. Speaking before the National Education Association, the governor recently advised, "The new financing needed must come largely from the Federal Government with state and local governments continuing to give the fullest possible measure of support." Before bringing the Federal Government into the education picture on any major scale, local communities have some homework to do. New ways must be found to make the money now spent do a better job. Just buying more of the current product with Federal dollars will not accomplish the basic task of recruiting better teachers and of securing better teaching from them.

Some distinction must be made between scholars and tradesmen as well as between students interested in academic subjects and those intent upon vocational training. Teacher salaries at present are too low for scholars and, in many cases, too high for the kind of tradesmen who operate as instructors in the schools. Many duties now assigned to teachers are a waste of the abilities of those who are truly competent in their fields of study. Those duties could as well be performed by non-professional assistants and by films, tapes, and T.V. There is a hierarchy in every secondary school administration but none at the operating level where it would make more sense. As long as teachers of chemistry are paid as much as instructors in cooking, dressmaking, and beauty care, very few able chemists will teach. As long as a teacher of American History is expected to monitor study halls and chaperone dances, few able historians will take the job. There is no more reason why a teacher who is a jack-of-all-duties should earn the salary of a professional scholar than that the community should expect to get an educated child to come out of a school which wastes the time of a competent teacher by making him a lunchroom referee and a roll taker. As in a hospital there are doctors and attendants, so in schools there should be specialists who operate on students' minds and assistants who render other less critical care.

On the matter of teacher talent and how it is used the Rockefeller Brothers Report has made pertinent comment: "Perhaps no profession has suffered such a general neglect of specialized abilities as that of the teacher. Teachers at the pre-college level tend to be handled as interchangeable units in an educational assembly line. The best teachers and the poorest in a school may teach the same grade and subject, use the same textbooks, handle the same number of students, get paid the same salaries, and rise at the same speed to the same ceiling. Clearly, if the teaching profession is to be made more attractive, this will have to be changed." It will not be changed as long as school administrations and the public at large regard the scholar as a fuddy-duddy and staff their schools with the cheapest facsimile on the market.

Nobel Prize physicist Harold C. Urey knows what it takes to produce a genuine scientist. In his opinion adult citizens had better develop a new respect for the mind or "possibly our unintellectualism is something which could kill us all." "It seems to me," says Dr. Urey, "that the population of this country has a considerable predilection for trusting essentially stupid people and mistrusting those who are brilliant." The renowned nuclear theorist is appalled by an educational system which treats the poor student to the same fare as the conscientious and able. "Many parents don't wish to have junior's precious ego exposed to the realities of life. They will pack his ego, and their own incidentally, in cotton and never face the fact that he is not an Einstein because he is a darling." One effect, he says, is to fill the colleges with students whose background and study habits are so poor that "most should never have gone to college."[11]

John F. Gummere, headmaster of William Penn Charter School in Philadelphia, is in favor of modifying present compulsory education codes so that children are not forced into schools "when they are incapable of further education." In agreement with others who have wondered what to do with those who do not want to study or cannot, Dr. Gummere has suggested that "something has to be done, indeed, for those who are ineducable, even by the lowest of academic standards; but let us not call what is done 'high school work.' I suggest we call it 'off-street parking' or something else which actually describes it." The whole educational system, he believes, has been distorted by "the 'felt-need' fraud according to which the teacher was not supposed to teach anything the student didn't think he needed."[12]

In this age of increasingly complicated technology, there

is a genuine demand for a greatly magnified and more serious program of vocational training. Since a very large proportion of present youth is headed for employment in the skilled crafts as adults, it is important to develop the most able technicians possible in courses designed for the purpose. Here again the instruction should be by persons who are fully qualified and competent in their trades and who should have worked at them with a high degree of success before coming into the schools to teach. Some critics of the present school system have expressed the opinion that vocational courses should be eliminated. Former president of Harvard University, James B. Conant, thinks differently. To him such courses are the very reason many students at comprehensive high schools "are committed, and see purpose." It would be a disastrous mistake to assume that only the academic subjects should be taught in elementary and secondary schools. Serious vocational training is highly necessary and top standards of instruction are equally important, but it would be folly to think that a school could hire a first-class instructor in chemistry for the same price that it could employ an expert machinist. The school, no less than society at large, must recognize the market place and the prices that are paid for various types and qualities of ability.

To compensate for the higher salaries that would have to be paid for professional scholars and skilled artisans, schools should adopt time-saving devices to relieve the specialists of all extraneous chores so that they may concentrate on instruction. Only the most meager beginnings have been made in the use of electronic devices. Tape recordings, moving pictures, and television have thus far been used as gimmicks or frills for the most part; but there is no reason why they could not handle much of the basic exposition and drill that are necessary in all teaching. Encyclopedia Britannica Films of Wilmette, Illinois, has produced a moving picture that presents a full-year high school course in physics. The instructor is no less than Dr. Harvey E. White, Professor of

Physics at the University of California. It is so organized that it can be run for 162 half-hour sessions. It has a format that calls for thirty-minute lectures on Monday, Wednesday, and Friday of each week and for laboratory sessions of the same length on Tuesday and Thursday. This one film, which represents an investment of a half-million dollars in talent and mechanics, is undoubtedly the best organized, most highly refined course in high-school physics ever presented. To suppose that anything comparable could be offered "live" by the average secondary school today would be foolishness. Such a film could carry the major job of exposition for all classes in a community school system. Under such circumstances a very large high school or several smaller ones could pool their budgets to hire one or more expert physicists whose full-time job would be to tutor the students through supplementary question-and-discussion periods to make certain they grasp the material. This would definitely not be a task that an amateur "fill-in" could perform, but considering the number of students who could be serviced it would justify employment of top-flight specialists. The machine operator could be anyone—even the kind of instructor who now teaches from a textbook which he himself may not understand.

Tape recordings are now widely used for routine drill in foreign languages, allowing a competent teacher to spend full time upon problems which develop and upon special exposition which is best done in person according to student progress. At the University of Delaware it has been found that as many as one half of the students of a foreign language are able to learn as much in one year with electronic laboratory equipment supplemented by expert teaching as previously was possible in two years by traditional methods. As explained by Professor Elbert D. Turner, Jr., "Language is an art which must be practiced." In a laboratory which provides devices for private listening and recording it is possible to gain as much oral practice in eight weeks as could be had formerly in two years. As Professor Turner announced in a report to the alumni of his university, "The reason for this will become apparent if you will think back to your own Delaware language courses which met, in all probability, three fifty-minute periods a week, not more than fifty such class meetings per semester, over a period of two years. Assuming a class size of twenty-five and that the teacher devoted no time to roll call, explanation, correction or testing, and called on every student every day (assumptions which you will recognize as unrealistic) your maximum opportunity for practice in the spoken language was one hundred minutes per semester—or a total of four hundred minutes or about six hours and forty minutes in two years."[13]

The main purpose of films, television, recording devices, and other electronic equipment is to make more efficient use of student and teacher time and of classroom and laboratory space. The purpose is not to eliminate the teacher but to eliminate the incompetent instructor and to justify the employment of a genuine expert because such an expert would be more efficiently used. The machines can be run by low-cost assistants. Such new implements will not alone revitalize the school system but they could make it possible to do a better job for more students on reasonable budgets.

Not all students are interested in or capable of academic work beyond certain elementary levels of literacy. The time of expert scholars should not be spent on those who do not have capacity or interest. It is not the job of schools to equate cooking and dressmaking with algebra or history because some students and parents want them to. If mothers have failed their daughters in the rudiments of housekeeping, there is no reason why high schools should offer to substitute for them because "home management courses help future parents to plan time and energy wisely—an important factor in this era of working wives." If this kind of instruction were turned over to a machine in the name of scholarship, it would probably blow a fuse.

Compulsory academic education beyond the point of literacy is quite unnecessary. The competitions for jobs, prestige, and wealth in adult society are sufficient to illustrate the serious value of school work. For those who cannot see the light the community can and should offer opportunities in trade shops and home economics institutes staffed by craftsmen, where the academic subjects would not be taught. Practical supermarket arithmetic and television English can be picked up without high-paid instruction.

THE CONSERVATION OF MAN

The typical suburban residential district has no precedent. It has come suddenly from nothing into full development. It may be a collection of subdivisions stocked with look-alike dwellings sprung into existence beside a highway and located between two or more shopping centers. Its only library is likely to be the magazine and paper-back section of the local drugstore. After a few brief mechanical earthquakes it has settled down and its space is all filled in to the last lot. From now on, until it wears out, nothing new is likely to happen unless an expressway is thrust through it. As a rule its site has no particular natural feature to distinguish it or give it purpose such as a river, a lake, an ocean harbor, or a mountain pass. There are no resources or production agencies in its vicinity with which it is intimately related such as farms, forests, minerals, or power. Its business is to be a commuters' bedroom and a dining room rather than to be a town with all the crosscurrents of activity and mixing of talents and resources that a town used to be. Gone is the old-fashioned village or small town which derived character from the opportunity everyone had of seeing adult craftsmen, merchants, and professionals going about their daily work.

The modern residential community is an occupational desert except for door-to-door salesmen, the trash collectors, newspaper boys and a few deliverymen. While this is economically acceptable, it contributes to cultural suicide. In such communities sons do not see their fathers at work. Thus they grow to young manhood with no very clear idea of the different kinds of jobs adults do to earn a living or how the adult world functions. The most important duty of their future life remains a mysterious abstraction, often until they are irrevocably committed. The student's ambitions and career aspirations develop in a vacuum pierced only by suggestions of a guidance counselor who gets his hunches from a battery of tests. The normal zestful desire to do something or be something in particular which one has seen with his own eyes is likely to be uncultivated while it is overshadowed by desires for income, security, and extracurricular fun only because these are now more concrete than the job by which the young will eventually earn them. Unless the schools, either in academic subjects or through true vocational instruction, give the student a thorough, expert command of some field of knowledge or technique they will simply prepare him for frustrations that no amount of "life adjustment units" will ease.

CHAPTER 12

Preventive Engineering

Peter Cooper Village is not, as its name might suggest, a quaint colonial settlement overlooked by the Twentieth Century. It is the prototype for an ultra-modern people-packing technique. The "village" covers a dozen square blocks of midtown Manhattan with gigantic brick monoliths. To soften the austere character of its thousands of monotonous human cubicles some trees have been planted in its streets and courts. These tokens of greenery seem somewhat incongruous, dwarfed as they are by the massive hulks of masonry around them. Yet in their own small way they reassure urban man that he has some living company in his world of stone.

One resident of Peter Cooper Village is particularly interested in these trees. He has noted with concern that their effect is gradually being offset by more and more traffic signs erected on steel posts. According to him this expanding forest of metal notices threatens to obscure the natural. It is already impossible to look at a tree without being advised that there is "No Parking," "No Parking This Side of Sign," "No Parking—Taxi Stand," "No Standing," "No Standing This Side of Sign," "No Parking 11 A.M. to 2 P.M. Tues., Thurs.," "No Parking 11 A.M. to 2 P.M. Mon., Wed., Fri.," etc. In a single two-block stretch there were, at last count, sixty-seven signs proclaiming eighteen vital civic messages. If these signs are not already enough to dumbfound the most insistent tree watcher, perhaps that oversight will be corrected—there is still room for a few more and the city's Department of Traffic seems well supplied with ammunition.

Doubtless the kind of ingenuity that created Peter Cooper Village and its clutter of curbside admonitions will find additional ways to make a limited amount of space provide somehow for an unlimited supply of people. It is a prediction of things to come upon a planet which seems deliberately headed for quantity rather than quality. While there are many devices by which humanity could still create a pleasanter, more adequate environment than that provided by Nature, they are not likely to be used because they would require the agreement of whole communities before they could be successfully applied. The world is now too thickly populated for crusading individuals to make much of a dent in the total arrangement of things. The sheer inertia of the human mass is too great for a single citizen to alter; so it is quite an achievement if he can just crawl off into a corner and do a reasonably good job for himself and his family. The bitter intensity of everyday competition between men of all classes for a better income and a nicer way of life is hard evidence that it is easier to supply the world with people than to supply people with the things of this world. Steel, subject though it is to rust, will probably outlast the living tree.

While it would be simpler to plan parenthood than to plan communities to accommodate more parents, very little real progress is made in that department. In fact prolific human breeding is sometimes encouraged by nations and factions within nations as a stratagem through which it is hoped eventually to outnumber and overwhelm rivals. If the individual family, in its own self-interest, will not plan to limit its size in order to attain a higher standard of living, it is rather futile to expect a community, whose members are less intimate, to plan effectively the environment. Like charity, planning might well begin at home. Without some exercise in forethought and co-operation there can be no preventive engineering either at the family level or on a community scale. Without vision, and the skill to implement it, society will have to depend, as it does now, upon hindsight and low-grade fumbling that does some patch work after trouble has developed.

This is a hard comedown for a nation which in its pioneer stages was guided by engineers and statesmen with insight and long-range plans. America's railroads, for example, were built by a generation of preventive engineers who conceived and built rights-of-way that to this day are the most efficient routes over which to haul interurban mass traffic. Even in the wilderness era of our history, when the future patterns of settlement and commercial exchange were less predictable than now, these engineers constructed guidelines that generated growth and power rather than frustration. In contrast, today's patched-up highway network, which suffers from marginal friction and jammed intersections, is typical of year-to-year improvisers who practice civic butchery because they have no fundamental concepts of the kind of landscape they are tinkering with or what kind of physical environment modern America should strive to create. There is piecemeal excellence in modern engineering beyond anything previously known, but it is offset by an appalling ignorance of the total environment that it is changing. The engineer or the politician who is concerned only with the design of a specific structure and not with the impact it will have on the design of the whole community, is only a proficient journeyman—he is not a master craftsman.

Planning without political follow-through is a futile waste of time just as political decisions without planning can be ruinous. Either the two go together on a high plane of quality or the result is a bungled job. The low level of liaison between planners and politicians on the national scene was rather ludicrously exposed a short while ago by a proposal to set up a gilt-edged *Committee on National Goals*. As conceived in a presidential directive, this committee was to be created to define long-term development objectives for the nation. Nine months after conception its birth had not taken place. Apparently the reason for miscarriage was that neither the idea nor the way it was to be promoted was well thought through. Even though the Federal Government manages an $80,000,000,000-a-year business, it declined to dip into its own pockets for the $3,000,000 needed to float this new committee that ostensibly was to plot a future course for 180,000,000 people. A commercial company doing a tiny fraction of that business with just a few million customers would either spend $3,000,000 a year to chart its way and define its goals or get lost in the heat of today's competition.

For some fuzzy reason it was believed that the glittering name of this committee-to-be would impress private foundations so that they would rush into the breach with a supply of funds and eggheads. Among the private sponsors of research presented with a prospectus were the Carnegie, Ford, Rockefeller, and Sloan foundations. Apparently all withheld their cash although they displayed interest in the idea. The weakness, it seems, lay in the government's inability to propose the kind of clear-cut definition of responsibility and purpose for its project which all research foundations expect of those to whom they make grants. Having tapped the U.S. Treasury so easily for so long, the bureaucrats found it too difficult to define a program of research that would measure up to competitive private standards. As President Eisenhower indicated later, the problem seemed to be to lay "this whole matter out so that everybody will understand it." Anybody reading the usual sort of government prospectus would heartily sympathize with the President. If just to set up a committee intelligently is now considered a severe task in the Washington atmosphere, it would be nothing less than phenomenal if those responsible for defining national goals ever were able to go into action without fantastic fumbling and procrastination. The committee was finally appointed in early 1960 but even then its own purpose had not been clarified; so it seemed as remote as ever from its own goal of financial support.

To perform a reasonable job of preventive engineering it is essential to view the national landscape in both comprehensive and detailed terms as to its resources, the technologies at hand, and the quality of life that it is envisioned Americans might live. Without a kind of planning which is guided by such knowledge from local through state and national levels, there can be only a hit-or-miss development. The most serious problems of environmental organization in the early days of our nation were on the frontier. Then the big task was to get people settled. Today the oversettled metropolitan areas are the prime centers of conflict and disturbance. The restless movement of one rootless citizen in five to a new residence every year, juvenile delinquency, and racial tensions in central cities where whites move out and colored move in—these and more are symptoms of man's poor adjustment to the place and people where he lives.

The sheer physical spread of modern metropolitan complexes magnifies the problem of the proper development of their space. The New York metropolitan area extends into the states of New Jersey and Connecticut. The Philadelphia metropolitan area includes parts of Pennsylvania, Delaware, and New Jersey. The Chicago metropolitan area includes parts of Illinois, Wisconsin, Indiana, and Michigan. The Pittsburgh metropolitan area overflows from Pennsylvania into Ohio and West Virginia. The Washington metropolitan area includes counties in Virginia and Maryland which adjoin the District of Columbia. Since cities are the legal offspring of states and subject to state regulations, it is obvious that jurisdiction is divided in the very localities where a single authority with a strong hand is most critically needed. Not only are metropolitan areas commonly partitioned among states but often the state capitals are blissfully removed from the centers of major growth and difficulty. Albany, the New York capital, senses nothing of the Empire City's troubles except by remote contact. Springfield, Illinois, looks out upon cornfields while Chicago is smothered in smog; Pittsburgh and Philadelphia may writhe in distress while Harrisburg admires the Susquehanna River and the Appalachian Mountains. Little does Dover know about Wilmington, Madison about Milwaukee, or Annapolis about Baltimore. These accidents of political geography invite repercussions upon planners and plans that are of the utmost importance.

Metropolitan areas are come-latelies compared with farm districts; thus they are often at a disadvantage in state legislatures, where representation is commonly based on patterns of population density and distribution long out of date. At the state level powerful farm minorities, far removed from the scene of urban strife, may easily obstruct appropriations to aid city majorities. Democrats may control the biggest urbanized area while Republicans rule the countryside or vice versa. Whatever the party labels, the conflict of interests does damage to planning and to budgets for public works and services that might otherwise aid metropolitan districts. With the Federal Government almost completely out of the picture except for liberal handouts of cheap advice, the dreary task of tussling with the realities of modern metropolitan life falls upon local units of government which are the poorest in revenue and least able to do the monumental job at hand.

The National Planning Association has proposed that if serious trouble is to be avoided there should be far-reaching changes in the future allocations of Federal funds to local communities. As the Association sees the picture, the Federal Government during the postwar period quietly eased itself out of major responsibilities for public services while unloading those former obligations onto states and local communities which are less able to foot the bill now than they ever were. As an example, in 1959 the Federal treasury spent $8.1 billion on non-defense goods and services for the people while the combined expenditures of states and local governments were $43.3 billions. Back in 1948 the ratio was $12.8 billion Federal to $22.6 by state and local governments for the same goods and services. Thus Washington, which now collects more revenue than it did in 1948, bears less than one sixth the cost of public goods and services while over a decade ago it shouldered more than one third of the burden. In 1959 the Federal Government spent more money just to stabilize farm prices and farm income than it spent on aids to public health, welfare, education, highways, urban renewal, public housing, national parks, and the management of forests and wildlife. While there are valid arguments for parts of the farm-support program, they are no better than those that have been presented but ignored for Federal aid to metropolitan areas and the urban citizen. Somehow or other the little man who pays most of the tax bill has been forgotten by the big man who collects it.

Although funds are vitally important to planning and the execution of plans in metropolitan areas, very little could be accomplished without co-operative effort at all levels of political authority. In a way it is putting the cart before the horse to clamor for more spending on more public projects until there is some willingness on the part of cities, suburban towns, counties, and states to pool their prerogatives so that a single unified form of metropolitan government could take basic problems in hand and deal with them as though there were no boundaries of political jurisdiction. When political control is fractionated and competitive within a single geographic area such as a metropolitan district, any disposition to co-operate is likely to be undermined by wrangling for the power to tax and spend. The professional politician, like any other professional, is in business to succeed and dominate his field. His reputation is established by his ability to acquire power; so he is not likely to surrender it lightly.

Today the budgets of America's major cities are larger than the budgets of many states. The principal metropolitan area in a state may have a larger population than all the rest of the state put together. It is rather silly that sons who have grown taller than fathers should still be dressed in knee pants and instructed by their parents as to which girls they may go out with. New York City has seriously thought of asking for separate statehood. It claims that its parent has reserved to itself the best sources of revenue while it is stuck with problems more difficult to solve than anything known to Albany.

As matters stand it is far more expensive to provide proper public services to eight million inhabitants in an area such as New York City, which is cluttered and cramped for space, than it is to service a similar number of persons distributed over the wide territory of the Empire State. In theory this situation should be reversed because theoretically dispersion should be more costly to deal with than concentration. Mass markets for public services should promote civic efficiency just as mass markets for automobiles have promoted industrial efficiency. But it must not be forgotten that in theory the environment would be as well planned as the assembly lines of Detroit, whereas in fact it is not. Without preventive engineering in the arrangement of space and services in metropolitan areas, people, like molecules, will generate more heat through friction the more tightly they are packed. It is no wonder that in a growing number of congested cities the municipal crankcase is smoking and the bearings are about to burn out.

Despite the fact that America has developed a greater number of urban complexes than any other nation, we have not yet learned how to organize these strange new assemblies of people to reduce overhead and improve public services.

If the same kind of engineering skill could be applied to metropolitan planning and development as is now applied to other mass production processes in our economy, then our cities would be the cheapest and most desirable places to live. In government, as in industry, efficiency is the product of good technicians directed by able management. Unless the divided authority of political management in sprawling metropolitan areas is consolidated so that there is a single line of authority rather than several bosses each of whom issues orders, markets services, and collects bills without co-ordination, then civic corporations are likely to go even deeper into the red. It is time that public enterprise adopted some of the methods of private enterprise to which it owes its support.

Possibly some of the reluctance of states to surrender their whips to upstart offspring is that occasionally the behavior of cities in their own province of authority develops doubt in the parental mind. Plagued as New York City is with a thousand modern ills, it recently chose to direct its ingenuity toward the solution of a problem that has not been resolved since first it stumped the ancients. With proper ceremonial fanfare including photographers and reporters, Sanitation Commissioner Paul P. Screvane, together with officials of the Mayor's Committee to Keep New York City Clean, inaugurated a $500 flower-decked comfort station for dogs at the corner of York Avenue and 92nd Street. While Mr. Screvane acknowledged he was not convinced that the city's 272,000 licensed canines could all be economically accommodated in this elite fashion, he thought the experiment worth a try. Fortunately before the Board of Estimate could vote to go all out in favor of man's best friend, the dogs themselves struck against this bureaucratic threat to their freedom. While the Sanitation Department waited in vain for signs of appreciation, the Fire Department continued to enjoy undiminished popularity.

THE COMING AGE OF THE METRO

Ever since the physical city began to spill over its own jurisdictional boundary to scatter industries, residences, shops, stores, and people into the open space of adjoining towns, counties, and states, there has been no central metropolitan authority to guide or regulate growth, zone land, plan and supply public services, or tax equitably. Anarchy has reigned where there has been the greatest need for unified control. If the city did not do a good job before it became too big for its breeches that was its own fault. If it cannot do a good job now it has an excuse. In the Baltimore metropolitan area there are ten distinct governments managing one thing or another. While this may seem like a prelude to managerial bedlam, actually Baltimore is conservative. Metropolitan Boston has 112 political bodies operating on the local level. Some are outside the central city; others are autonomous entities within it. Buffalo has 155. Chicago, never known to slouch, has 954 governing units with rights to collect taxes or sell bonds and do things for or to people. New York, as might be expected, upstages all others with its own 1074. Why it should require 705 authoritative administrations to run the Philadelphia metropolitan area is anybody's guess. San Francisco is operated by 401. Even the District of Columbia, which complains that Congress will not give it independence, has 67 and St. Louis has an even 400. Not since Humpty-Dumpty fell off the wall and elections replaced the divine rights of kings have all the mayor's men been so distressed as they are now, trying to restore reasonable jurisdictional form to a politico-geographic omelet.

For a big-business people who once believed that "to govern best is to govern least," it might appear the worm has turned and that government has become the biggest of all big businesses with a steadily mounting roster of employees. However, all actions provoke reactions. On July 22, 1957,

Miami, together with 25 other Florida communities in its gravitational field, decided by popular vote that they had had enough of competing and overlapping public authorities. To simplify their political life, discharge superfluous office holders, reduce other expenses, and co-ordinate civic troubles, the citizens chose to establish America's first united metropolitan government and futuristically dubbed it "Metro." Metro did not receive a warm welcome from many of the 7600 entrenched bureaucrats who had previously run things in the 26 separate communities. An effort soon was launched to emasculate the new government through a charter amendment prescribing that the autonomy of individual municipalities should not be "infringed upon, disturbed or interfered with." However, this bold show of selfishness was defeated at the polls 73,958 to 49,469 despite the fact that Miami's garbage trucks and other city vehicles carried campaign posters pleading "Vote Yes." Quipped the Cleveland *Press*—which has plugged for a Greater Cleveland authority —"Looks as if nobody wants Metro in Miami but the people."

According to Metro's top executive, O. W. Campbell, the new supercity, which takes in Dade County, will not displace all local government. He believes, "Some things can best be done in the neighborhoods. If we were to get one big government, city hall would be more remote than Washington as far as services are concerned. Metro will do the region-wide things that individual municipalities can't do."[1] Specifically, Mr. Campbell thinks Metro can establish a uniform traffic code and consolidate nine independent buslines to provide better service for present fares. Good water and sewage services, he believes, can best be engineered on an area-wide basis. Assessors are already at work to equalize property evaluations. A zoning plan is expected to emerge and a central purchasing agency will be established. All of these problems are the sort of thing every community must wrestle with, but they become more complicated when physical fusion of built-up space takes place on a mass scale as it does in all growing metropolitan areas.

If such a new form of government as Metro holds the answer to new efficiencies, the question may be asked, Why is it not more popular? Thomas H. Reed, who has made a specialty of metropolitan surveys, thinks the states are responsible. In a paper presented to the National Municipal League he observed, "In dealing with this critical and momentous problem the states have so far played an inglorious role. They have for the most part adhered slavishly to their traditional policies with regard to the structure of local government." By rather freely granting rights of incorporation to small communities, without much regard to their arrangement in space, the states have paved the way for multiplicities of authority in what are now becoming thickly settled, contiguous urban districts. According to the 1957 census there were 3422 municipalities in the nation's 174 metropolitan areas—an average of twenty for each locality where one could do a better job.

To undo this error Dr. Reed believes, "The states must provide a means of bringing about metropolitan integration which cannot be thwarted by the penny-wise opposition of a local clique or wrecked on the shoals of suburban particularism. No other agency than the state can accomplish the reorganization of the structure of local government necessary to a solution of the metropolitan problem. It is unreasonable to expect the municipalities of a metropolitan area, with their highly individualized interests and habits, to agree on any form of union which it is believed will cost any of them either higher taxes or diminished prestige. Their conflicts of interest can be resolved only by a higher and impartial power." The Miami Metro came into being, Dr. Reed believes, because "the proposal was submitted to the voters of the area as a whole" and did not grow by piecemeal annexation.

If there is any place where urban growth has slipped its

leash, it is in and around the national capital itself. Despite
the combined talent of congressional committees, the state
legislatures of Virginia and Maryland, and all the high-brow
know-how employed by the counties, cities, and towns which
surround the District of Columbia, no one has figured how
to bring order out of a chaos that grows more baffling with
each rise in population. Although Washington is the beacon
that beams light into the darkest corners of the underdeveloped earth, illuminating pathways to technological progress,
it has not been able to draft a functional floor plan for its
own people in their own living room. Within view of the
Pentagon, the logistic nerve center of the Western World
where the speedy transportation of ten million troops could
be calculated at the slip of a slide rule, the 14th Street bridge
over the Potomac is snarled in a traffic jam every workday
afternoon of the year, and this has been going on for two
decades.

Although its population has skyrocketed for the past
twenty years without let-up, the Washington metropolitan
area has not yet settled down to the serious business of planning its own future in a rational way. It still does not know
how to quarter people without creating both urban and
suburban slums as fast as old ones are torn down. It has
perennial trouble with water supply and sewage disposal.
The more expressways it builds the more congested they
become. Having had one of the best electric trolley systems
anywhere, it is dismantling it to clear the way for more automobiles. While Washington is renowned for its old parks,
newer outlying residential areas take shape without them
and there is talk of charging citizens for visits to the zoo.
Schools are overcrowded; taxes mount; garbage collections
only once a week are commonplace. Apparently snafu has
become respectable and everything would be easier if a
million people would just relax and enjoy their tour of duty.
While this may be a good prescription for the hardened
bureaucrat who knows little should be expected from either

a civil servant or a political master, the rest of the country which foots the bill cannot be so easily appeased.

The problems which confront the Washington metropolitan area are not basically different from those known to two hundred other big cities around the country which are boxed in by suburbs. These human aggregates look to the Washington situation for practical solutions. They want to be shown how to solve their problems in the only kind of currency that counts—concrete example. This expectation that Washington should act is not unreasonable. It is part of the function of a capital city to be a showplace of national pride and respect. Certainly it should not be a prize example of frustration. The American metropolitan area, as it has developed in the postwar period, is truly a new phenomenon in the annals of the human habitat. It baffles our best minds and it puts the stigma of delinquency on a sizable segment of the next generation. It is imperative that a responsible Federal Government should make a real effort with all its resources and political influence to work out a solution just as it has tried to solve its military problems and its agricultural problems— by research and, above all, by action. A crisis confronts the American people. Their very own communities are threatened from within by shabby decay, congestion, cultural deterioration, and mounting debt. It is time that Washington looked to its own for more than revenue lest this, too, become an underdeveloped country.

The closest the Washington area has come to organizing a metro was to establish in 1957 the Washington Metropolitan Regional Conference, which is a permanent but loosely informal association of representatives from every jurisdiction in the District of Columbia and its built-up vicinity. These leaders in the affairs of various local governments have pledged themselves to seek agreement on ways to solve problems of mutual concern. Unlike Miami's Metro the WMRC is not a government and it has no authority. It is a club for discussion and the interchange of ideas and good will. Initiated at the suggestion of District Commissioner Robert E. McLaughlin, it does make possible, as he says, "a forum of cordial co-operation among officials who, a few months ago, were not even acquainted."[2]

The WMRC started off in an atmosphere of conviviality and hope by asking that all local governments accept in principle the ideal that all new growth should be so controlled as to keep sewage out of a significant section of the Potomac River. Thus far the mutual suasion behind this sanitary truce has had some beneficial effects. The Conference has also attempted to get standard interjurisdictional taxicab fares and agreements on handling public health, hospital, and welfare services. The ambition of those who look to WMRC as a way to reduce the waste and agony of unco-ordinated metropolitan sprawl is that the delegates to the Conference will see the light on such specific issues as highways, zoning, and parks. Then, it is anticipated, they will go back to their own legislative bodies and plug for a program that will benefit the whole area as well as the individual segments. To the political realist this Pollyanna, fraternal-lodge approach must seem pathetic.

The attitude of Maryland's former Governor Theodore R. McKeldin toward the suggestion of something stronger than WMRC has been made quite explicit. Said he, "There is a tendency among peoples and governments to shed their most troublesome problems by turning them over to higher authorities . . . I cannot, however, accept the surrender of autonomy by local jurisdictions to a super-government in a region."[3] Quite obviously the coming age of the metro will be postponed until politicians in strategic positions such as the state house are ready to play the midwife. Major General Louis W. Prentiss, chairman of the Federal City Council's policy committee, is outspoken in favor of the metro approach. He recognizes the importance of a firm chain of command in a battle for any difficult objective when there is a possibility that the weak-kneed might back out if the going gets rough. General Prentiss has observed that "a single, overall, area-wide authority is needed to co-ordinate and direct regional programs affecting metropolitan growth. Its powers and responsibilities could be spelled out by means of an interstate compact commission. To date, solutions have been impossible due to the confusion, overlapping of authority and rivalry. For too many years, efforts to resolve this confusion have been stymied by inaction and lack of recognition of the importance of an area-wide approach. This approach can never be taken until there is established a workable, overall authority."[4] These are blunt words and strong medicine, but the patient is too sick to be treated with coddling and gumdrops. General Prentiss has laid the facts of metro's political life on the line. The community which flinches from his advice is headed for chronic trouble.

Until there is some kind of metropolitan-area programming with precise plans for total land use, people will have to rely upon individual community zoning and the courts to protect property values and to guard residential neighborhoods from invasion by undesirable construction. Arlington, Virginia, which is ensnared within the Washington metropolitan net, is under severe pressure by apartment, industrial, and commercial interests to release land in residential neighborhoods for these other uses. To preserve its residential character Arlington forbids the building of apartments in many places, but investment syndicates are not above challenging these restrictions in court. Recently suit was brought against the county by parties who sought to build $8 million worth of high-rise apartments in a protected neighborhood. In a decision upholding the county, Circuit Judge Walter T. McCarthy declared that Arlington was within its rights to tell new residents and developers to "go elsewhere."

In his rejection of plaintiff's appeal Judge McCarthy summed up the situation in forceful style. "It is undoubtedly true," he said, "that the petitioner in this case can gain wealth by having the property zoned the way he wants to.

But it appears to me that that possibly results in a kind of osmosis or a blotting up of the potential wealth of the whole neighborhood into his area . . . There is no question that the pressure of 'the explosive population' is beating down upon Arlington County . . . So the question is, does Arlington have a right to say to the metropolitan area, 'We shall not supply your demands—go elsewhere.' I am inclined to think it does. I think it has a right to set up the character of the development that will take place within it, and to say, if it wants to, that notwithstanding any of the great metropolitan demand for apartments or for commercial or industrial areas, that our people don't want that kind of development, and we are not going to have it here."[5] Most people in Arlington felt relieved when this decision was announced. If there were to be no metro to organize an orderly growth of the region, at least the little county caught in the middle had found a way to do something for its own.

THE ORGANIZATION OF METROPOLITAN SPACE

While improved area-wide jurisdiction is desirable if metropolitan areas are to grow and function rationally, it would be folly to think a new political organization could completely change old habits of land utilization. It is undoubtedly true that a metro such as Miami's could institute efficiencies and could plan and zone for the total region in a co-ordinated way. The improvements which it promises are worth striving for, but the problem which stumps present governments and will stump Metro whenever it gets going is lack of positive control over the use of space within the community. Let there be no mistake about it, the power to zone and to issue building permits is not the power to control the actual organization and development of land. Yet such power is positively necessary in order to cope with the intricate task of wisely locating people, industry, transportation arteries, commercial centers, recreational facilities, water reservoirs, schools, and all the other physical entities that make up a modern metropolis.

Space is not just a commodity for speculation and trade. It is the one precious, absolutely limited, irreplaceable, and non-transferrable element of the habitat. Of all other substances that go to make up a metropolitan environment the few square miles it occupies are its most vital possession. How that space is used will affect the lives of generations. It will influence the vitality of commerce, the cultural level of the people, the tax rate, and the general quality of daily living. Political administrations can be changed by elections. Old buildings can be replaced with new ones. But space cannot be stretched, exchanged, shrunk, or moved. What a community does with this one ingredient of its existence will affect its vigor, utility, and beauty for all human time.

Metro, to save its own neck, will have to go into the real-estate business—not to make money, or even to save money, although that would be nice. Metro will have to become a landholder, a land planner, and a land dispenser for the most vital reason of all—to assure itself of the proper organization of space. Let us assume, which is not at all preposterous, that in the next century all two hundred of America's present metropolitan areas quadruple in population. The chances are they will more than quadruple in size since suburban sprawl absorbs more room per capita than urban concentration. What will those new giant agglomerations of people look like? What will they be like to live in, work in, move around in, relax in? Realistically, unless the preventive engineer, who designs so as to avoid trouble, takes over from the surgical engineer, who knows only how to use the scalpel, the whole community will be fit for the psychiatric ward. Even now it is reported that 17,000,000 Americans are mentally ill—roughly one in ten. The anguish of some is expressed in the behavior of the hostile teenager and the emotionally disturbed criminal. The torment of the majority is reflected in shrunken lives and social bitterness. The environment that intensifies psychological stress will breed a tense and callous people.

The main reason that the citizen of today's urbanized area finds streets and highways too narrow, intersections clogged by buildings, parks too few, slum neighborhoods in cities, suburbs too remote from the job, scarcities of industrial sites, schools without playing fields, the natural beauty of landscape desecrated by unsightly buildings, billboards, and junk yards, is due largely to the fact that communities have not taken a strong hand in the rational allocation of space. Without the actual possession of land, at least long enough to plan its use in detail and to write specific restrictions into all deeds to guarantee that use will conform to plan, a community cannot be master of its own shape. Zoning at best is but a set of general rules for developers. Zoning is not platting. It is not design. It is not specific space allocation and therein lies the rub.

It would be unconstitutional and ethically wrong for a metropolitan community to survey the outlying farms on its rim and to tell one landowner arbitrarily he might construct apartment houses and to tell another that according to plan his place is to become a public park. This would be equivalent to handing one man a chance for fabulous profit while skinning the other man alive. The only equitable way in which a metropolis could plan its growth fairly would be to buy all the space it will need for all purposes for years to come. It should buy this land at the prevailing market price and put it into its own space bank. Only then should its preventive engineers set about to plan in detail how that space should be used as the community grows. Their sole criteria should be the capabilities of the land and the diverse needs of the community. Though the funds required would be substantial they would be recovered, in part, through sales to private developers of those spaces allocated to homes, industries, and commercial establishments. The community itself would have priority for all public needs—thus it would be assured of a functional skeleton and not a heap of mismatched bones.

A Federal Government which can afford a multi-billion-dollar program to put agricultural land in a soil bank in times of surplus should be able in this period of emergency to advance ample funds to cities for space banks. Of course the present capital-gains tax on real estate, which is really the product of local community growth, should go not to the Federal treasury but to the communities to help them purchase lands from these space banks for public uses. With its future space thus held in a sort of safe-deposit vault, a metropolis would presumably make withdrawals only for use according to the instructions of its preventive engineers, whose job it would be to know exactly where and how much should be allocated to every civic purpose, both public and private, as the population increases. In this way it should be possible to expand without congestion and to create an environment of both beauty and utility.

On a very small scale the Federal Government has already started something along this line and the first reaction seems to be enthusiastic. Boulder City, Nevada, is a town of 3500 which grew up with Hoover Dam and Lake Mead. It was Federal property and Federally administered until 1959 when an act of Congress gave it powers of self-government. Along with the powers of jurisdiction went a gift to the municipality of all its land. Even more important, the community was also given title to thirty-two square miles of undeveloped land around it. According to the terms of the gift the new city council must draft an over-all plan for the future use and subdivision of the whole thirty-two square miles. What the community does not need for public purposes will be sold eventually to private developers. Rapid growth of population and industry is guaranteed because of the almost limitless supply of water and power from Hoover Dam coupled with the delightful recreational advantages of Lake Mead.

City manager Curtis Blyth expressed local sentiment when he once said, "I think the Southwest is the growingest area in the country. There's going to be no stopping it for many years to come." Blyth believes that the town's biggest job is to develop wisely its thirty-two square miles of real estate. "We want to get the best planners we can to come here and do it right. We have complete control, and we're starting with a community that already has been built by plan." Mayor Robert Broadbent, a local druggist, agrees with his city manager. "We can't compete with Las Vegas," says Broadbent. "So we're going to try to be something else. We can offer a clean city, good recreation, opportunity, good schools . . . It's going to be fun to be around for the next few years."[6] It would be fun for anybody to be around for a lifetime in any community that could provide ever-increasing economic and cultural opportunity and that seemed likely to grow more beautiful with time.

APPENDIX

Sources of Quoted Material

Chapter 1. Competitions for Space

1. *The New York Times,* May 24, 1959
2. *The New York Times,* June 20, 1959
3. *The New York Times,* November 30, 1958
4. *Wilmington* (Delaware) *Morning News,* May 27, 1959
5. *The New York Times,* November 13, 1957
6. *Wilmington* (Delaware) *Journal-Every Evening,* April 13, 1959
7. *The New York Times,* April 14, 1959
8. *The New York Times,* October 23, 1958
9. *The New York Times,* September 6, 1959

Chapter 2. Urban Space

1. *The New York Times,* March 3, 1959
2. *The New York Times,* July 18, 1959
3. *Time* Magazine, December 22, 1958
4. *The New York Times,* July 15, 1959
5. Letter to *The New York Herald-Tribune,* December 11, 1958
6. *The New York Times,* May 22, 1959
7. *The New York Times,* June 30, 1959
8. Letter to *The New York Times,* July 7, 1959

Chapter 3. City Planning

1. Pine, John B. *The Story of Gramercy Park,* 1831-1921. Gramercy Park Association, New York, 1921. p. 9.
2. Worcester (Massachusetts) *The Daily Telegram,* March 13, 1957

3. *The New York Times,* June 19, 1959
4. *The New York Times,* August 18, 1958

Chapter 4. Suburbia

1. *The Philadelphia Inquirer,* July 11, 1959
2. *The Philadelphia Inquirer,* July 11, 1959
3. *The New York Times,* March 21, 1959

Chapter 5. Suburbia—Continued

1. *The New York Times,* August 30, 1959
2. *The New York Times,* March 20, 1958
3. Sears, Paul B. "The Inexorable Problem of Space." *Science,* January 3, 1958. Article based on speech at Indianapolis, December 28, 1957.
4. *The New York Times,* March 2, 1959
5. *The New York Times,* July 1, 1959

Chapter 7. The Farm as Space

1. Norton, E. A. "Vanishing Crop Land." Reprint from *Journal of Soil and Water Conservation,* Vol. 11, No. 4, July 1956.

Chapter 8. Space and Circulation

1. *The New York Times,* November 13, 1959
2. *The New York Times,* November 13, 1959
3. *The New York Times,* May 23, 1957
4. *The New York Times,* October 20, 1959
5. *The New York Times,* March 21, 1957

Chapter 9. Parks and Playgrounds

1. Washington (D.C.) *The Evening Star,* December 3, 1959
2. *The New York Times,* July 28, 1958
3. *Wilmington* (Delaware) *Journal-Every Evening,* Associated Press release.
4. Martha's Vineyard (Massachusetts) *The Vineyard Gazette,* May 2, 1958
5. *Wilmington* (Delaware) *Journal-Every Evening,* April 1, 1960

6. *The New York Times,* June 1, 1957
7. *The New York Times,* August 8, 1959

Chapter 10. Covering the Water Front

1. *The New York Times,* August 30, 1959
2. *The New York Times,* August 16, 1959
3. *The New York Times,* October 3, 1958
4. *The New York Times,* December 6, 1959

Chapter 11. Space Between the Ears

1. *Time* Magazine, November 25, 1957
2. *The New York Times,* December 11, 1957
3. *Time* Magazine, November 25, 1957
4. *The New York Times,* November 25, 1959
5. *The New York Times,* November 24, 1959
6. *The New York Times,* November 24, 1959
7. *The New York Times,* January 15, 1959
8. Washington (D.C.) *The Evening Star,* January 6, 1960
9. *The New York Times,* June 30, 1959
10. *Wilmington* (Delaware) *Journal-Every Evening,* January 17, 1958
11. *Wilmington* (Delaware) *Journal-Every Evening,* November 30, 1957
12. *The New York Times,* March 9, 1958
13. *The University News,* University of Delaware, Winter 1955-1956

Chapter 12. Preventive Engineering

1. *Wisconsin State Journal,* May 10, 1959
2. Washington (D.C.) *The Sunday Star,* November 24, 1957
3. Washington (D.C.) *The Sunday Star,* November 24, 1957
4. Washington (D.C.) *The Sunday Star,* November 24, 1957
5. Washington (D.C.) *The Evening Star,* December 2, 1959
6. *Wilmington* (Delaware) *Journal-Every Evening,* January 14, 1960

INDEX